THE TIME OF MONEY

CURRENCIES

New Thinking for Financial Times

Melinda Cooper and Martijn Konings, Series Editors

The Time of Money

LISA ADKINS

Stanford University Press

Stanford, California

Stanford University Press
Stanford, California

Printed in the United States of America on acid-free, archival-quality paper

Library of Congress Cataloging-in-Publication Data

Names: Adkins, Lisa, 1966– author.
Title: The time of money / Lisa Adkins.
Description: Stanford, California : Stanford University Press, 2018. | Series: Currencies | Includes bibliographical references and index.
Identifiers: LCCN 2017060459 (print) | LCCN 2018000391 (ebook) | ISBN 9781503607118 (ebook)| ISBN 9781503606265 (cloth : alk. paper) | ISBN 9781503607101 (pbk : alk. paper)
Subjects: LCSH: Speculation—Social aspects. | Finance—Social aspects. | Money—Social aspects. | Time—Social aspects. | Economics—Sociological aspects.
Classification: LCC HG6015 (ebook) | LCC HG6015 .A35 2018 (print) | DDC 306.3—dc23
LC record available at https://lccn.loc.gov/2017060459

Cover design by Angela Moody
Cover art: Shawn Hempel/Adobe Stock
Text design by Bruce Lundquist
Typeset at Stanford University Press in 10/15 Janson

Contents

Acknowledgments

This book has been written over a number of years, and across this time my work has benefited from the input, feedback, and encouragement of trusted colleagues and friends. I would especially like to thank Pertti Alasuutari, Vikki Bell, Dick Bryan, Patricia Clough, Rebecca Coleman, Jane Elliott, Nick Gane, Ros Gill, Elizabeth Humphrys, Turo-Kimmo Lehtonen, Celia Lury, Derek McCormack, Marsha Rosengarten, Simon Susen, and Iris van der Tuin. I would also like to thank the two readers of the manuscript for Stanford—Ivan Ascher and Silvia Federici—whose insightful comments enabled me to improve the manuscript immeasurably. Thanks also to Fiona Sim for her thorough copyediting of the manuscript and to Tanya Carney for her assistance in the preparation of figures.

While writing this book I have had the opportunity to present different elements of my research at a number of institutions, including the Social Theory Centre at the University of Warwick; the Department of Sociology at City University of London; the Department of Gender Studies at the University of Lund; the Research Centre for Gender and Sexuality at the University of Amsterdam; the Department of Philosophy, History, Culture, and Art Studies at the University of Helsinki; and the Helsinki Collegium. In addition to those colleagues already named above, I would like to thank Jo Littler, Tuija Pulkinnen, Rebecca Selberg, Sigridur Thorgeirsdottir, and Marguerite van den Berg for extending those invitations.

Research for this book has been enlivened through invitations to present at particular conferences and workshops. I would like to highlight the workshops organized by the Social Studies of Finance Research Network at the University of Sydney, who generously included me in their activities across a number of years. I would also like to acknowledge invitations from the organizers of "Futures in Question" at Goldsmiths, University of London; "Intersections of Finance and Society" at the City University of London; the Crossroads in Cultural Studies conference at the University of Sydney; "Debt, Experience and Critique" at the University of Warwick; and "Debt: Philosophical and Cultural Perspectives" at the University of Helsinki.

The completion of this book was ultimately made possible by extended fellowship periods in Finland associated with my Academy of Finland FiDiPro award. I wish to thank Risto Kunelius of the University of Tampere for his tremendous support and for creating a welcoming environment. During my time at Tampere I have had the pleasure of working with my research team and associated scholars from across Finland, particularly Johannes Kananen, Susanna Paasonen, Susanne Soederberg, Liu Xin, and Hanna Ylöstalo.

I am very grateful to the two editors of the Currencies series—Melinda Cooper and Martijn Konings—and thank them for their support and encouragement and for pushing me to make this a much better book. Their own work has served as a source of inspiration across the years in which this book was written. Finally, my biggest thank-you goes to Maryanne Dever, who spent countless hours discussing the ideas on which this book is based and always believed I would get it done.

Chapter 5 of this book draws on research funded by the Australian Research Council ("Employment Activation and the Changing Economy-Society Relation," Discovery Project 150101772) and the Academy of Finland ("Social Science for the Twenty-First Century," FiDiPro Award 282955 and 282970).

THE TIME OF MONEY

The Time of Money
An Introduction

The Time of Money is concerned with some of the most universal features and problems evident in finance-led post-Fordist capitalism: mass indebtedness, financial turbulence, economic crises, austerity, underemployment, unemployment, wagelessness, wage repression, in-work poverty, crises of livelihood, precariousness, and emptied-out futures. I argue that these features and problems are by no means incidental to contemporary capitalism (and hence cannot be remedied by any simple program of reforms) but are intrinsic to its very dynamics and operations. In this book I suggest that what unites these features and problems is a logic of speculation, a logic that is both at the heart of contemporary capitalist accumulation strategies and guides and directs the dynamics of social formation, even though its forms—from the schedules and calendars of household bill and debt payments through to demands that the unemployed always stand ready for work—may appear to be disconnected, disparate, and dispersed. As a mode or system of accumulation, the logic of speculation is dominated by the generation and production of surplus via financial channels, and especially by movements and flows in and of money. This book will detail, however, how speculation cannot and should not be limited to financial practices and financial exchanges alone, since a logic of speculation is also at issue in regard to everyday, mundane forms of money. As a mode or system of social organization, the logic of speculation involves the emergence of forms of life that are characterized not by equilibrium states and stasis but by disequilibrium, disproportion, and asymmetry. Households whose debts outstrip the probabilities of repayment, wages that do not cover the costs of life, and work that does not pay are all at issue here, as are forms of practice attuned not to the reproduction of labor but to the optimization of payment. This book will suggest that, as a mode of social organization, the logic of speculation must be recognized not simply to have replaced a previous social order in a totalizing fashion, but as emergent and as subsisting alongside other modes. One feature of the logic of speculation is the active translation of existing cartographies of the social into the topographies of speculation.

In proposing that the logic of speculation must be understood both as a mode of accumulation centered on finance and money and as a specific mode of social organization, *The Time of Money* is necessarily making a further claim, namely, that the logic of speculation must be understood as a rationality that defines the telos of action. This book will suggest that what unites the two modes of speculation—that is, what precisely constitutes the logic of speculation *as* a rationality—is temporality. Indeed, the logic of speculation should be understood to concern a specific form of time. This is a time in which pasts, presents, and futures do not flow chronologically or in sequence but are open to a constant state of revision. This is also a time in which events cannot necessarily be foreseen but unfold in unpredictable ways. I suggest that it is along the flows of this indeterminate and nonchronological time that strategies to generate surplus via money and finance subsist, and it is the nonsynchronous tempos and rhythms of this time that mark the distinctiveness of a mode of social organization ordered by a logic of speculation. This book, then, is not only about money, finance, and emergent forms of social organization—it is also about time.

In *The Time of Money*, I suggest that the indeterminacy of speculative time should not be confused with a fragmentation or individualizing of time. As Elizabeth Freeman (2010) and Miranda Joseph (2014) have recently reminded us, time binds. Specific time universes bind people, spaces, and things together in a manner that enables coordinated action to take place—a point on which sociologists of time would most certainly agree. But more than this, specific time universes organize people and their actions in such a way as to maximize their capacities toward productivity. This latter was made dazzlingly clear by E. P. Thompson in his 1967 essay on the significance of the sociotechnical device of the mechanical clock. As Thompson noted, the mechanical clock afforded coordinated modes of action and life forms that organized and disciplined people and their practices to maximize their productivity—and especially their laboring productivity—for industrial capitalism.[1] But while Thompson suggested that the clock bound people and their actions to a mode of production centered on the direct extraction of surplus value from the human laboring body, in this book I outline a rather different scenario. I suggest that in the time of speculation (or the time of money) a range of sociotechnical devices—schedules, contracts, and timetables—bind people and their practices to a mode of accumulation centering on the generation of surplus from flows of money, including from flows of everyday money. Certainly, this involves specific laboring forms and laboring practices, including sporadic, intermittent, and uncertain forms of wage labor (as well as particular forms of employment contracting). But the logic of speculation does not center itself on laboring forms alone, precisely because the generation of surplus is centered on and in flows of money that are not contained in or by the coordinates of work or labor. In the time of speculation, what is critical instead are modes of practice through which the capacities of people in regard to flows of money can be activated and maximized. This includes the maximization of capacities in respect to payment streams flowing from households and capacities in the leveraging of volatile wages and other forms of income for mortgages, personal loans, and other forms of personal debt. At issue in regard to the sociotechnical devices of speculative time, therefore, is the affordance and organization of modes of practice that maximize the productivity of entire populations in regard to the creation of surplus from the nonchronological and indeterminate movements or flows of money.

It is important to make explicit that some analysts of present-day money and finance would balk at the idea put forth here that surplus value is generated from flows of money. This is because such analysts tie surplus creation to labor power, that is, to value-creating labor in the wage-labor relation, and understand finance as a process of making money from money that is parasitic on the creation of surplus from labor (see, e.g., Chesnais 2014; Fine 2010; Lapavitsas 2009).[2] In this book, I illustrate how neither modern-day labor nor modern-day finance approximates to these descriptions. I stress how the critical site for the creation of surplus in present-day finance-led capitalism is not wage labor but the everyday payments that households make to ensure their existence and how this concerns both poor and more affluent households alike. Through the mundane provision of streams of contracted payments to service mortgages and pay credit cards, utilities, and other household bills, households provide income streams to financial institutions and service providers that are sold on to finance markets. In turn, these contracted payments contribute to the creation of liquid assets in the form of securities in global finance markets. In this way, households are playing a critical role in the creation of financial securities, their viability, and their profitability. In recognition of this role, the process of the creation of liquid assets (securities) has been described as a "coproduction" between households and finance capital (Bryan, Rafferty, and Jefferis 2015).[3] It is through this mundane, albeit contracted, coproduction that households must be understood as incorporated into the production of value and as providing the conditions of possibility for the profitability of securities trading. Throughout this book, I highlight how this coproduction is organized and maximized through a set of devices that attune people and their practices to the nonchronological, indeterminate movements and flows of everyday money. I highlight, in other words, how this coproduction entails the opening out of practices that are speculative in form.

In assembling this intervention regarding speculation as a rationality, and especially as a form of time, this book draws on recent social and cultural theory, particularly recent feminist theory, on time and temporality. Such theorizing has precisely opened out how time can be understood as not necessarily flowing in one direction or another or proceeding in chronological sequence. Feminist theorists such as Rebecca Coleman (2008, 2010, 2014, 2016), Elizabeth Grosz (2000, 2004, 2010), and Iris van der Tuin (2015) have, for example, argued that it is precisely such a nonchronological time that can account for the movements of objects such as bodies as well as habits, sensations, and feeling states. It is on this body of work, as well as on adjacent work on temporality in cultural theory, cultural anthropology, and the philosophy of history, that I draw to map the features of speculative time. But also strongly in play throughout this book is social theory—unsurprisingly, since *The Time of Money* is concerned not only with speculation as a form of time but with speculation more broadly as a mode of social organization. Here my sources are wide-ranging and include figures from both classical and contemporary social theory. Thus, I engage with the classical social theory of Marx and Simmel as well as the contemporary social theory of Bourdieu, Nowotny, Feher, and Deleuze.

In many ways these figures may seem to be at odds with one another, especially when one considers that classical social theory was concerned with an entirely different social formation from that of today. Certainly, classical social theory was not engaged in any direct sense with a logic of speculation as both a mode of accumulation centered on money and a mode of social organization; that is, it was not concerned with speculation as a specific rationality. Marx, of course, did discuss speculation as a financial practice, and specifically speculation on money in money markets as constitutive of a specific form of capital, namely, what he termed fictitious capital. His explicit writings on speculation were, however, limited to this financial practice alone. Nonetheless, despite any direct or unequivocal engagement with speculation as a rationality, in this book I elaborate how classical figures such as Simmel and Marx have both an ongoing and renewed relevance in regard to certain features of this rationality. Simmel's writings on money, for example, especially his writings on money as a social form, find particular relevance when money operates not as a substance with fixed properties but as an in-motion, multidimensional surface. I also discuss why no consideration of the logic of speculation can proceed without acknowledging a debt to Marx, not least because of his understanding of industrial capitalism as comprising and operating by an extractive logic, especially a logic of the extraction of surplus value from laboring bodies, a logic that organized strategies for the creation of surplus value and configured social relations and social formations. Moreover, Marx made clear that to ensure both economic and social existence, people must enter into these relations and cannot subsist outside of them.

Marx, then, understood the extractive logic of industrial capitalism to operate precisely as a rationality. In proposing that the logic of speculation operates as a rationality, my debt to Marx is clear, although across the chapters of this book I propose that rather than through the extraction of surplus from laboring bodies, the axes of coordination of the logic of speculation concern the creation of surplus from the flows and movements of money.

As well as indicating how the logic of speculation necessitates recognition of the ongoing and renewed relevance of certain strands of classical social theory, *The Time of Money* also elaborates how this logic presents certain puzzles or problems for social theory, both classical and contemporary. I detail how such problems stretch particular forms of social theorizing to certain thresholds or limit points. These problems include money that cannot be represented, unemployment that demands labor, futures that might never arrive, wages that have no anchor, and money and debt that exist not as quantity, volume, quantum, or substance but as heterogenous processes that permanently and pervasively surround life. I suggest that these problems not only demand attention but also require social theorists and sociologists to rethink certain assumptions. These include but are by no means limited to assumptions regarding practice, temporality, labor, and money. I make clear how, in turn, such assumptions are fuelled by adherence to particular models of social organization and social formation within social theory, especially models designed to capture equivalence, fixed properties, determinacy, and the quantum of substances. Across the chapters that follow, I trace how the relevance of such models is being displaced—albeit unevenly—through the emergence of social forms whose dynamics involve unpredictability and indeterminacy. It is by means of a mapping of these dynamics that the problems posed for social theory by the logic of speculation can be made explicit and be addressed. It is, in other words, against these dynamics and these problems that social theory must be set and put to the test.

To elaborate the logic of speculation as a rationality, I engage, then, not only with allied bodies of work on time and temporality but also with various strands of social theory. Since I propose that as a rationality the logic of speculation operates not only as a mode of social organization but also as a mode of accumulation that centers on movements and flows of money, I also necessarily engage with a further body of work, namely, literature on money and finance. I draw in particular on recent literature from the studies of finance, especially those that have drawn attention to the ways in which finance does not stand discretely outside of society but how the logics of finance are increasingly present and thoroughly embedded in a wide range of domains historically designated as social (see, e.g., Allon 2015a; Cooper 2015; Cooper and Konings 2015; Konings 2015). I also draw on literature within the social studies of finance that has paid serious attention to the proliferation of financial instruments as well as to their operations. This includes literature that understands financial instruments as ordering devices, that is, not as benign instruments but as devices that actively intervene in the world (see, e.g., Esposito 2011; Mackenzie 2007; Nesvetailova 2015; Zaloom 2009). With reference to these bodies of work, as well as to literature that has recorded the shifting political economy of finance and finance markets, including financial expansion and the shifting political economy of consumer and household finance markets (see, e.g., Aalbers 2012; Konings 2010; Mehrling 2005; Panitich and Gindin 2005), I outline the dynamics of the generation of surplus from indeterminate flows and movements of money. Drawing on these bodies of work, I also consider how key sociotechnical innovations in regard to money and finance have afforded this form of surplus creation unprecedented intensity.

These sociotechnical innovations critically include the process of securitization, that is, the transformation of assets via legal and financial instruments into liquid securities (including asset-backed securities) that can be sold and traded on finance markets. While securitization is often understood to involve trading on assets (goods and commodities) that underlie securities (such as derivatives), throughout this book I stress how it is critical to understand that securitization entails a separation of securities—a separation achieved by means of securities contracts—from the ownership of assets that underlie them (Bryan and Rafferty 2014; Bryan, Rafferty, and Jefferis 2015; Poovey 2015). This separation means that securities trading does not concern trading on values (e.g., the value of houses) that exist in an external relation to securities and on which the value of securities rests, but instead concerns trading on securities themselves (e.g., the contracted payment streams that comprise home mortgages). In turn, securities consist of the attributes of the objects and subjects of securities contracts, including the attributes of contracted payments. These attributes are bundled together in risk-related tranches and traded. What is critical to take away from this is that the pricing (or value) of a security does not relate to the price of any underlying assets. Instead, it is determined by the bundling and trading of various attributes of money that comprise the securities themselves. It is also critical to understand that to talk of the process of securitization is to necessarily invoke a process in which the relations between money and value are at stake. It is important to understand as well that financial innovations such as securitization were, from the 1970s onward, US centered; in concert with the adoption of monetarist and neoliberal policies on the part of the US government, such innovations enabled American finance to emerge as the center of financial power, that is, as the center of financial expansion and finance-led accumulation (Gindin and Panitich 2012; Panitich and Gindin 2005; Panitich and Konings 2009). This process has taken place by way of complex webs of institutional linkages and associations with, for example, the practices and institutions of American finance thoroughly embedded in what have now become global financial markets.[4]

Across the chapters that follow I discuss how the process of securitization is not only central to the intense productivity of money and finance in regard to capital accumulation but integral to a range of critical developments in the political economy of money, including in consumer finance markets, that is, markets for mortgages and personal loans. These developments include expansions and extensions to these markets as well as transformations to mortgages and other forms of consumer finance products. They also include transformations to the calculus of consumer borrowing and, in particular, the emergence of what I term in this book a calculus of securitized debt. This calculus embeds debt and borrowing not in the probables of repayment but in the possibles of servicing debt, that is, in the possibles of payment. It is these transformations, I suggest, that are at the heart of the explosion of debt and indebtedness, including debt that outruns working and lived lives and debt that if indexed against income can never be repaid. Thus, I point to how mass indebtedness as a surround to life is hardwired into the process of the creation of surplus through the movements and flows of money. But more than this, I suggest that it is in these sets of transformations that the productivity of populations in regard to this mode of accumulation is harnessed and maximized, not least via the schedules and rhythms of securitized debt.[5]

As this suggests, and as I have already adumbrated, I do not limit the generation of surplus from the flows and movements of money, or the speculative logic that is at its heart, to specialist financial exchanges alone. Nor do I suggest that this mode of the generation of surplus is contained within differentiated sites such as finance markets. Instead, I suggest that a logic of speculation in regard to money is "everyday." *The Time of Money* is therefore not only concerned with the operations of the logic of speculation in ordering and organizing the capacities and movements of money and trading on money in roving finance markets (including trade on the movements of asset-backed securities), but also with how the logic of speculation orders and organizes everyday mundane money. Two forms of everyday money in particular will be considered: first, as suggested in my discussion above, household and personal debt; and second, the money exchanged for labor power, that is, money in the form of wages.

In focusing on these forms of everyday money, the book draws inspiration from writers in the discipline of cultural studies (Allon 2010, 2014; La Berge 2014a, 2014b; Martin 2002, 2013) who are concerned with how accumulation via money and finance does not operate at a distance from everyday lives or ordinary worlds but yields a distinct set of everyday practices, routines, and habits.[6] Fiona Allon (2010, 2014), for example, has described an everyday culture of finance operating in owner-occupied households. Here, not only do homeowners see homes and dwellings as assets to speculate on, but the very location of the home as an asset gives rise to a distinct set of practices—such as financial management and accounting—that form part of the routines of everyday household life, in fact constitute a form of household labor. Research such as Allon's documents, then, how everyday life is being reordered and rescripted in the context of accumulation via money and finance. Indeed, her research points to a broad and wide-ranging process of the embedding of a rationality of accumulation via money and finance in everyday life. With startling foresight, in

2002 Randy Martin named this process the financialization of daily life.[7] In this context, it is important to register that such insights draw on and align with a longer tradition in the disciplines of sociology and cultural studies that, through figures such as Benjamin, Simmel, de Certeau, and Gramsci, locates the everyday and the mundane as critical conjunctural scenes or sites for the investigation of socioeconomic and sociopolitical phenomena, and especially social and political change (Hall 1978, 1979, 1980; Highmore 2002, 2011; Williams 1989 [1958], 1961, 1977). My focus on everyday forms of money in this book is, then, to an important extent indebted to work in cultural studies on the financialization of daily life and in broader terms to this longer tradition in sociology and cultural studies concerning the everyday. While this longer tradition has often been called upon to look to the everyday as a site of inventiveness and especially resistance to dominant orders and modes of representation, my concern with the everyday in this book is of a rather different order. Specifically, my concern is not to trace resistance in the ordinary or in the poetics of everyday life but to understand how, through everyday money, the productivity of populations in regard to a mode of accumulation centered on the generation of surplus via the movements and flows of money is harnessed and maximized.

In assembling its line of intervention regarding the logic of speculation, *The Time of Money* therefore has a number of key touchstones or points of reference: feminist theory, social theory, the social studies of finance, the political economy of finance and of finance markets, and cultural analyses of the everyday. To lay out this intervention, I proceed across a number of cases or case studies. These, however, are more than cases in a dry technical or methodological sense; rather, they are zones or sites of intensity in regard to the logic of speculation. They are zones or sites in which a logic of speculation is actively displacing a logic of accumulation and social organization based on principles of equilibrium, stability, and stasis in which pasts, presents, and futures proceed chronologically and in sequence. The sites or zones I include here are finance markets, state-led austerity programs, household and personal debt, wages, and state-led programs that seek to activate the labor of the unemployed and underemployed. These sites, moreover, do not simply host or house a logic of speculation; their dynamics and characteristics unfold with it.

Read in sequence, the chapters that follow could be understood to chart a set of unfolding events leading to and flowing from the 2007–8 financial crisis. That is, they could be read as recording a set of practices that led to a rupture and a set of wide-ranging and devastating consequences ensuing from that rupture, including sovereign debt crises, the rolling out of state-managed programs to address so-called spending deficits, plummeting wage rates, spiraling household and personal debt, home repossessions, rocketing unemployment rates, and expansions to underemployment and precarious employment. My strong contention in this book is that phenomena that are so often identified as outcomes of the global financial crisis—that is, as outcomes of a rupture or break in an otherwise normal state of affairs—are in fact permanent features of contemporary capitalism. They must be understood in terms of the dynamics of the logic of speculation, whose historicity is longer term than the financial crisis and its aftermath, and moreover, is still unfolding. Rather than being a temporary postcrisis aberration, wage stagnation, for example, predates the financial crisis and results from a long-term restructuring of money and the relationship between money and labor. And while the securitization of assets (and especially the trade in securitized subprime mortgages) is often understood as being at the very heart of the financial crisis, in this book I understand securitization as being connected to longer-term shifts in the operations and dynamics of finance markets, money, and the design and operation of financial products, especially consumer finance products. Indeed, notwithstanding the crisis of liquidity in 2007–8, the process of securitization has continued apace, although in regard to mortgage markets in particular, banks and financial institutions such as the European Central Bank now encourage what is rather euphemistically termed "high quality" securitization. Indeed, I propose that even mechanisms and measures that ostensibly appear to have been designed to deal with problems that the global financial crisis unfolded and to return us to a more stable and secure state of affairs are in fact fundamental to the logic of speculation. Austerity measures and programs, for example, should be understood as provoking and extending a political economy of debt, that is, as operating to further enroll the productivity of populations in the generation of surplus via movements and flows of money.

In setting out its key lines of intervention, I therefore necessarily engage with and disrupt a series of commonplace, popular, and well-rehearsed assumptions regarding the financial crisis and its aftermath. These include the assumptions that the financial crisis was the outcome of reckless and irresponsible actions on the part of financial traders, banks, and financial institutions; that trading in and on money involves trade in fictitious forms of capital adrift from the real economy and real value; and that trading on money is destructive of the future. They also include the assumptions that redistributions of resources, especially redistributions of money, can redress exacerbating forms of post-financial-crisis inequality; that mass debt empties time of creativity and possibility; that reconnecting wages to the value created by laboring activities can counter wage repression and stagnation; and that the post–financial crisis era has returned us, or will return us, to previous forms of socioeconomic existence, especially to a range of undesirable states, both real and imagined. What is so fascinating about these assumptions from the point of view of my concerns in this book is that so many of them center on issues of time and temporality: for instance, the closing down of time, backwards movements in time, and the hollowing out of the potentiality of time. Indeed, as I detail in Chapter 1, in the context of austerity, mass debt, and rising unemployment, the post–global financial crisis era has witnessed demands for time itself. One question that this book seeks to address, therefore, is how and why concerns about our current juncture are so often articulated as concerns about time and especially as concerns about inappropriate movements of time and/or uses of time. I conjecture that, in part, it is precisely because the logic of speculation is opening out a specific temporal universe that disquiet about the present is so often expressed as a concern over time.

Chapter 1 begins the exploration of the logic of speculation by way of a focus on finance markets. It addresses the claim that at the heart of the 2007–8 financial crisis lay unregulated and excessive speculation on the part of finance traders and finance houses, an excess often understood in terms of a normative (and I would add, following the insights of queer theorists such as Lee Edelman [2004], a heteronormative) account of time. Here, traders, banks, and financial institutions stood accused of trading on the future at the expense of the present. This narrative of time degeneracy, moreover, structured and fuelled (and continues to fuel) a range of protests and political mobilizations in the post–financial crisis era. By focusing not on the actions of traders but on movements and flows of money in financial markets, I show that at issue in regard to finance markets, and specifically post–Bretton Woods agreement finance markets, is not a trade on the future but a shifting relationship between time and money. In such markets, time is not a simple vessel through which money flows and moves; rather, money and time merge together. I describe how this shifting relationship between time and money is linked to the so-called deregulation or liberalization of money and finance, especially to the floating of the price of currencies (particularly the US dollar) and interest rates. Here, then, I begin to lay out the distinct temporality of the logic of speculation and how channels for profit lie in the movements of this time. In this context I ask what forms of social theory can engage with this time. I suggest that a possibly surprising candidate for such an engagement is Pierre Bourdieu—not the Bourdieu of capital and fields, that is, the Bourdieu of social substances, but the more phenomenological Bourdieu, the Bourdieu of practice.

In Chapter 2, my attention turns to state responses to the financial crisis and the recessions that followed. I attend particularly to programs of austerity, that is, to programs ostensibly designed to cut state budgets, debts, and deficits via reductions in public spending, wages, and prices. My focus is on austerity policies in the UK, especially on the widespread claim made on the part of a range of social progressives that such measures—and especially cuts to public spending—are contributing to an intensification of and extension to already existing forms of social inequality. Taking feminist debates on austerity in the UK as a case in point, I elaborate on how strategies of redistribution—and especially the redistribution of money—have been proposed as a tactic to redress such deepening inequalities. Yet through a consideration of how the capacities of money have shifted in a context of pervasive financial expansion, I ask, Can money deliver social justice? To pursue this question, I revisit the demands of the UK's women's liberation movement, particularly the assumption at play in these demands that money both measures and distributes justice. I suggest that while such assumptions were relevant at that moment (i.e., during the last gasps of the Fordist-Keynesian era and at the threshold of a dynamic set of changes that would unfold a post-Fordist global order in which the logic of speculation dominates), transformations to the capacities of money (i.e., transformations to what money can do) now leave its injustice-remedying capacities in doubt.

But more than tracking the shifting capacities of money—a transformation that I characterize as involving a shift away from money serving as a universal broker of equivalence and privileged measure of value toward money operating as a value in and of itself—in this chapter I also propose that recognition of this shift necessarily demands an entirely different understanding of austerity. Specifically, instead of programs to cut debt, and especially sovereign debt, austerity must be understood as provoking more debt, and especially more personal debt; that is, austerity must be understood to involve a political strategy through which the economy of debt—and the operations of money as a value—is being extended, an extension that enrolls the productivity of populations in the generation of surplus via the movements and flows of money. This chapter therefore not only outlines transformations to money as central to the logic of speculation but also begins to articulate the enrollment of people in modes of practice in which their productivity regarding the creation of surplus from money is both activated and expanded.

This enrollment is confronted more directly in Chapter 3, where my attention turns to mass indebtedness, especially to the schedules and rhythms of securitized debt. That is, here I address the issue of the temporality of securitized debt. Against the widespread view that the time of mass debt undermines the potentiality and creativity of time, I outline the time universe of securitized debt and the binding of people to this time. This, moreover, concerns a binding to nonchronological time, or what I term here speculative time or the time of speculation. I elaborate how central to this time and this binding is the operation of the calculus of securitized debt, a calculus concerned not with the probable but with the possible, and in particular, not with working lives of repayment but with lifetimes of payment. I outline, therefore, how the calculus of securitized debt not only concerns working populations but also the jobless, the job seeking, the unemployed, the wageless, the underemployed, and the potentially employed.

I detail how the calculus of securitized debt not only continuously seeks income streams across whole populations but also affords variable and adjustable schedules of debt whose very variability is fundamental to the generation of surplus via indeterminate movements and flows of money. Moreover, these variable schedules activate the capacities of populations in regard to that variability, especially capacities in regard to the payment of the possible. I set out how these schedules open out modes of practice that maximize the productivity of populations in regard to the generation of surplus from the movements of money. Here, then, speculation as a mode of accumulation and speculation as a mode of social organization collide. Moreover, they do so via everyday money, that is, money paid by every-day households to service debt. But more than this, I point to the ways in which, in regard to everyday securitized debt, an active translation of social cartographies into topographies of speculation is at play. I elaborate how at issue in regard to everyday securitized debt is a double movement relating to the social: the calculus of securitized debt both works on the social and transforms it, turning social attributions into distributed financial attributions or risk exposures. I suggest that this movement is critical for any un-derstanding of how the calculus of securitized debt is rewriting the social, not as a closed field or substance but as open to continuous processes of disassembly and reassembly.

In Chapter 4, I consider a further form of everyday money, namely, wages or money paid in exchange for labor. It is well documented that, in the Global North, wages are stagnant. Indeed, a pervasive gap has opened out between what labor earns and what it needs to spend, with indebted laboring now a ubiquitous and entrenched standard. In this chapter I de-scribe how, to date, these features of wages have been connected to a broad range of processes, including the expansion of precariousness as both a form of work and a way of life, attacks on social reproduction, new forms of the extraction of surplus, the dismantling of the social wage, and a general-ized intensification of the powers of capital vis-à-vis labor. I also consider a range of strategies that have been proposed to tackle the problems as-sociated with wages, strategies that cohere around seeking to anchor value expressed in the money form in labor—that is, in reconnecting value with labor. In this chapter I elaborate how these strategies sidestep and bracket broader transformations to the capacities of money, transformations that render money an unstable and unpredictable measure of any value, including value that might or might not be constituted by labor. I lay out how such transformations to the capacities of money have rendered money an in-motion surface that does not and cannot represent the value of other things in any straightforward fashion. Such transformations to the capacities of money demand a focus not on what wages should measure or comprise and/or, *pace* Marx, on wages as the price of labor, but on what wages can do or might do, that is, on their potentiality. In this chapter I therefore map how the logic of speculation involves not only transformations to the capacities of money but also a reworking of the relationship between labor and money. This reworking means that any analysis of wages should focus precisely on what wages are, namely, money, and in particular on how wages serve as an access point to what money might or might not set in motion. Critically, what is at issue in the reworking of the relationship between wages and labor is not a repression of the waged worker but rather the replacement of the free laborer—who must exchange his or her labor for a wage and who strives to accumulate human capital in an attempt to maximize that exchange—by what Michel Feher (2009) has termed the speculative subject. Extending Feher's thesis, I suggest that this is a subject who must speculate not only on his or her (stagnant) wages *as money* but on his or her whole life and lifetime. At stake in the reworking of wages from the price of labor to wages as money are therefore major transformations to the social.

In the fifth and final substantive chapter of this book, my attention turns more directly to the question of the labor. Perhaps paradoxically for a chapter concerned with labor, my focus is on unemployment, not least because in the present, by means of a set of coordinated sociotechnical interventions targeted at the jobless and the wageless, the relationship of unemployment to employment is being rewritten, while at the same time a restructuring of labor is taking place on the very ground of unemployment. Operating under the banner of employment activation, these interventions command unemployed populations to participate in a range of activities, including work and work-like activities. As I make clear, what is critical in regard to these activities is that they not only render unemployment a site of busyness but also demand that the unemployed always stand ready for work, even if employment never arrives. Indeed, just as their precariously employed counterparts stand patiently but restlessly in the hope of waged work that is never guaranteed, the unemployed stand in perpetual readiness for work—whether waged or unwaged—whose arrival cannot be predicted or foreseen. And just as employment increasingly concerns a set of events that take place in unpredictable ways, unemployment concerns a set of variable events that might not even take place. At issue here is a restructuring and rewriting of labor organized by the logic of speculation, a rewriting that activates and opens out the capacities and productivity of the wageless and the jobless in regard to events that have not yet happened and might never do so. In this chapter I describe how this rewriting of labor both erodes historical distinctions between employment and unemployment and ties and binds unemployed populations to the logic of speculation through the command to adapt to the possible, that is, to the movements of indeterminate speculative time. While activation regimes have previously been identified as operating as a policy analogue to flexible labor markets, I suggest that they should properly be identified instead as a policy analogue to the creation of surplus via the indeterminate movements and flows of money, not least because of their opening out of modes of everyday practice that are speculative in form.

In this chapter I also highlight how the developments it charts—especially the making productive of unemployment—might be identified by many social scientists as involving the process of economization, that is, the folding of the economy into society. This is especially so for a certain strand of post-Marxist thinkers who have identified the process of economization as concerning a movement of laboring and value-producing activities away from the formally productive sphere and their dispersal across the social body. I make clear, however, that in their focus on the extraction of value from laboring activities located in the social body, such analyses entirely miss how a logic of extraction has been replaced by a logic of speculation—indeed, how understanding the making productive of unemployment in such a register would be to entirely sideline the activation and maximization of the productive capacities of populations in regard to this logic.

There is one further matter at issue in this chapter: how the post–financial crisis era has been and continues to be understood to evidence how the generation of surplus via finance and money is corrosive and disruptive of the social order. Thus, one recurring diagnosis of this era is that accumulation via finance and money is inherently unstable and that this instability threatens to return us, or has returned us, to previous forms of socioeconomic existence, especially to undesirable past states of being. A range of commentators have, for example, pointed to the ways in which increases in unemployment since the financial crisis, and especially increasing rates of job loss for women, threatened a return of the exclusionary sexual contract of the Fordist-Keynesian era—indeed, to "send women back to the kitchen." As I make clear, such sentiments thoroughly bypass transformations to labor that have taken place across post-Fordist economies since the late 1970s, including how interventions in regard to unemployed populations work to position all potential workers, including all potential women workers—no matter what their circumstances—as always needing to work. I elaborate how, rather than returning us to a previous social order, such commands form part of the terms of an emergent sexual contract. Across a number of chapters in this book, I discuss how the contours and coordinates of this contract are at issue not only in interventions targeted at unemployed populations but in broad-scale transformations to the management of life and economic growth, including in shifts to the political economy of money. I indicate, in particular, how the coordinates of this contract are implicated in extensions to consumer finance markets, transformations to finance products, and the shifting capacities of money itself.

Rather than charging the accumulation of surplus via finance with being corrosive of the social order and/or marking the return of previously existing social forms, this book views it as unfolding a particular social world, indeed, as involving a specific mode of social organization that yields particular social forms. In making this claim it aligns itself with the work of a number of scholars who have rallied against the view that the expansion of finance has disordered and destabilized the social and instead recognizes that one of the most important challenges facing the social sciences today is the development of understandings of the penetration of money and finance into human life (Allon 2015a; Bryan and Rafferty 2014; Cooper and

Konings 2015; de Goede 2015; Martin 2002, 2015). In positing that the logic of speculation operates as a rationality—that is, as both a mode of accumulation and a mode of social organization that are united by time—this book should be understood as contributing to this broader project. In the chapters that follow I seek to add substance and life to these claims.

CHAPTER 1

Money on the Move

The global financial crisis and its aftermath, including ongoing economic turbulence and recession, sovereign debt crises and continuing state debt emergencies, unemployment and underemployment, and punishing (and increasingly embedded and institutionalized) austerity measures, have rendered the lives of increasing numbers of people precarious and vulnerable. This is witnessed not only in rising unemployment and underemployment rates (International Labour Organization 2015) but also in welfare and public service cuts, unmanageable household and personal debt, wage freezes and cuts, plummeting pensions, tax increases, and ongoing labor market reforms that are eroding the rights of the employed and the potentially employed and further entrenching the contingent and precarious contract of contemporary capitalism. Little wonder that one of the refrains heard across debt- and austerity-hit territories in the post–financial crisis era has been—and continues to be—"no future." In Spain, for example, a protest movement emerging after the financial crisis organized under the banner of Juventud Sin Futuro (Youth Without a Future). The self-defined precarious movement is disillusioned by a range of issues: skyrocketing youth unemployment rates (which have stood for some time at over 50 percent [Eurostat 2015]); ongoing government spending cuts; the privatization of education; labor market and labor law reforms; the prospect of a whole lifetime of unemployment and/or precarious employment; insecure housing; and last, no guaranteed retirement income. Prevailing socio-economic conditions, the movement maintains, are dispossessing Spain's youth of a future. Juventud Sin Futuro, therefore, rallies against the disappearance of the future as a horizon of possibility and hope. Its participants also demand mobilization and action against the ongoing process of dispossession. Juventud Sin Futuro may have no home, no job, and no retirement, but according to one of their slogans, they have no fear and refuse to become a lost generation (Juventud Sin Futuro 2011).[1]

It is not only Juventud Sin Futuro that decries diminished prospects or the absence of a future. In early 2012, at protests in Greece against the ongoing debt crisis and parliamentary approval of tough austerity measures, one protestor commented: "I wish I could hope for a better future . . . but Greece is just living day to day" (in Kakissis 2012). Another protestor proclaimed, "It's like the end of the world" (ibid.). And while protestors condemned emptied futures, a young Greek woman—interviewed by a journalist reporting for *The Guardian* newspaper—observed: "The previous generation didn't think so much about the future. They grew up dreaming

Figure 1.1. "Sin Casa, Sin Curro, Sin Pensión, Sin Miedo," 2011. Photograph: Dominique Faget / AFP / Getty Images. Used with permission.

of having work, money, a home and family and educating their children and here we are educated . . . but with no work or money. . . . [T]here is no way you can have dreams or make plans" (in Smith et al. 2012). Fears regarding an absent or hollowed-out future were also expressed at 2012 protests against labor reforms and ongoing spending cuts in Spain. One protestor said he was protesting because he was "worried about his grandchildren's future" (in Goodman 2012). Another said she was protesting against the employment practices of commercial businesses: "[T]hey offer you internships for one year and then fire you without severance pay. There is no future for young people here" (ibid.). According to another protestor, who at the time was employed as a university researcher: "[C]ontracts are getting worse every year. They [the government] say they want to invest in the future while cutting research budgets. They're not looking to the future but to the next election with cuts dictated from Brussels" (in Day and Cobos 2012). And while hundreds of thousands of people protested against the hollowed-out, precarious, and compromised futures brought about by labor market reform, in an ironic twist the Spanish prime minister Mariano Rajoy remarked that "[w]hen we designed this reform we were thinking of the people who are out of work, who see no future" (ibid.).

Cancelling the Future

While desires and demands for better futures might be seen as leitmotifs of the post–global financial crisis era, they should nonetheless be treated with caution. This is so not least because, as Lee Edelman (2004) has argued, desires for better futures are very often structured by what he terms a reproductive futurism and yearnings for a heteronormative social order.[2] Such futures, Edelman notes, are invariably imagined and conceived through heteronormative figures, including the figure of the innocent child. While such a reproductive futurism is clearly at issue in the cries of "no future" in post–financial crisis Europe, evidenced in the mobilization of the figure of the child to make such declarations, what is also of interest, and perhaps not incidentally, is the idea that the global financial crisis and the events that have unfolded from it have interrupted the proper flow of time, especially a time in which pasts, presents, and futures flow chronologically and in sequence, or to put it another way, that the global financial crisis and the events that have unfolded from it have dispossessed (and continue to strip) people of a future, especially a future that flows from the present and operates as a horizon of hope and possibility. Declarations of no future heard across austerity-hit and debt-torn Europe should thus be understood not only as protests against forbidding socioeconomic prospects but as declarations regarding the improper flow of time. This is, of course, not to suggest that the lives of growing numbers of people are not increasingly precarious, or to suggest that socioeconomic inequalities, especially those based on wealth, are not intensifying (Piketty 2014).[3] Rather, it is to draw attention to how concerns about the lived present in the post–financial crisis era are often expressed as concerns about (and as demands for a different) time, especially concerns about the improper flow of time or, perhaps more precisely, about interruptions to the proper flow of time, in particular the flow of the future and its relationship to the present.

In this context, it is important to register that the historicity of such concerns cannot necessarily be reduced to the post–financial crisis era alone. Indeed, reducing concerns about the emptying out of the temporal form of the future to the post–financial crisis era would be to sidestep analyses suggesting that at issue may in fact be a long-term process that cannot be tied to a particular set of socioeconomic events or to any particular mode of experience relating to socioeconomic position or positioning. Franco Berardi, for example, suggests that, in the contemporary present, the future is over. He posits that the twentieth century was the "century that trusted in the future" (Berardi 2011, 17). Fuelled by the experience of capitalist economic growth, especially by the experience of apparently limitless growth, as well as by the machinery of industrialization promising the endless transgression of limits, Berardi suggests that the idea of the future, and especially a progressive future, was central to the energy and principles of the twentieth century. The future, he maintains, reached its peak in the second part of the nineteenth century and the first part of the twentieth, when it became not simply a belief but "true faith" (ibid., 18). Indeed, he notes how political action was reframed in the light of this faith in the future. Thus, all of the different families of modern political theory—from liberalism to anarchism—share one certainty: "notwithstanding the darkness of the present, the future will be bright" (ibid.).

Yet while the future fuelled economic, social, and political action in the twentieth century, the future—Berardi maintains—is now over. The slow cancellation of the future got underway, he claims, in the 1970s and 1980s, a time when the perception of the future began to shift and a postfuturist mood began to emerge. Thus, in 1977 British punks adopted what at the time seemed to be a nonsensical cry of "no future." This perception of the future, Berardi says, is now a generalized condition. We do not, he asserts, believe in the future in the same way. Of course we know that a time after the present is going to come, but "we don't expect that it will fulfill the promises of the present" (Berardi 2011, 25). Our postfuturist mood, he continues, is based on the awareness that the future is not going to be bright. Yet, crucially, this postfuturist sensibility is not one that has simply emerged in light of or in response to problematic external events or moments of crisis. Thus, a postfuturist sensibility cannot be explained with reference to events such as economic crisis, climate change, or natural disasters that have blighted, interfered with, or interrupted the flow of the future and its relationship with the present. On the contrary, rather than concerning crises that have temporarily and violently cut agents loose from the future, the emergence of a postfuturist sensibility concerns a *shift in time itself*.

Berardi understands this shift to concern a colonization of the domain of time, or what he terms the colonization of the mind and perception, a colonization that has ensured that the future has collapsed. The collapse of the future, he argues, is "rooted in the acceleration of psychic and cognitive rhythm" (Berardi 2011, 23), an acceleration entangled with changes to capitalism and especially with how "the whole psychosphere of the human being becomes subject to the movement of capital, now operating at digital speeds" (Genosko and Thoburn 2011, 5). For Berardi, therefore, the collapse of the future is tied to the ways in which the capacities of capital to assemble and orchestrate labor have not only extended spatially but also intensified along a temporal dimension. Hence, while more and more workers are precariously employed on temporary, short-term, sporadic, and intermittent bases, work and production increasingly involve the elaboration of constantly moving fractal entities assembled only at the exact moment they are required. Today's firms are interested mainly in these moments, but the entire working day of laborers is "subjected to this kind of production, pulsating and available, like a brain-sprawl in waiting . . . [b]lackberries and mobile phones ever ready" (ibid.). Workers are therefore in a state of constant expectation, or in stand-by mode, not knowing exactly when or if they may be required but nonetheless existing in a continuous state of restless availability.

It is these long-term shifts in capital accumulation, especially an intensification of the capacities of capital to assemble and mobilize labor in time, that, for Berardi, account for the closing down of the temporal form of the future—indeed, that have opened out an eternal present in which the future cannot be known or sensed and is beyond the grasp of human intervention. The future has, in short, closed down because capital requires workers to exist in a never-ending present. Understood from this point of view—that is, in terms of a long-term process of the closing down of the future—the cries of "no future" heard across austerity-hit and debt-loaded Europe should not necessarily be understood as evidence of forms of critique or as demands for different forms of time but as expressions of the eternal present of postfuturism, a present in which the future—or more precisely, the time after the present—can no longer deliver on hopes, promises, or dreams. Indeed, understood from this point of view, a postfuturist mood should not be attributed to or associated with the dispossessed—for instance, the unemployed, the precariously employed, mortgage defaulters, or the homeless—but understood as a generalized condition. As will become clear in what follows, such an understanding raises particular questions and challenges for prevailing understandings of the future and especially for claims that the global financial crisis concerned an excessive orientation to (and trading in) the yet-to-come. While this understanding raises such questions, however, I will also suggest in this chapter that Berardi is mistaken in his diagnosis of the shutting down of the temporal form of the future, not least because the context of financial expansion has witnessed a shifting relationship between time and events.

Trading the Future

While Berardi insists that the temporal form of the future as a plane of hope and possibility is over, and one implication of his analysis is that the post–financial crisis era should not be located as synchronous or coterminous with the emergence of a postfuturist mood, a frequently rehearsed (and popular) account of the financial crisis and its aftermath suggests that the financial crisis did, in fact, concern specific mutations to time. This is an account, however, that does not foreground a closing down of the future but instead an excessive orientation toward the forthcoming, to future-oriented action and future events—an orientation that is deleterious to and destabilizing of the lived present. At issue here is how financial practices, especially the practices and instruments implicated in the global financial crisis, have been (and continue to be) understood to constitute a trading of the future: specifically, as involving a betting on future events—a betting (and bets on those bets) on events that have not yet taken place and might never do so, a trade that is assumed to take place at the expense of the present. Since the financial crisis, finance traders, dealers, and finance capital more generally therefore stood accused, and continue to stand accused,[4] of creating an unstable and compromised present due to irresponsible and excessive speculation on the future. At stake in particular here is alleged excessive and reckless speculation on not yet realized (albeit anticipated and calibrated) gains on the net worth of future income or payment streams. In volume 3 of *Capital* Marx refers to such forms of predicted (but not yet realized) gains, along with the bets placed on them, as fictitious capital. Bubbles of fictitious capital, so the story goes, inevitably reach a limit point and burst when claims on not yet existing value (or claims on the future) begin to excessively outstrip already existing or "real" surplus value.

Accounts of such excessive trading on the future abound. Thus, shortly after the financial crisis, Vicanne Adams, Michelle Murphy, and Adele E. Clarke declared that the economic recession (or Great Recession) that unfolded from the crisis was "sparked by finance capital's delirious trade in futures and risks" (Adams et al. 2009, 254). Robin Blackburn described such trade, and especially the anticipation of gains before they have been realized, as being due to aspirations on the part of finance engineers to

"move the world without securing the land on which they stand" (Blackburn 2008, 84). Indeed, along with a range of commentators, Blackburn
paralleled the global financial crisis to the 1929 Wall Street crash.[5] He
suggested that, just as the latter was fuelled by the bursting of a speculative bubble centered on property bonds, in 2007–8 "speculative financial
instruments based on property mortgages . . . also collapsed" (ibid., 93).
This account of the global financial crisis as the outcome of excessive (and
accelerated) speculative activity—of an excessive and unchecked trade on
the future—is one that has continued to have traction in the post–financial
crisis era. François Chesnais, for example, recently described the global
financial crisis as concerning a "feverish attempt to make money without
the intervention of the process of production" (Chesnais 2014, 79). He
concedes that since the financial crisis, the "growth of the notional value
of fictitious capital . . . has been spectacular" (ibid., 78), but nonetheless—
and given that Chesnais positions this value as fictitious and not real—he
suggests that within the mass of this fictitious capital lies "the threat of
new episodes of major worldwide financial crisis" (ibid., 73). Indeed, for
Chesnais (and despite apparent evidence to the contrary) the trade in and
value of fictitious capital will inevitably falter when claims on the future
excessively outstrip real surplus value. While Chesnais points to the threat
of new financial crises immanent to trading on the future and always already existing structural limits on speculation set by the real economy (see
also Thompson 2016), in a systems theory register Elena Esposito likewise
notes how finance capital and finance markets trade the future (Esposito
2011, 1). But whereas writers such as Chesnais and Blackburn locate unfet-
tered speculative practice as central to this trade and build-ups of bubbles
of fictitious capital as posing immanent threats to the present, if not full-
blown crises, Esposito elaborates on the significance of complex financial
instruments and especially derivatives (including options, swaps, and forwards) in this process, especially in post–Bretton Woods agreement global
finance markets.

I will come back to the idea that financial value and finance capital are
fictitious and somehow less real than other forms of value and capital in
later chapters, and I will return to the significance and capacities of financial instruments in post–Bretton Woods agreement finance markets later

in this chapter. For now, however, I want to reflect a little more on the idea that financial trading—that is, speculative practices (and especially those practices widely posited to have culminated in the global financial crisis)— involves an excessive trade in and orientation to the future. I want to consider, in particular, the manner in which this understanding of financial practices and of the 2007–8 global financial crisis shares much in common with—and might be productively located in terms of—a broader strand of thinking within the contemporary social sciences and humanities. This is a strand of thought that posits that the present is characterized by an intensification in anticipatory ways of life or in states of anticipation. Adams, Murphy, and Clarke (2009) make this connection explicit in their proposition that the trade in futures and risks by finance capital makes plain that our current moment is defined by a state of anticipation, a thinking and living toward events that have not yet taken place and might never do so. As this suggests, at issue here is not merely practices in finance markets on the part of traders and dealers and/or the operations of financial instruments, but a generalized state of anticipation.

Indeed, across a range of disciplines a number of socioeconomic phenomena have been identified as evidencing such a generalized state of anticipation. In addition to speculative financial practices, these include consumers mortgaging their futures in the form of indebtedness to secure commodities in the here and now (Law 2009); farmers obtaining credit on the basis of what might happen to their crops (Adams et al. 2009); company and organization valuations not made on the grounds of present assets but on those of events yet to come (Marazzi 2007); calculations of the value of workers and workforces not made on the basis of existing skills, experiences, and capabilities but on their potential ability or ability to deal with events that have yet to take place (Adkins 2008; Beckert 2016; Sennett 2006); the emergence of consumer preferences that are anticipated before they have been chosen, via the predictive algorithms of big data (Amoore and Piotukh 2015); the advent of anticipatory policy and legal instruments that endeavor to both predict and preempt events that have not yet taken place (Amoore 2013; de Goede 2012; Kerr and Earle 2013); and the creation of liquidity (and profits) via financial tools and devices in relation to events yet to come (Esposito 2011).

Significantly for my concerns here, such anticipatory practices are very often identified and understood in negative terms. Adams, Murphy, and Clarke (2009), for example, display such a stance in a set of reflections on strategies of refusal in regard to anticipation, while Richard Sennett argues that the shift in skill from embodied and accumulated capacities to potential ability that he describes not only raises the specter of uselessness but also deprives people of a sense of narrative movement, of the accumulation of experience and connections between events in time. It also "eschews sensate impressions, divides analyzing from believing, ignores the glue of emotional attachment, penalizes digging deep" (Sennett 2006, 121–22). As such sentiments suggest, accounts of increasingly anticipatory forms of life often carry with them a set of normative assumptions regarding time (as well as social ordering). These include the assumption that the future should be at some distance from the present (or that a boundary should exist between the present and the future); the conjecture that the future can (and should) be protected via prudent action in the here and now; the assumption that the future should not be traded as a resource in the present (i.e., that the future should not be commodified and/or colonized); and the supposition that the future should not determine or govern the present. In her discussion of the global financial crisis, Elena Esposito makes such normative thinking explicit when she asks: "Why was it wrong to sell one's own future and those of others in the present?" (Esposito 2011, 157). Her response to this question is that in making use of the future in the present—a process she refers to as de-futurization—finance markets limited (and continue to limit) the future as an opening and a space of possibilities.[6] As a consequence, she claims, the present "has less available future" (ibid., 181). Indeed, she calls for what she terms a "conscious (and empirically appropriate) use of time" in finance markets (ibid., 186), one that rather than closing down the future via present use allows for relatively open possibilities via the embrace of (regulatory) techniques that do not allow for excessive de-futurization. We might then add to the list of normative assumptions made by writers concerned with anticipatory practices and modes of life the supposition that the future should stand in an appropriate ratio and volume to the present, that is, that the present have an appropriate quantity of future available to itself.

As I will make clear in Chapter 3, it is not only Esposito who positions the operations of finance markets and the process of financialization more generally as closing down the possibilities of time and especially of the future. For now, however, I want to highlight two further assumptions at play in accounts of increasingly anticipatory modes of life. The first of these is that the present, or more precisely, a certain version of the present—one in which, on Sennett's account, experience can be accumulated and connections can be made between events in time—is being destroyed by a specific relationship to the future, namely, by the injunction to anticipate. For Sennett, then, a constant looking to the future creates a present that not only is deprived of any narrative potential but also cannot and does not promise or provide any form of security. The second assumption is the idea that the injunction to think and live in the direction of the future is relatively new, or at the very least, has intensified in our current moment.

In highlighting this string of assumptions about time, and in particular, assumptions about how time should flow and how the future should stand in relation to the present, I seek to do more than draw attention to their operation in accounts of anticipatory modes of life: in addition, I want to make clear just how problematic such assumptions are when put side by side with many sociological accounts of time. They pull against, for instance, the account of time provided by Berardi, especially his account not of a present being destabilized by an excessive orientation to the future but of the opening out of a never-ending present. They also pull against Helga Nowotny's influential account not of a present under threat, undercut, or destroyed by the future but rather of a loss of temporal horizons. In particular, they challenge Nowotny's thesis of the disappearance of the category of the future and the emergence of what she terms an extended present. Central to the disappearance of the future, Nowotny maintains, is the emergence of a present geared to accelerated innovation, a present that "devour[s] the future" (Nowotny 1994, 11). Thus, she notes that a range of technologies and sociotechnical devices have increased the permeability of the boundary between present and future by facilitating temporal uncoupling and decentralization. Such technologies and devices also produce different models of time, and in particular, generate presents that are detached from linearity. Indeed, as Nowotny remarks, with the end of an age in which the belief in linearity and progress were maintained by the time structure of industrial production, "the category of the future is losing much of its attractiveness" (ibid.).

The parallels between Nowotny's and Berardi's accounts of time are obvious. But for my purposes, what is important to draw out here is not only how these accounts raise questions about the assumption that the present is being undercut by the future, but also that as substantive sociological accounts of time, especially of the changing boundaries between the past, present, and future and thus of shifts in and to the categories and experience of time, they challenge some of the fundamental presuppositions regarding time found in accounts concerned with the rise of anticipatory modes of life. Specifically, rather than assuming where the boundaries between past, present, and future should be or how time should be experienced, Nowotny's and Berardi's accounts alert us to how these boundaries and experiences might change—in short, how these are preeminently sociological, rather than normative, issues. In fact, Nowotny's and Berardi's accounts make clear that to make such normative assumptions regarding time is to close down the sociological imagination—indeed, to assume that time itself should (and does) remain the same. I have already mentioned that I will go on to challenge the view that the temporal form of the future has been shut down; notwithstanding this point of contention, however, Berardi's and Nowotny's accounts are significant in that they act as powerful reminders that the movements of time can in no way be taken for granted and that there is no necessarily correct or proper direction or path along which time should flow, including the relations between the present and the future.

Anticipation: Time in the Making

It is, however, not just in substantive sociological accounts of temporal change but also in social theory that we can find challenges to the assumptions regarding time found in accounts of intensifying anticipation. While not particularly celebrated for his work on time, such challenges can be found in the work of Pierre Bourdieu, especially in his insistence that the future is not a contingent possibility (a possible, which might or might not happen), or a distant horizon separated from the present, but always already present in the here and now.[7] The future, for Bourdieu, is therefore always already there. Bourdieu insists that the future is always inscribed in the immediate present because agents are ordinarily immersed in the forthcoming, or more precisely, agents practically and pre-reflexively anticipate the forthcoming as a routine part of practice. The future is therefore always existent in the present because practice for Bourdieu—following Husserl (1931)—is protensive in character. Indeed, Bourdieu suggests that a pre-reflexive aiming at the forthcoming is the most common form of the experience of time, although this experience is itself paradoxical, since, similar to the experience of the self-evidence of the familiar world, time does not offer itself to be felt or sensed and passes largely unnoticed. According to Bourdieu, then, time is for the most part unexperienced.

The ordinary practical anticipation of the forthcoming that Bourdieu proffers is particularly clear in the case of emotions, through which the body sees the forthcoming—the oncoming car or threatening dog—as something already there or irremediable. Bourdieu describes how, in such instances, "the body is snatched by the forthcoming of the world" (Bourdieu 2000 [1997], 208). Yet, beyond these instances of fear, he claims that similar processes are at work in mundane practice. In a game of football, for example, a good player positions her- or himself not where the ball is but where the ball is about to land. In this case, the forthcoming is not simply a possible but is already present in the configuration of the game, including the present positions and postures of teammates and opponents.

For Bourdieu, however, the inscription of the future in the immediate present is not a simple given of practice;[8] rather, it is constituted in the relationship between the habitus and the social world, and more precisely, in the relationship between the dispositions, durable habits, and schemes of appreciation and action with which agents are endowed, together with the tendencies of social fields. For Bourdieu, as has been well explained elsewhere, fields are only fully viable if their logics are durably embedded in the dispositions of agents operating within them (Bourdieu 1977 [1972]); thus, fields can only exist insofar as the pre-reflexive dispositions, habits, and schemes of agents are aligned with the objective principles of fields. Such schemes, Bourdieu writes, are "the product of incorporation of the structures and tendencies of the world . . . [and] make it possible to adapt endlessly to partially modified contexts, and to construct the situation as a complex whole endowed with meaning, in a practical operation of quasi-bodily anticipation of the immanent tendencies of fields" (Bourdieu 2000 [1997], 139). It is, then, because agents are incorporated in the world, that their dispositions are open to the very structures of the world—indeed, that dispositions are the incorporated form of those structures—that enables a routine, pre-reflexive, and practical anticipation of the future. And this is so because in the relationship between habitus and field, the future is inscribed as an objective potential or trace in the immediate given. "What is to be done" is defined in the relationship between the structure of expectations constitutive of a particular habitus and the structure of probabilities, which is constitutive of a given social space (a social field).

Bourdieu illustrates the practical anticipation of the forthcoming with reference to a variety of exemplars, but particularly relevant to my concerns in this book is the description of anticipation in the economic field that he provides in *The Social Structures of the Economy* (Bourdieu 2005 [2000]).[9] In line with his general theorization of social space, Bourdieu posits that to operate in the economic field, agents must be endowed with the habits and dispositions of that field, that is, with dispositions engendered by the incorporation of the experience of constant or recurring situations that are adapted to new, but not necessarily unprecedented, situations. Such engendering provides a practical mastery of situations, including situations of uncertainty, since the habitus "grounds a relation to the future which is not that of a project, as an aiming for possible outcomes . . . , but a relation of practical anticipation . . . grasping time-to-come as a quasi-present (and not as a contingent future)" (ibid., 214). By virtue of the regularities inscribed in the recurrent games that are played out in it, the economic field therefore offers a predictable and calculable future, and agents acquire in it transmissible skills and dispositions (sometimes called "routines") that form the basis of practical anticipations that are at least roughly well founded (ibid., 196).

Thus, just as agents operating in other fields practically anticipate the forthcoming, for agents in the economic field the future is always already there in the immediate present, allowing agents routinely to anticipate the yet-to-come. Yet, and following Mark Granovetter's (1985) insistence that economic action is always embedded in networks of social relations,[10] Bourdieu warns that this practical anticipation of the future in the economic field—the grasping of time yet-to-come as a quasi-present—should not be understood to involve a rational calculus of risk as neoclassical economics would suggest. Indeed, Bourdieu maintains that while economic orthodoxy will always reduce the practical mastery of situations of uncertainty to a rational calculus of risk, construing the anticipation of the behavior of others as a calculation of the intent of opponents, understanding economic action and especially the practical anticipation of the future as engendered by the habitus—collective, historical, and unconscious structures—throws the calculating agent of economic orthodoxy into radical doubt.[11]

I will return to the issue of time and the economic field, and especially time in relation to post–Bretton Woods finance markets, but it is important for now to reflect on how Bourdieu's understanding of time and temporalization raises challenges to accounts of increasingly anticipatory ways of life. A number of issues stand out here. First, Bourdieu's insistence that ordinary action is anticipatory and that the future is already inscribed in the immediate present raises questions around the assumption, found in accounts of increasingly anticipatory ways of life, that the injunction to anticipate is relatively new and specific to our present moment: for inasmuch as ordinary action is necessarily anticipatory, how can it be claimed that action attuned to the forthcoming is specific to the present? Second, Bourdieu's understanding of the inscription of the forthcoming in the immediate present surely also questions the assumption, found in accounts of the injunction to anticipate, that the present is being undercut or destroyed by the future. For if, as Bourdieu claims, the forthcoming is always and necessarily inscribed in the present—that is, if the present contains the future—how can it be claimed that the forthcoming can undercut and destabilize the present? How, for example, can the forthcoming undercut the accumulation of experience and compromise connections between events in time, as Sennett maintains, if the forthcoming is inscribed in those very practices?

Third, Bourdieu's account of time must also make us question the normative assumptions in accounts of the injunction to anticipate that the future should be at some distance from the present, that a boundary should exist between the present and the future, and that the proper sequence of time is one in which the present precedes the future. If the forthcoming is already present in the configuration of the game, how can such claims be upheld? How can we, for instance, uphold the claim that the proper sequence of time is one in which the future is at a distance from and comes after the present, when the future is already inscribed in ordinary practical action in the here and now?

Yet perhaps the most significant—and fourth—challenge that Bourdieu's understanding of temporality raises to accounts of increasingly anticipatory ways of life is the insistence that time is not an entity that simply passes. Specifically, for Bourdieu, time is not a simple medium through which, or a vessel in which, events take place, nor does time operate externally to subjects and their actions. Far from practice simply taking place *in* time, for Bourdieu practice *makes* time. In short, Bourdieu insists that "practice [is] temporalization" (Bourdieu 2000 [1997], 206). This insistence is of some significance when we consider that in accounts of ways of life that are increasingly anticipatory, time and events (or practice) tend to be separated out. Thus in Sennett's account of the undercutting of the present by the forthcoming, the present under threat is one in which connections can (and should) be made between events in time, that is, a present in which time operates and proceeds externally to events. Yet for Bourdieu events (or practices) do not only take place in time, they also make time. The future, for example, is not separate from or an external horizon to practice but, inasmuch as agents are endowed with the habitus adjusted to the field, is routinely constituted in practice. And while we can make use of Bourdieu to problematize the idea of a present in which time is external to events, the very notion of practice as temporalization also makes it clear that the futures at issue in accounts of increasing anticipation—including the so-called traded, mortgaged, contracted, and indebted futures at issue in the global financial crisis—are not preexisting blocks of yet-to-come time that have been subjected to a set of morally questionable practices (trading, contracting, and mortgaging) as critics of the injunction to anticipate tend to assume. Whereas critics of anticipatory forms of life presuppose not only the latter but also that the future is and should be a separate horizon from present practices and events, Bourdieu's notion of practice as temporalization alerts us to the fact that traded, contracted, and mortgaged futures are necessarily constituted in the present, that is, are necessarily immanent to and unfold from the very practices of trading, contracting, and mortgaging themselves.

Bourdieu's account of practice as temporalization, however, does more than problematize the idea that the future has been or can be traded, and that, by implication, the recent financial crisis concerns such a trading. It highlights a further normative assumption at work in critiques of the injunction to anticipate. Specifically, both Bourdieu's claim that to perform practical acts is precisely to temporalize—to make time—and the implications of this claim for recent economic events, namely, that practices such as trading, mortgaging, and contracting do not stand outside of time or colonize existing futures but craft futures, make clear that critics of the injunction to anticipate are (problematically) objecting to the entanglement of economic practices with issues of time and temporalization and demanding their separation. Indeed, we might speculate that the desire to separate out present and future on the part of such critics concerns precisely such a demand.

It is not only Bourdieu's social theory that permits us to speculate that this is the case, however, but also the range of voices heard following the financial crisis that explicitly objected to the entanglement of economic practices with time and demanded their disentanglement. "Don't mortgage our children's future," a US Republican senator barked in a response to the then Democratic government's post–financial crisis economic stimulus plan (Sanford 2009); in responding to the economic crisis, do not "mortgage the future," the Bank for International Settlements warned governments, banks, and consumers (Long 2009); "We've got to stop this Government before they bankrupt our economy and bankrupt our children's future," the then opposition leader of the UK Conservative Party, David Cameron, pronounced in regard to the Labour government's postcrisis bank recapitalization (Cameron 2009); while a journalist for *The Times* claimed that the future has been mortgaged by "insane spendaholics," whom she named as the then UK Labour government (Cavendish 2009). Clearly it was not only financial traders and dealers who stood accused of entangling economic practice and time but banks, governments, and consumers as well.

Time Is Money

In response to such demands to separate out economic practice from time, we might, following Bourdieu, point out that economic practice—inasmuch as it is practice—will always be entangled with time, a point made incontrovertible by industrial capitalism, where abstract labor time is the unit of exchange and (as a consequence) time is money (Adam 1994; Hassan 2003; O'Carroll 2008; Weber 1930 [1905]). Specifically, for capitalist industrial production, not only do rates of profit relate to rates of speed in production (where doing things faster and more efficiently produces increases in profits),[12] but those rates are also measured in units of the clock—in abstract, quantitative, homogenized, and reversible units of time. Indeed, in the case of industrial capitalism, such time is hegemonic (Giddens 1981; Postone 1993; Thompson 1967). Moreover, it is precisely measurement in terms of abstract units of labor time that enables exponential rates of exchange specific to industrial capitalism. Indeed, the abstraction and quantification of labor into units of time, or the conversion of living labor into exchangeable abstract equivalents, is the very process that generates exponential rates of exchange and enables the extraction of surplus from human labor. In industrial capitalism, the exploitation of labor is therefore centered on the exploitation of time. Little wonder, then, that in the history of industrial capitalism, stand-offs between capital and labor have centered paradigmatically on conflicts over time, including struggles concerning duration (the length of the working day), intervals (nonworking time), and pace (rates of production).

Yet while we might posit—following Bourdieu—that economic practice will always concern temporalization, the centrality of abstract time to the process of the accumulation of capital in industrial capitalism also raises important challenges to his theorization of time. One of these challenges is well rehearsed and relates to how Bourdieu's general social theory fails to confront the dynamics of capitalism. This is the case despite it being a theory of different forms of capital that Bourdieu posits to comprise accumulated labor. At no point, however, does he elaborate the specificity of capitalist capital.[13] He therefore fails to specify what differentiates capitalist capital from other forms of capital that he describes. As a consequence, he fails to elaborate the process of abstraction and quantification of labor into units of standardized time, that is, the process of conversion of living labor into abstract exchangeable equivalents, a process that is both paradigmatic of and specific to capitalist social relations. Hence, whereas in Marx capitalist capital is understood as homogenous abstracted labor time, for Bourdieu it is simply conceived of as accumulated labor. As Craig Calhoun (1993) has argued, understanding capital simply as congealed labor will never allow us to capture the specificity of capitalist capital—of how and why capitalism is able to constantly expand its reach and transcend its own limits and boundaries—since it is unable to grasp the extraordinary levels of convertibility encountered in capitalism, levels of convertibility that are constituted precisely in the very process of the production of abstract universal equivalents. Jon Beasley-Murray (2000) has also observed that Bourdieu ignores the process of abstraction specific to capitalism, especially the conversion of living into abstract labor. While Calhoun is concerned that ignoring this process brackets the exponential rates of exchange specific to capitalist capital, Beasley-Murray is concerned that it amounts to a refusal to engage with the process of the production and accumulation of surplus value specific to capitalism, a refusal that amounts to a failure to confront the exploitation of human labor power characteristic of and inherent to industrial capitalism.[14]

But we might add to this and say that Bourdieu's general failure to elaborate the hegemony of the clock for the case of industrial capitalism not only leads to a failure to confront the dynamics and specificity of capitalist capital but confounds his insistence that time should not be understood as operating externally to subjects and their actions, as "a thing with which we have a relationship of externality, that of a subject facing an object" (Bourdieu 2000 [1997], 206). This is so because, as a form of time, abstract clock time is arranged exogenously to practices and events, acting paradigmatically as an external measure of events, witnessed in measures such as production rates and targets, profit ratios and predictions, working-day and working-break lengths (Gilbert 2007). And it does such measuring in abstract, quantitative, reversible, homogenous units. Contrary to Bourdieu's understanding of practice as temporalization, in clock time phenomena and time are, in other words, separated out. In the universe of the clock, events do not make time but take place *in* time. Bourdieu's failure to recognize and elaborate the hegemony, operations, and characteristics of clock time for industrial capitalism therefore not only—as Calhoun and Beasley-Murray observe—limits the ability of his social theory to capture the dynamics and specificities of capitalism, but also—inasmuch as clock time operates externally to the events it attempts to measure—throws his account of time, of practice as temporalization, into radical doubt.

So we have, or at least appear to have, a set of contradictions in regard to both Bourdieu's understanding of time in general and time and economic practice in particular. On the one hand, as I have already suggested, Bourdieu's understanding of practice as temporalization permits us to cut through and problematize various normative assumptions concerning time: that time should flow in one direction or another, for example, or that there should be a certain sequencing of time—for instance, that the future should operate as a distant horizon vis-à-vis present practices and events. In addition, Bourdieu's understanding that anticipation is a mundane (and necessary) feature of practice also warns that a degree of caution may be required regarding the claim that ways of life are increasingly anticipatory. The notion of practice as temporalization also allows us to problematize the view that economic practices should (and can) be held at a distance from time and therefore to question the view—expressed by all manner of voices in regard to the global financial crisis and its aftermath— that the future can be colonized, traded, or commodified. Hence, as I have argued so far in this chapter, Bourdieu's understanding of time helps us to understand that, far from existing at a distance from economic presents, futures must be understood as immanent to economic practices, including practices of mortgaging, trading, and contracting.

Yet while Bourdieu's understanding of time permits us to develop these kinds of insights, we might, on the other hand, reasonably ask to what extent they are destabilized by his sidestepping the time of the clock and its hegemonic status in industrial capitalism. Does the bracketing of an abstract and external or extensive form of time, one that, moreover, is at the very core of the logic and dynamics of capitalist accumulation, mean that Bourdieu's social theory may remain apt and germane for grasping issues of symbolic and cultural value but a rather blunt instrument in regard to economic practices, especially capitalist economic practices? Writers such as Calhoun and Beasley-Murray certainly understand this to be the case. But while it may be correct to state that Bourdieu ignored and bracketed the hegemony of the clock, and in so doing sidestepped a form of time that has radical implications for the status and relevance of his notion of practice as temporalization, scrutiny of the relationship between time and contemporary economic practices, especially financial practices, suggests that this bracketing may not be fatal. In fact, the nature of this relationship would seem to suggest that, even though it may well be the case that Bourdieu's social theory shot wide of the key dynamics and processes of industrial capitalism centered on the extraction of surplus from labor power, for present-day finance-led capitalism—a capitalism whose dynamic and drive centers on the generation of surplus via financial channels and the movements and flows of money—it has a surprising amount of traction. Financial practices indicate a diffusion of the hegemonic status of clock time and the emergence of a form of time more akin to the conception of temporality found in Bourdieu: a form of time that is not simply a vessel for events but one in which time and events proceed together. The relationship between time and current economic practices suggests, in other words, that while Bourdieu's social theory will never be a key resource for understanding the dynamics and processes of industrial capitalism (and will always frustrate the sociologist who seeks such an application), greater traction can be found for present-day capitalism, one that centers on the dynamics of finance and money.

Money Is Time

Consider, for example, the case of financial prediction. For many, financial prediction and related practices such as economic foreseeing and forecasting are increasingly blunt instruments, not least because of the novel forms of value yielded by contemporary capitalism that are not easily captured by such techniques (see, e.g., Marazzi 2007). Indeed, the global financial crisis—widely reported as unpredicted and unexpected,[15] that is, as not amenable to instruments of prediction and foreseeing—indicates that this view may well hold water. Yet we can modify this view when we consider that in practices such as prediction and forecasting the relationship between time and events is not necessarily fixed but open to change and flux. In her discussion of a specific predictive financial instrument, namely, the yield curve of the US Treasury, Caitlyn Zaloom (2009) makes such a shifting relation between time and events particularly clear. Zaloom charts a shifting relationship between time and money (specifically bundles of government securities), one where rather than standing outside of money, mapping and measuring its movements, time is increasingly fused with it.

The yield curve of the US Treasury maps the future value of US bonds, that is, the future value of US Treasury debt securities (or bonds). It is a device for understanding risk and time in the US Treasury market and offers such an understanding by mapping treasury yields, that is, the relationship between interest rates and the time to maturity of treasury bonds. The latter are packages of credit categorized as equal in quality but with different calendar dates of maturity. The yield curve is used as a benchmark for the future value of other forms of market debt, including the setting of mortgage rates. Indeed, the yield curve acts as a barometer of general economic well-being and economic prospects. It is, as Zaloom makes clear, "a widely used indicator of economic strength" both in the US and internationally (Zaloom 2009, 247), which central bankers, investors, and other financial market participants watch "like hawks" (Christophers 2017, 63). As such, the yield curve is a device that "offers a way to understand the market's collective assessment of the future" (ibid.).

While, as Zaloom describes, yield curve analysis existed in the 1960s, its true significance emerged in the 1970s and 1980s. This was a period of major transformations to global finance (Cooper 2010; Dymski and Kaltenbrunner 2017; Konings 2016; Mehrling 2005; Panitich and Gindin 2005). These transformations are critical to the arguments of this book, so it is important to set them out here. As Martijn Konings (2010) has elaborated, at issue in these transformations, initially centered in the US, was (and continues to be) a reconfiguration of financial relations, a reconfiguration involving the extension and expansion of the capacities of both the state and citizens to fund debts and deficits.[16] The expansion in capacities to shoulder debt has turned on the breaking down of the standardizing and equilibrium-seeking impulses of Keynesianism (including the institutions and regulations of the Bretton Woods agreement),[17] and the emergence of a range of new institutional arrangements and infrastructures focused around the expansionary dynamics and multiplier effects of credit debt. Critical to these developments have been the promotion and management of financial expansion by the Federal Reserve Bank (and subsequently by other major central banks and banking agencies); the floating of the US dollar (and the subsequent floating of a whole host of currencies); the floating of interest rates; the securitization of credit (and especially of mortgage and consumer credit); the (associated) intensification of the capital-yielding capacities of securities and other financial instruments; the extension of creditworthiness to populations previously deemed risky and/or uncreditworthy; the repression of wages; the emergence of contingent employment contracting as a permanent condition of wage labor; income volatility; cuts to state-provisioned forms of income; the development of new forms of financial products and services; and the emergence of novel financial instruments, as well as new forms of commercial financial institutions, including those with integrated financial functions.

As this suggests, the expansion of the capacities of both citizens (especially of households) and states to shoulder credit-debt involves a broad-ranging set of embedded institutional arrangements. As a consequence, financial expansion cannot be taken to be a short-lived, ephemeral, or unstable development that can be halted and/or reversed by means of a program of reforms that seek to discipline or regulate finance markets, banks, and other institutions of credit. This is the case even if the crisis of liquidity in 2007–8 is taken into account, the aftermath of which not only saw state bailouts and recapitalizations of private banks and the further embedding of the securitization of credit, but also state-led strategies in the form of austerity programs to expand and extend the capacities of populations to shoulder yet more debt. In other words, the post–financial crisis era has witnessed a further expansion of finance and a further articulation of its infrastructures (Mirowski 2013).

In regard to the US Treasury yield curve and the shifting relationship between time and events, in this set of financial reconfigurations the floating of the prices of the US dollar and interest rates in the 1970s is critical. Prior to this shift, as Zaloom explains, treasury bonds had been dealt as "discrete packages of time" (Zaloom 2009, 252). Financial traders were assigned to separate markets dealing in two-, five-, and ten-year bonds. Hence, for a two-year bond, traders "bought and sold the security looking at the risks that lay in the economy to the point of the bond's expiration" (ibid., 253). In short (and while Zaloom herself does not explain it in these terms), when the prices of dollars and interest rates were relatively fixed, time and bonds, or parcels of profit-yielding debt, were held as separate entities, with bonds moving in and through time and time acting as an external measure of both yield (or profit) and bond duration.

The floating of the price of the US dollar and interest rates, however, rewrote the relationship between time and money, or more precisely, between time and profit opportunities on state debt securities. Rather than acting as an external measure of financial objects and their movements, time became both part of those very objects and an object or event in and of itself. Zaloom describes, for instance, how, as the market floating of price-setting took place and on receipt of the company's first computer, a mathematician working at a New York bond house used it to calculate the prices of bonds and even fractions of bonds and began trading on the basis of these calculations. Such calculations connected bonds that were previously traded as separate entities (as, e.g., two- and ten-year bonds). Moreover, in forging such connections, these calculations generated opportunities to exploit "the relationships between future points in time" (ibid.). In short, the calculations generated "profit making opportunities from temporal relationships" (ibid., 252). Indeed, such calculations should be understood as techniques that, in the post–Bretton Woods era, have contributed toward amplifying and intensifying the productivity and profitability of financial securities along with that of other financial instruments.

At issue in such techniques and the extension of the profitability of bonds was, however, not a making profitable of temporal relationships and coordinates that stood in an external or exterior relationship to the securities, but a transformation of the very materiality of securities themselves.

In connecting previously discrete and closed objects moving in and being measured by time and generating profit opportunities via such connections, these techniques transformed securities into what Zaloom describes as "a continuum of moments," a transformation that, in turn, opened out multiple and expanding possibilities in regard to profit.[18] The market floating of prices and the trading practices this floating afforded therefore *temporalized* securities. Instead of moving in time, securities were transformed into temporal forms, and it was precisely this process of temporalization that presented opportunities to capitalize on securities in novel ways. The floating of the prices of the US dollar and interest rates therefore not only extended and intensified the profitability of securities, but this extension forged a new relationship between time and phenomena in finance markets. Indeed, in post–Bretton Woods agreement securities markets, time itself emerged as an object of innovation and invention. Thus, we might propose that, contrary to the case of industrial capitalism, where time is money, in post–Bretton Woods finance markets, money is time.

This last point is crucial, for it allows us to explicitly confront how the practices and actions of financial trading and contracting, as well as those of governments and other key agents involved in the process of the reconfiguration of finance, have not concerned a simple trade, commodification, colonization, or use of preexisting futures in the present but rather transformations to time itself. To be exact, in post–Bretton Woods securities markets, time has ceased to operate as an external vessel for practice and has increasingly merged with phenomena and events. And here we find resonances with Bourdieu's understanding of time. For just as Bourdieu insists that time is not a "thing" in which events take place (that time is not something that simply "passes") and that practice is temporalization, in securities markets objects (such as securities) have become forms of time. The time of these objects (including their futures and their presents), moreover, is constituted in the very techniques and practices of those markets, practices that in turn have opened out the time of securities to innovative strategies for the creation of profit. Critically, therefore, this shift in the time of securities is not one where futures have been closed down or used up in a relentless search for profitability or the pursuit of profit via finance. Instead, the merging of time with events means that securities have their own temporal profiles, including futures and presents, which are open to constant contestation and recalibration.[19] Understood in this way, then, the yield curve should not be taken as a map of predicted or projected futures of securities—that is, of the yield of securities in time—but instead as a mapping of the very temporal profiles of securities themselves.

We have in Bourdieu, then, a perhaps unlikely figure for thinking through some of the reconfigurations at issue in the expansion of finance. While we may rightly feel frustrated by his lack of attention to the hegemony of the clock in the case of industrial capitalism and his lack of concern with the centrality of clock time in the transformation of living into abstract labor, paradoxically his understanding of time appears to offer much purchase for the key practices driving the accumulation of capital today. To be sure, Bourdieu had little if anything to say about time and financial practices. In an undeveloped aside in *The Social Structures of the Economy* he did, however, note how (what he termed) the liberalization and deregulation of finance tended "to eliminate the time differentials that separated various national markets" (Bourdieu 2005 [2000], 224). While this comment was made in the context of a discussion on the political creation of what he termed the global market, nonetheless it is suggestive that he understood—at least implicitly—that financial expansion related in some way to the restructuring of the time of finance markets, a restructuring I have described as a shift from the hegemony of the clock to practice as temporalization. This shift raises significant challenges to attempts to understand the expansion of finance (including the intensification of the profitability of securities) as well as the practices implicated in the global financial crisis via externalist and/or normative theories of time. Indeed, I would suggest that financial expansion and the practices it entails may be far better addressed and understood not in terms of wrongdoings to time that should be corrected by returning the future to its rightful place, but as concerning a transformation to time, and in particular, transformations to the time of money.

In closing this chapter, it is important to reflect on a further sense in which Bourdieu is a rather unlikely figure to mobilize for engaging the processes implicated in the reconfiguring of financial relations. This concerns his aforementioned commitment to the social embeddedness school of economic sociology associated not only with Mark Granovetter (1985) but also with Karl Polanyi (2001). While this school has served as a sociological foil (and at times almost as a reflex) against the claims of neoclassical economics, especially to challenge the view that economic action is utility maximizing and calculative, the foundations of the embeddedness school have recently been shaken by three developments. The first has come in the form of a science and technology studies–styled economic sociology.[20] Here, Michel Callon (see, e.g., Callon 1999; Callon, Millo, and Muniesa 2007) has challenged the embeddedness school to take the matter of calculative action seriously and to refrain from positioning such action as a fiction. The possibilities for calculative action, Callon maintains, are fashioned by infrastructures and devices of calculation. Such assembled material devices, he argues, give calculative activity a shape. Calculative action is, therefore, not a fiction but a material possibility configured in and by the assembly of sociotechnical devices. Calculative activity is not, however, an ahistorical universal of action, but is variable, configured, and framed.

The second and related development concerns a repositioning of the relationship of economics to calculative activity itself, and more particularly, a reframing of economics as standing not in a representational but in a performative position vis-à-vis such activity (see, e.g., Mackenzie, Muniesa, and Sui 2007). Here, then, rather than as fictional or as a benign descriptive science, economics and its techniques—including its calculations, algorithms, and measuring devices—must be understood to intervene in the world, including in the operations and dynamics of finance markets (Mackenzie 2007). Indeed, the linking of previously discrete securities via the techniques of mathematics and their transformation into a continuum of moments might well be understood in such a performative register (see also Christophers [2017] on the performativity of the yield curve).

Finally, while these developments challenge the fictional and illusory status ascribed by the embeddedness school to the utility-maximizing, human capital–seeking, calculative subject of neoclassical economics, there is a further challenge, albeit from a rather different direction, by an environment that demands not a capital-accumulating but a speculative subject. This is a subject attuned not to the accumulation of capital or to struggles for rights to claim ownership of capital (including the ownership of labor power) but to speculation, especially speculation in regard to flows of money across whole lifetimes. It is also a subject whose everyday practices are speculative in form. The activation and expansion of such speculative capacities will be the focus of discussion in subsequent chapters, but for now it is enough to say that if the fictional status of the utility-maximizing, capital-pursuing, calculative subject has been challenged by the first two developments I have outlined here, then the logics of financial expansion have put the embeddedness school and neoclassical economics (especially the standoff between them) firmly in their historical place.[21] Indeed, these logics suggest that in regard to the empirical world, the relevance of both is reaching certain limit points.

CHAPTER 2

Austere Times

I suggested in Chapter 1 that in post–Bretton Woods agreement finance markets the relations between time and money have been rewritten. I elaborated how, rather than moving through and in time, financial objects such as securities should be understood as forms of time. I also made clear how this rewriting of the relations between time and money has contributed to the opening out of the intense productivity of financial securities—indeed, how this process has led to novel and expanded opportunities for the generation of profit via finance. I proposed therefore that expansions to finance from the 1970s onward have, in part, entailed transformations to the time of money in finance markets. I also made clear how these transformations should be understood to challenge the view that expansions to the generation of surplus via finance (including any crises that such expansions may entail) involve wrongdoings to time. These transformations should not, for example, be understood to involve inappropriate uses of the forthcoming at the expense of the present or a closing down of the temporal form of the future. Instead, I stressed how at issue in regard to financial expansion is a reworking of time, a reworking in which presents and futures do not stand in an external relation to financial objects but in which such objects have their own time.

I will continue my explorations of the changing relationship between time and money in Chapter 3, where my focus shifts from finance markets to personal and household debt. In Chapter 2, however, my attention will be focused on state-led austerity programs, that is, on programs comprising sets of policy measures designed to cut state budgets, debts, and deficits through reductions in public spending. Austerity has been widely embraced, promoted, and authorized by a range of political and financial institutions (including the International Monetary Fund [IMF] and the European Central Bank [ECB]), as well as by national governments, ostensibly as a counter to the global financial crisis and especially the sovereign debt emergencies to which the crisis has given rise. Against this understanding, I suggest that austerity should be understood as a political strategy through which the economy of debt is being actively expanded and extended. This expansion further enrolls the productivity of populations in the generation of surplus value via the movements and flows of money. But in addition to putting forth this understanding, I also interrogate the widely held assumption on the part of a range of progressives that austerity programs are actively extending and exacerbating already existing forms of socioeconomic inequality and that such inequalities can be redressed by strategies to redistribute resources, including money. I suggest that what such redistributive strategies fail to consider is how, in a context of long-term financial expansion (or, as it is often termed, financialization), the capacities of resources—and especially the capacities of money—have shifted. They fail to acknowledge in particular that financial extension and the generation of surplus through financial channels has involved a transformation of the material capacities of everyday money. This is a transformation that leaves the justice-distributing potential of money in doubt. In this chapter, as well as offering an analysis of austerity, I therefore map these shifting capacities of everyday money.

Austerity Bites

In the wake of the financial crisis and the sovereign debt crises that followed the bailouts and recapitalizations of banks,[1] as well as the collapse in the yield of assets (especially of sovereign bonds) and the application of quantitative easing policies,[2] a number of states have adopted and actively pursued austerity measures and programs. Indeed, in the face of exces-

sive indebtedness and debt defaults to large banks and other financial institutions, for some Eurozone states (notably Greece, Ireland, Portugal,
and Spain) fiscal austerity measures have been imposed on them by their
creditors (the European Union [EU], the ECB, the IMF, and the European
Stability Mechanism [ESM]) as part of economic adjustment programs.
Now, more than ten years on from the crisis, other European member
states such as Finland, in concert with the EU and especially the European
Commission, are actively pursuing austerity agendas focused on cuts to
state spending and state-sponsored cuts to wages. As this latter implies,
while the pursuit of austerity marches on (and does so especially in Europe), and while such policies have very often been framed as common-
sense responses to the global financial crisis and its aftermath, there is no
necessary relationship between austerity programs and the financial crisis.
The promotion and pursuit of austerity in Europe should in fact be understood as part of a broader political project of structural reform being
aggressively pursued by key institutions of the EU (including the ECB and
the European Commission), as well as by the post–Washington Consensus
institutions, including the World Bank and the IMF. While making ap-
peals to increasing economic competitiveness and increasing employment
(i.e., to economic growth), this is a project that rests on policies aimed at
decreasing real wages, liberalizing employment protection, and creating
low-paid and unpaid jobs (Regan 2014). This is also a project, as I will
elaborate in Chapters 4 and 5, that is implicated in major transformations
to socioeconomic forms, including the ongoing reform of welfare states,
the transformation of the relationship between wages and value, and the
rewriting of the relationship between unemployment and employment.

As well as being embedded in the broad political project of structural
reform, many of the key ideas and tropes informing contemporary austerity agendas, including frugality and a fear of state debt, were present at the
very inception of economic liberalism, as Mark Blyth (2013) has elaborated.
Blyth also documents how austerity thinking informed US and UK economic policy-making in the Great Depression of the late 1920s and 1930s.
While essential to the structural reform agenda of contemporary neoliberalism, it is therefore important to recognize that austerity is not coterminous with the contemporary era. Despite this, Blyth insists that a range of

problems in today's socioeconomic environment—the ongoing and endlessly contorting debt crisis in Europe, persistent unemployment in the US,
skyrocketing unemployment and underemployment rates (especially youth
unemployment rates) in Europe, incipient mass poverty in Greece, and the
contraction of middle-class privileges and opportunities in the US—are
united by austerity. What these problems have in common, he argues, is
their supposed cure: "austerity, the policy of cutting the state's budget to
promote growth" (Blyth 2013, 2).

Echoing the 1920s anti-austerity sentiments of John Maynard Keynes,
especially Keynes' critique of policies of devaluation as a strategy to promote growth, Blyth has one simple message about austerity, namely, that
as a plan for promoting growth it does not work. In this understanding, he
is by no means alone (see, e.g., Streeck 2014). But Blyth also argues that
the burden of present-day austerity falls disproportionately on the poor
and specifically on the financial-asset poor. Drawing on the language of
securities contracting and trading, he describes present-day austerity as a
"class-specific put-option," one that is "written on the majority of asset
poor OECD citizens" (Blyth 2013, 258). By this, Blyth means that the
dynamics of austerity, especially the transformation of private into public debt that foreshadowed the rolling out of austerity measures, has effectively drawn the financial-asset poor into a project of bailing out and
reliquidating the assets (the loans and mortgages) that banks had sold
and contracted out for trade on finance markets. Contemporary austerity, then, should not be confused with a project that simply benefits
(or bails out) financial institutions and financial elites. Instead, austerity
should be understood as a project that benefits the financial-asset rich,
especially that part of populations holding contracts on mortgages, loans,
superannuation, and other assets that are traded on finance markets. Blyth
estimates the asset rich to comprise the top 30 percent of the income
distribution in OECD countries. Moreover, he maintains, these bailouts
were and continue to be paid for by people who are not only asset poor
but also "rely on government spending and public goods" (ibid., 259), that
is, on the very spending and goods that austerity policies cut. The result,
Blyth argues, is that the poorest segment of society "is forced to pay out
on an insurance policy that they never agreed to guarantee, and for which

they never received a single insurance premium from the holders of the bailed (i.e., insured) assets" (ibid.). As free insurance for the top end of the income and asset-distribution spectrum, contemporary austerity must therefore be understood as a class-based political project, or in Blyth's terms, a class-specific put option. While the Keynesian state insured its populations, the future of finance capital and the asset rich is therefore now insured via the asset poor, whose conditions of existence are themselves being undercut through the annulling of the protective functions of the state.

Blyth is not the only scholar to identify austerity as an inequitable and socially regressive policy regime. A range of observers have suggested that austerity not only constitutes a "class-specific put-option" but is socially regressive along other lines as well, including those of race and gender. In the UK, for example, where austerity policies have been in operation since 2010, many feminist voices have claimed that austerity affects women more harshly than many men and extends and intensifies socioeconomic inequalities organized along axes of gender (see, e.g., Elson 2013; European Women's Lobby 2012; Karamessini and Rubery 2013; Pearson and Elson 2015; Women's Budget Group 2016). Here it is typically stressed that austerity measures—and especially cuts in public expenditures—are disproportionately and adversely affecting women, particularly as employees and as users and providers of state-provisioned services (see, e.g., Annesley 2014; Fawcett Society 2013; Women's Budget Group 2012, 2016). Cuts in public sector jobs and freezes in public sector wages, for example, are widely understood to be disproportionately affecting women because of their concentration in public sector jobs. To take one paradigmatic example of such an assessment, in a 2012 roundtable discussion[3] on the UK's austerity measures, Scarlett Harris, a Trades Union Congress women's equality officer, reported that more women than men were losing jobs in local authorities, that job cuts in the public sector were leading to increases in women's unemployment and underemployment, and that 73 percent of those subject to public sector pay freezes were women (Harris, in Steans and Jenkins 2012, 5–7).

In the same roundtable discussion, Anna Bird, a member of the Fawcett Society,[4] declared that while the pay gap between men and women had been slowly closing, austerity measures mean that "women's incomes will shrink and more women will live in . . . poverty" (Bird, in Steans and Jenkins 2012, 10). Indeed, Bird suggested that over the "next few years, we will see a number of indicators of women's equality and rights going backwards." She continued: "[W]e need to remember *why money matters*—it affords women the ability to exercise control and choice over the world around us. An independent income affords us autonomy, bargaining power, financial control. Women's voice and choice will be diminished" (ibid.; emphasis added). Discussing alternatives to austerity, Bird went on to suggest that instead of a program of cuts there needs to be economic policy that provides a coherent vision for the future on welfare, employment, and public services, policy that delivers for women and "prevents time from turning backwards" (ibid., 30). To this point, a further participant in the roundtable, Maureen Connolly, added, "[M]ore and more people do not accept that there is no alternative. I believe our focus needs to be on shaping an effective voice for women's interests. . . . I believe we can provide clear evidence and arguments, we can show that economic and social policies are ideologically determined not inevitable. We can show that redistributive mechanisms will impact on the majority of people, all in the interests of transferring resources from the richest to the poorest" (Connolly, in Steans and Jenkins 2012, 31).

In this roundtable discussion, we find a number of motifs and axioms common to analyses of women and austerity. Indeed, many of the ideas at play in the roundtable discussion are in broad circulation and amount to what might be understood as a feminist common sense in regard to the politics of austerity. Thus, across a range of both academic and more policy-oriented discussions, similar sentiments regarding the adverse and deleterious effects of austerity on women can be found (see, e.g., Annesley 2014; Elson 2013; European Women's Lobby 2012; Fawcett Society 2013; Karamessini and Rubery 2013; Women's Budget Group 2012). Yet while these sentiments are echoed across a range of policy discussions, reports, and academic literatures and have come to constitute something of a consensus position, they are nonetheless underpinned by a number of interrelated assumptions that, for the purposes of this chapter, are important to make explicit.

In the roundtable discussion,[5] five such assumptions are at play. First, as already underscored, is the idea that austerity measures are intensifying and extending already existing inequalities; thus, rather than rewriting or modulating the socioeconomic field and especially the distribution of inequalities, austerity is assumed to be continuous with longer-term processes, especially processes of the formation and distribution of socioeconomic inequality assembled along the axes of gender. But in addition to the view that austerity measures extend and intensify existing inequalities, a resource-based model of socioeconomic inequalities is put forth. Here the volume and distribution of resources such as money, income, and wages, as well other resources such as public and quasi-public goods and services, are assumed to be central to the making of socioeconomic inequalities.

The second key assumption is therefore that socioeconomic inequalities are inherent in resources and their distribution. The third assumption is that, as well as being central to the making of inequalities, the volume and distribution of such resources are measures of inequality. Wage freezes or wage decreases are, for example, assumed to correspond to or at the very least to indicate potential increases in inequality. Moreover, and fourth, this resource model of inequality leads the roundtable contributors to embrace a redistributive notion of justice.[6] Hence, for participants in the roundtable discussion, socioeconomic injustices are to be addressed via the redistribution of resources. As one contributor to the roundtable suggested, redistributive mechanisms that transfer resources "from the richest to the poorest" can be put to work to address current (as well as longer-term) injustices and serve as an alternative to austerity.

The fifth key assumption, which is critical to my concerns here, relates to resources themselves. Specifically, in the roundtable discussion the resources deemed most significant in the socioeconomic field—money, income, wages, and publicly provided goods such as welfare services—remain relatively unexamined. Thus, the materiality of these resources—what they can do and what they cannot do—remains unscrutinized. Indeed, it is assumed that only the volume and distribution of such resources are of significance in the process of the making of inequalities; as such their properties and capacities remain bracketed. Even when hints toward the properties and capacities of such resources are made, it is assumed that such capacities have somehow remained the same or at the very least do not require new forms of analysis. Thus, rather than analyzing what such resources do and might be unable to do in the here and now, or analyzing how and why resources may be entangled with the processes of making social inequalities in the contemporary present, we are asked instead to simply remember or recall how and why such resources are important. We are asked, for example, to "*remember why money matters*" (Bird, in Steans and Jenkins 2012, 10; emphasis added). Such a process of remembering, it is maintained, will enable us to recall that money matters for women because it affords choice, autonomy, bargaining power, and financial control. It is thus implied that if there is a problem in the analysis of resources and their entanglement with social inequalities, it is simply that we have somehow forgotten why resources matter, a forgetting that can be remedied by a process of remembering. Remembering will, moreover, remind us that resources matter—and in this instance, that money matters—because they have properties that afford women all manner of social goods, such as autonomy, control, and choice, that may work toward achieving all manner of redistributive ends and goals.

It is worth observing that this incitement to remember and to deploy the device of remembering to produce adequate feminist analyses of austerity resembles one key narrative identified by Clare Hemmings (2011) as driving and structuring contemporary feminist theory: that of a knowing return to the axioms and maxims established by forms of feminist analysis produced in a previous era. As Hemmings argues, this narrative typically compels feminist theory to return to the era that closed at the end of the 1970s, in which feminism was characterized by activity, clarity, and focus, and in particular by a focus on issues that "really" mattered: the economy, socioeconomic inequalities, constraint, and justice. Inasmuch as the roundtable asks us to remember this era, it may therefore be understood to exemplify not only key feminist sentiments on austerity but also broader currents in contemporary feminist theory and thinking.

But in recalling such modes of analysis we might ask, Can resources such as money, wages, income, and property be understood to unproblematically deliver social goods in today's crisis-ridden, austerity-hit, and thoroughly financialized reality? And can a redistribution of resources redress socioeconomic inequalities in that reality? Moreover, is a process of remembering sufficient for the analysis of resources in that reality? I would suggest the answer to all of these questions is by no means certain or clear-cut, not least because what resources are (and more importantly, what they can do) has shifted in a seriously consequential fashion. Moreover, this shift in the capacities of resources implies that far from being a matter of remembering, the analysis of resources—including which resources matter and how and why they matter—can in no way be taken for granted but must concern an ongoing process of open investigation. To elaborate why such openness is necessary and to map shifts in the coordinates and capacities of resources, I shall offer an analysis of money. In so doing, I take up the challenge thrown down by the roundtable discussion on women, the crisis, and austerity by addressing the question of how and why money mattered to the UK's second-wave women's liberation movement.

Why Money Matters I: Measurement and Equivalence

To begin this process of remembering, I first recall three of the seven demands of the UK women's liberation movement, demands made in the early 1970s: equal pay (later articulated as a demand for equal pay for equal worth); equal educational and employment opportunities; and legal and financial independence for all women. In recalling these demands, I am not suggesting that a process of remembering can substitute for analysis. Rather, I am recalling these demands to highlight how at that juncture—that is, at the last gasps of the Fordist or Keynesian era and the dawn of the dynamic set of transformations that would unfold a post-Fordist global order now dominated by the generation of surplus via finance—the UK women's movement demanded resources including money in the form of wages, education, and jobs. But this was not a simple demand for access to resources; it was also a demand that these resources be distributed equally. In short, there was a double movement in these demands, of both access and distribution, or more accurately, of both access and redistribution, a redistribution that was required in the context of large-scale socioeconomic inequalities. In struggles for the realization of these dual demands, all manner of sociotechnical devices were invented, designed, and redesigned, including legal, political, and policy devices. And as part of this project, all manner of metrological instruments were put in place in attempts to measure these dual ends, particularly to measure the distribution of resources.

Yet there is something far more interesting about these dual demands than struggles in and around their measurement and realization. This concerns the relationship between the resources to which the women's movement demanded access and notions of justice. Money serves as an excellent case in point. Money mattered to the women's liberation movement because it was understood to be a resource that could—if distributed equally—deliver social goods to women, especially the control, autonomy, and independence taken to be crucial to the achievement of justice. Money, and especially its equal distribution, was therefore viewed not only as a key measure of justice but also as a justice-giving substance or material. Yet we might ask how and in what way the substance of money can deliver such outcomes—that is, how can money deliver socioeconomic equality or parity? Put somewhat differently, how—or under what circumstances—can an equal distribution of money be assumed to deliver socioeconomic justice in the form of equality? Moreover, we might ask how and why there was such certainty that a redistribution of money could deliver these ends. Why, at this historical juncture, was there so much faith in money, including money in the form of wages, as an injustice-remedying material, or more precisely, as an equality-making material?

To make these assumptions (i.e., that the distribution of money not only can act as a measure of justice but also in and of itself can distribute justice) requires taking for granted that money has certain properties or characteristics, or works in particular ways. Specifically, it assumes two properties of money. First, it assumes that money acts as a measure of something, or more precisely, that it can act as a measure of other things, in this instance as a measure of both equality and inequality. Thus, it assumes that one property of money is measurement: that money can measure. Second, and relatedly, in assuming that money can deliver justice, or more precisely, that it can—by means of a fair distribution or redistribution—deliver equality or parity between things, it is assumed that money can mediate between things to produce such parity or equivalence. Thus, it assumes not only that money performs measurement but that it can mediate between things to produce equivalence, equalization, or sameness.

Crucially, these are the very properties of money that classical social theorists such as Georg Simmel (2004 [1907]) and Karl Marx (1983 [1867]) recognized as being those of money in capitalism. As elaborated in Chapter 1, a key feature of capitalism is exponential growth and the endless transgression of limits. This is achieved as a result of the extraordinary levels of convertibility and commensurability encountered in capitalism. These levels of convertibility are constituted in the process of the production of universal equivalents. Money is critical in the production of such equivalence, since within capitalism money acts as the universal medium of exchange. That is, money is the universal mediator between things, allowing the noncommensurable to become commensurable, nonequivalents to become equivalents, and the singular to become reversible. And this is so because money converts the concrete and particular—or use values—into exchange values. Thus, money as the universal mediator between things creates commensurability. Critically, money is more than a medium of exchange; it also measures. As Simmel made clear in *The Philosophy of Money*, "the form in which money exists for us is that of mediating exchanges *and* measuring values" (Simmel 2004 [1907], 203; emphasis added). More specifically, money is the measure of exchange; it permits the precise measurement or calculation of equivalents and hence enables exchange. Without money and its measurement of equivalents, there can be no exchange (Lash 2007). Money thus converts singularities—or the concrete and particular—into commodities, or use values into exchange values. And to do so, money measures in abstract, standardized, numerical, interchangeable units.

While these properties of money are very well documented in the sociology and philosophy of money, what is of interest from the point of view of my concerns in this chapter is how these are the very properties that the 1970s women's liberation movement sought from the resource of money in their quest for justice. More precisely, in the assumption that money can not only measure justice but also distribute justice in the form of equality—that is, act as an inequality-remedying and parity-producing substance—the women's movement asked that money do what it already did. Specifically, the women's liberation movement asked money to measure or act as a unit of account and to mediate between things to produce equivalence, commensurability, and sameness, that is, to produce a process of equalization. The women's movement thus asked not for a transformation of money or its properties or for different kinds of money,[7] but that money extend its properties of measurement and equivalence to remedy socioeconomic inequalities arranged along axes of gender. The demand for such a process of extension was politically efficacious, not least because (and as Simmel observed) one feature of a money economy is precisely the expansion and extension of the scope of exchange, even as that expansion contributes to a flatness of everyday life.

My point here is that a process of remembering or recalling why money mattered to the 1970s women's liberation movement involves far more than a confrontation with demands for resources and their redistribution in the pursuit of socioeconomic justice. It also necessarily involves a confrontation with the very properties of those resources and the relationship of those properties to socioeconomic inequalities and justice. But in highlighting the properties of money, my point has also been to elaborate the very properties of resources, in this instance of money, that, if commentators on austerity are correct in their analysis of the persistence of already existing socioeconomic inequalities, should be at issue in the contemporary present. In short, if to analyze austerity we simply need to remember why resources such as money matter, then the properties of such resources as well as their relationship to inequalities and justice should have remained the same. Thus, money should still measure and still produce equivalence. Money should still act—or at least have the potential to act—as an inequality-remedying and parity-producing substance.

Why Money Matters II: Money as Value

But does money still matter in the same way? Have the capacities of money retained their relationship to socioeconomic inequalities and justice? Can money still remedy inequality and distribute justice? To address these questions, it is impossible not to confront ongoing financial expansion and financialization. Thus, it is impossible not to confront the process through which, as Greta Krippner defines it, "profits accrue primarily through financial channels rather than through trade and commodity production" (Krippner 2005, 174).[8] As indicated in Chapter 1, critical to financial expansion has been the process of securitization, especially the securitization of various forms of debt, including state debt.[9] In addition to securitization, a number of further features of the process of financial expansion are important to my concerns in this chapter. First, as underscored in the previous chapter, from the 1970s onward this mode or pattern of accumulation has developed apace. This growth is expressed in all manner of measures, including records of profits returned by financial assets and financial institutions (Ascher 2016a; Chesnais 2014; Crotty 2005), the proliferation of novel financial instruments (Bryan and Rafferty 2010), and the increasing autonomy of finance as a field (Bourdieu 2003 [2001]; van der Zwan 2014).[10] A second important feature of financial expansion is that it is not employment intensive. The intensification and growth in the production of surplus via finance therefore cannot be read off from changing employment patterns, especially from expansions in employment in particular sectors of the economy. This breaks with established indicators of shifts in the production of surplus and challenges the long-lived assumption that employment patterns are "hard" indicators of economic growth (Krippner 2005). In short, contemporary financial expansion confounds many established ideas regarding economic growth (and decline) as well as the relationship between economic growth and jobs, or more precisely, between the generation of surplus and wage labor. As I will elaborate in subsequent chapters, particularly Chapter 4, contemporary financial expansion involves the forging of a set of new relations between labor (especially wage labor) and value.

A third significant feature of financial expansion is that these developments have not taken place at a distance from everyday life but are thoroughly embedded within it (Allon 2010, 2014; Allon and Redden 2012; Martin 2002). As Fiona Allon has elaborated, it is not simply elite actors operating in the financial field who are oriented to speculative gains on assets, but actors in everyday life. As she puts it, "everyday life is increasingly framed as a space of investment yielding both financial and personal returns" (Allon 2010, 367). By "investment" Allon is referring quite literally to financial investment. Thus, she notes a pervasive cultural rationality that has seen the constitution of the individual as a citizen-speculator who is required to depend on the home in particular "as a site of accumulation and as an object of leveraged investment, not only for debt-fuelled consumption in the present but also as an asset base for investment in the future" (ibid., 368). A fourth significant feature of financial expansion is therefore the thoroughgoing embedding of a speculative rationality in ordinary, everyday life.

The fifth and final characteristic to note about financial expansion—and the most significant for my concerns in this chapter—is the transformation of money at issue in this process, and in particular, transformations to its capacities. Central to these transformed capacities is the rise of money not simply as a mediator, medium, or means of exchange but as a pervasive object of exchange in its own right (Amato, Doria, and Fantacci 2010). Thus, in financial markets, money does not act as the medium and measure of exchange but instead is exchangeable in and of itself as a commodity or product (Lash 2007). Historically, the trading of money for money and the generation of surplus from such trading is far from unique. We need only to look to the writings of Marx for evidence of the historical operations of money as a commodity. Here Marx (1981 [1894]) discussed the logics and dynamics of finance capital—including the operations of money markets—and what he understood to be the relationship between this form of accumulation and economic crises. But money as a commodity in the context of present-day financialization has a number of features that differentiate it from previous historical moments.

The first of these is that money as a commodity is *the* commodity through which the generation of surplus in contemporary capitalism takes place, especially (although not only) money in the form of securitized credit debt. Critical here are securitized home mortgages and personal loans. Notwithstanding the 2007–8 financial crisis and the central role that the crash of mortgage-backed securities played in the crisis of liquidity, these securities and in particular the income streams on which they rely continue to drive financial expansion, that is, the generation of surplus via finance (Allon 2015b; Konings 2010). Income streams from mortgages and other forms of consumer finance (and the contracts between financial institutions and the households that secure them) also link households directly to the operations of global finance markets. Serving as the asset base for securities trading, they position households as the anchor of finance-led capitalism; indeed, they locate the household as well as the attributes of households as the "frontier of financial expansion" (Bryan and Rafferty 2014, 895). In contemporary finance-led capitalism, the money that serves as the anchor for accumulation via finance and is traded *as* a commodity is therefore money that flows directly from households; in other words, households are central to the project of financial expansion and increasingly drive finance-led growth.[11]

The second feature of money as a commodity in present-day finance-led capitalism that distinguishes it from previous moments is that it is pervasive. Money as a commodity does not operate as such only in regard to specialist sites or specific kinds of exchanges but is omnipresent in everyday life. In this regard there is a critical issue to grasp: when money is a commodity, it loses its measurement function, especially its function as *the* measure or standard of value and equivalence. Put simply, when money is a commodity, it can no longer commensurate, or act as a general measure of equivalence, since rather than being a measure of value, it is a value in and of itself. So when money is a pervasive commodity, it can no longer function in any straightforward sense as an equivalence-producing mechanism or instrument.[12]

The third feature of money as a commodity that differentiates it from previous moments is that money as a product or commodity in the context of present-day capitalism is by no means straightforward. It is, for example, by no means the case that money in a singular form has simply become commodified. As Bryan and Rafferty (2006, 2007, 2010) have discussed, financial expansion has involved more and more monetary forms and, additionally, monetary forms with novel capacities and attributes. Paradigmatic for Bryan and Rafferty in this regard are financial instruments, especially financial derivatives. As they explain it, one of the key operations that derivatives perform is the breaking down of particular forms of conventional money—such as contractual credit-debt or bonds—into its constituent attributes, such as price and interest rate. Derivatives then bundle and trade these attributes in a range of combinations whose "possibilities . . . are virtually endless" (Bryan and Rafferty 2007, 141). In derivative trading, money therefore is not simply exchanged with money but in the very process of trading is transformed via an iterative process of dismantling, bundling, and rebundling, a process that is itself made possible by the separation of that trade from the ownership of any underlying asset or assets. Derivative trading is, then, transformative in regard to money. It transforms conventional money (as well as conventional assets) into spaces of possibility. In this context, money is defined less by fixed attributes or properties and more by what it might do: by what it might set in motion. As Bryan and Rafferty note, foremost in this process of setting in motion is a blurring of the conventional distinction between money (such as bonds) and assets or capital (such as equity or shares), with money taking on the characteristics of capital and capital taking on the characteristics of money. One outcome of the blending that derivative trading involves is therefore a merging of money and capital. As such, for Bryan and Rafferty, derivatives should be understood as commodities or as "money with commodity characteristics" (ibid., 153). At issue in finance-led capitalism, then, is not simply that money is no longer a straightforward medium of exchange and is now a pervasive product or commodity, but also that a material reconstruction of money has taken place such that money has become a space of possibility. Financial expansion should, in other words, be understood to involve a material reconstruction of the capacities of money.

Everyday Money

I will return to these changing capacities of money and especially their implications for analyses of austerity. For now, however, it is important to register not only that instruments such as derivatives set things in motion but that they do so typically in relation to contractual household and consumer debt, especially mortgage and consumer debt. That is, the money that is broken down into different attributes and traded in varying combinations via financial instruments such as derivatives on finance markets is typically money from income streams from various forms of contractual mortgage and consumer debt. It also includes money from income streams derived from other aspects of everyday life, including mobile phone bills, household bills (such as electricity and water bills), car repayments, and student loans. The money that financial instruments both work on and trade, and that is the lifeblood of finance-led accumulation, is therefore mundane everyday money: the money that citizens regularly pay on their mortgages, cars, personal loans, mobile phones, and household bills. By way of everyday payments, ordinary people and their run-of-the-mill money are consequently, as the subprime-mortgage crisis so violently evidenced, profoundly entangled with, dependent on, and exposed to the operations of global finance. It is this money-debt that is the subject and object of contemporary financial expansion. In fact, from the late 1970s onward, not only has consumer and mortgage finance gradually been extended to those previously deemed uncreditworthy and/or risky (Aalbers 2012; Allon 2014, 2015a; Ascher 2016a, 2016b; Bauman 2010; Joseph 2014), but this extension has taken place through the development of a range of new consumer finance products that, by means of a range of strategies, have also embedded finance—including financial calculation and accounting—into the routines and habits of everyday life. It is this process of embedding that Allon (2010, 2014) locates as critical to the emergence of the framing of everyday life—and especially the home—in terms of a space of financial investment and speculation; that is, this embedding is critical to the process that Randy Martin (2002) terms the financialization of daily life.

Yet while financial expansion and the generation of surplus via finance continues to demand and depend on (indeed, is anchored in) payment streams from household and personal debt and other forms of contracted payments, this demand hits a set of apparent contradictions in the conditions associated with wage labor, that is, in the very activity through which money for the payment of contracted household and personal debt must, for most people, be generated. Two issues are critical here. First, wage labor is increasingly contingent or nonstandard (Cooper 2012, 2015; Peck and Theodore 2012; Standing 2011); that is, wage labor is paradigmatically unpredictable, insecure, and sporadic. Second, wages for the past thirty years or more have been stagnant and repressed (Harvey 2010). Add to this the conditions of austerity, in which not only state services are being cut but also wages, and an assault—again, for the past thirty years or more—on state-provisioned incomes under the banner of welfare reform, and a critical question emerges: How, in such conditions, do households continue to provide the income streams that are central to the generation of surplus via finance? How, in fact, do households survive in such conditions?

The straightforward answer to both of these questions is: through more household and personal debt. In conditions of contingent or provisional employment contracting, state restructuring (including ongoing welfare reform), austerity, and repressed wages, average everyday citizens are funding their lives and their lifetimes by means of private debt. In so doing, they are, through necessity, directly contributing to the extension and multiplication of the extraction of surplus from money and finance. There is, however, much more to household survival than increases in the quantum of debt. The exposure of households to financial risk and their increased dependency on debt is one part of the story of transformations to the household in the context of a finance-led regime of accumulation, but it is only part of it. Households also have a further characteristic that is central to my concerns here: they are increasingly dependent on the wages and incomes of women, no matter how repressed, precarious, or volatile these wages and incomes may themselves be (see, e.g., Anderson 2012; Federici 2014; Folbre 2012; Fraser 2013; Fudge 2011; Roberts 2013; Sevenhuijsen 2003). This increasing dependency is, furthermore, the case for low- and middle-income women alike, and not only for households headed by women.

The increasing dependency of households on the wages of women relates to a broad set of transformations in regard to work and labor (as well as to the state) in which women's labor—whatever the circumstances of women themselves—has been enrolled in post-Fordist labor markets and the imperative of wage labor on an extraordinary scale. Across a range of literatures and disciplines, feminist scholars have recorded the centrality of women's labor to post-Fordist labor markets (Cooper and Waldby 2014; Fraser 2013; McDowell 1991, 2004, 2008; McRobbie 2007; Mohanty 2002; Morini 2007; Waldby and Cooper 2010). An extensive body of research has also recorded how the mass enrollment of women's labor in post-Fordist labor markets in part comprises waged work in highly precarious labor markets operating on a global scale that provision a range of socially reproductive services, from child care through elder care to domestic services (Anderson 2000; Andersson and Kvist 2015; Carrasco and

Domínguez 2011; Ehrenreich and Hochschild 2002; Hochschild 2000, 2012; Lutz 2011; Yeates 2004). As Sara Farris (2015) has noted with reference to the EU, the demand for domestic and caring services has continued to expand in a context of economic turbulence and uncertainty, particularly in the post–financial crisis era. Farris notes further, as do a range of other feminist writers, that such provisioning of services on the part of poor and migrant women in particular (especially in the form of privately provisioned child-care and domestic services) furnishes the conditions of possibility for more-privileged women to fulfill the demands of their own wage labor (Akalin 2007, 2015; Gutiérrez-Rodriguez 2010, 2014; Staples 2007). It also furnishes the conditions for such privileged women to attach themselves to a set of aspirational hopes about such work, despite the fact that such hopes may be destined to remain frustrated and unfulfilled (Berlant 2008, 2011; Gutiérrez-Rodriguez 2010, 2014; Gill and Orgad 2015; McRobbie 2015). As well as witnessing a flood of women workers into waged work, the post-Fordist labor market has therefore also set in play a complex set of dependencies and divisions between and among women.

The flooding of women into the precarious and contingent post-Fordist labor market, especially into waged work providing caring and domestic services, should in turn be understood to be related to transformations in the organization of social reproduction, especially transformations to social reproduction in national formations previously governed and organized by a Fordist-Keynesian social contract. At issue here is not only a withdrawal of the state from forms of social provisioning (such as health care, housing, education, elder care, and child care) and the privatization of the maintenance of life,[13] but a major transformation of the gender order. This is a transformation concerning the fade-out of the sexual contract of the post–Second World War Fordist era (or what Nancy Fraser [2013] has termed the industrial gender order) and the emergence of a post-Fordist sexual contract.

The emergence of a post-Fordist sexual contract is not tied to transformations to social reproduction alone. Its unfolding is also hardwired to the radical dismantling of the postwar consensus among capital, labor, and the state. This consensus had at its core the ideals of the heterosexual nuclear family, the family wage, and the male breadwinner and female dependency. It also had at its core the ideals of domestic femininity and a motherhood defined in terms of the occupation of the home, selflessness, and self-sacrifice. While these ideals were only ever available to some women, nonetheless they stood as powerful regulatory forces for all women in the postwar Fordist era (Barrett and McIntosh 1980; Lewis 1996; Wilson 1977). On the one hand, they stood as aspirations for many women, and as such were often a source of both pleasure and disappointment (Radway 1983). On the other, they were stringently policed and regulated not only in cultural terms but also institutionally: by employers, unions, and the state. Organized labor, in concert with employers, for example, ensured that for women who were waged workers, their wages remained depressed and lower than those of most men, while the operations of social policy ensured that women who fell outside the ideals of heterosexual marriage, domestic femininity, and motherhood did not gain the same access to many of those benefits given to women fulfilling or striving to achieve such ideals. In the postwar Fordist era, state provision for women (albeit usually indirectly) was therefore conditional upon attempting to fulfill the demands of financial dependency on the wages of men, domestic heterosexual femininity, and selfless motherhood. Little wonder that under these prevailing social and economic conditions the 1970s women's liberation movement demanded equal pay, equal educational and employment opportunities, and legal and financial independence for all women. Little wonder, too, that cries heard after the 2007–8 financial crisis for a return to Keynesian social and economic policies filled many feminists with horror and dismay.

At stake in post-Fordism, however, is an active rewriting of the relations among capital, labor, and the state and a new set of institutional arrangements and imperatives. The contingent contracting of post-Fordism is, for example, shaping the terms of a reworked labor market settlement "which is systematically skewed against the interests of labour—a downscaling and atomization of employment relations achieved in the context of transnationalizing employment relations" (Peck and Theodore 2012, 743). But as well as a recalibration of class relations, the post-Fordist labor settlement is also the scene of the roll-out of the post-Fordist sexual contract. The break-up of collective wage bargaining and wage setting, the end of lifelong employment, and the disassembling of employment contracts with attached rights and social provisions (and especially provisions for male workers and dependents) have, for example, dismantled the family wage and the male breadwinner ideal. An institutionalized adult worker model has replaced this ideal, a model in which all adults—regardless of their circumstances—are positioned as duty bound to work, or if not in employment, to be actively seeking and constantly prepared for the possibility of waged work. At the same time, income streams previously (although by no means universally) provided by the state as part of the social rights of citizenship (such as unemployment and retirement benefits) have become increasingly conditional and precarious.

These arrangements—enacted not only by employers in and through employment contracts and the terms and conditions of waged work but also by states via employment and social policies informed by structural reform agendas—are actively unfolding a new set of ideals for women. These include employment, wage earning, excessive attachments to waged work, intensive motherhood, and a rearticulated domestic femininity defined in terms of heterosexual intimacy and an entrepreneurial, investor attitude toward the domestic space and the work of social reproduction (Allon 2014; Freeman 2014; McRobbie 2015; Taylor 2016). Melinda Cooper (2017) has powerfully shown how the operation of such principles must be set and understood in terms of the wholesale reinvention and reinstitutionalization of the family and family values within post-Fordism. Through social and employment policies that have redistributed responsibilities for the maintenance of life away from employers and the state toward households (including interventions to halt wage increases), the family has been strategically reinvented via the tradition of private family responsibility, and especially the private bonds of family obligation.[14] Through this reinvention, the family has been positioned as the key institution responsible for the funding and provision of those goods that were previously publicly underwritten, including education, health care, child care, welfare, and retirement funding. The reinvention of family responsibility has, in other words, been central to the crafting of the post-Fordist economic order. If in Fordism the heterosexual family served as the locus of the reproduction of labor power and consumer demand, and did so in the context of a set of socialized obligations toward that very family, in post-Fordism the family is a self-sufficient economic unit or site of investment that funds itself through private debt and operates by means of a set of responsibilities and obligations toward itself carved by the lines of kinship.

The reinstitutionalization of the family through the reinvention of the tradition of private responsibility has, then, entailed its significant transformation. Critical among these transformations is not only the funding of the family's enterprises via debt but also the inclusion of women in the wage labor imperative, as well as the redefinition of the work of social reproduction as an entrepreneurial venture. What the equilibrium-seeking devices of Fordism sought to locate in separate spheres of action, the nonequilibrium devices of finance-led post-Fordism have therefore located along the same continuous plane. In this context, "good mothering" is defined less by the continual occupation of the home and the selfless performance of care and more by employment: to be employed is now the right thing to do for the benefit of children (McDowell 2008; McRobbie 2013). In turn, the domestic space is defined less as a scene of the labor of social reproduction working to replenish and maintain the laboring and social body and more as a site of investment and entrepreneurial possibility (Allon 2014; Federici 2014; Tadiar 2013; Taylor 2016). As Angela McRobbie has framed it, domestic, familial space has been recalibrated "in terms of an enterprise or small business led by the wife and mother who provides strong leadership and demonstrates the right kind of managerial skills" (McRobbie 2013, 135).

There are a number of issues that are important to highlight about the principles and ideals underpinning the reinvention of the family and the operations of the post-Fordist sexual contract. First, in a context of precariousness, contingent contracting, and repressed and volatile wages, these ideals and principles are as elusive as they are pervasive and regulatory. As a consequence, they involve their own distinctive forms of suffering for poor and more affluent women alike.[15] These include constant and exhausting labor, as well as specific feeling states such as guilt and shame and the fatigue of constantly deferred hope.[16] As Shani Orgad (2017) has elaborated for the case of employed middle-class women who are mothers, lived attachments to waged work meet the brutal demands of motherhood, especially the demands of intensive mothering, to become not only a source of exhaustion but of anxiety and ambivalence as well, and even of guilt and shame. Second, while these ideals and principles are in practice exclusionary and are so especially in terms of class and race,[17] they should also be recognized as drawing connections between women's lives in specific ways, even if on the surface such lives seem distant and removed. The lives of women in middle-income jobs who continuously train and update their skills to remain in and retain those jobs, and the lives of poor single mothers who work for state benefits and are commanded to become "work-ready," are connected through their incorporation into the wage labor imperative and in their being subjects of economic capacity in regard to capitalist growth. As I will elaborate in Chapter 5, in the opening out of whole populations to the command to work, out-of-work women are located as specific targets not only of the demand that they activate their labor but also of cuts to their state benefit payments. Paradoxically, such regimes do so in the face of a lack of life-sustaining jobs.

It is, then, in the context of this major restructuring of the gender order—a restructuring that is part of and not incidental to the rewriting of the relations among capital, labor, and the state constitutive of the post-Fordist condition—that the increasing reliance of households on women's (contingent, unpredictable, and repressed) wages for survival (for low- and middle-income households in particular) must be placed and understood. The "feminization of survival" (Sassen 2000) is integral to the conditions of post-Fordism. What is critical, however, about the reliance of households on women's wages in contexts where households do not earn as much as they need to spend is that it does not hinge on the volume or quantum of wages put to use as a mediator of exchange or measure of value. That is, it does not hinge on money that acts as and is valued for its properties in regard to mediating exchange and measuring value (as it does, for instance, in consumption transactions). Instead, it involves reliance on the leveraging of and speculation on wages to access securitized credit debt from banks and other financial institutions to finance everyday life and the very life of the household, including to finance and provide those goods that were previously underwritten by the state and employers. The dependence of the household on women's wages therefore involves reliance on attempts at maximizing repressed, contingent, and unpredictable wages by way of the multiplier effects of securitized debt. In putting everyday wages to work in this way—that is, as an asset to both access securitized mortgages, credit, and loans and to service this indebtedness via contracted payments—all indebted workers (and would-be indebted workers) are necessarily putting wages to work not as a mediator of exchange but as a commodity—a form of money that is a value in and of itself.

Two points are particularly important here. First, the leveraging of wages to access securitized debt indicates that it is not only in finance markets that money is put to work as a value. It shows how prevailing social and economic conditions demand that workers must speculate on their mundane money and put it to work as a value to set things in motion. Second, in this context, it is clear that what is significant about transformations to households in the post-Keynesian or post-Fordist era is that they have become dependent not simply on women's wages for survival but on what those wages can do or on what they can set in motion. Silvia Federici (2014) has astutely observed that entering into relations of securitized indebtedness places women in direct relations of dependency and subordination in regard to banking and financial institutions, that is, in regard to institutions of credit debt.[18] This observation forces a recognition that these relations of dependency and subordination should be central to any present-day analysis of the enrollment of the productivity of populations in the generation of surplus via the movements and flows of money. But in addition to such relations of dependency and subordination, the leveraging of repressed and volatile wages to access securitized debt thoroughly exposes women to what money might put in motion. Thus, and with little or no protection from the state or regulatory institutions, in leveraging wages to both access and service securitized debt, women and their households become fully exposed to what money might do on financial markets and to the risks of this exposure. While the financial crisis indicated that one of these risks is mortgage default and foreclosure, it is important to note that since the financial crisis, banks and other credit institutions have attempted to militate against such outcomes through the adoption of a range of techniques. These include the monitoring of household balance sheets and the development of new forms of payment and income insurance for households. What is critical about such techniques is that they do not attempt to reduce or banish exposure to financial risk; instead, they work to ensure that households can withstand and tolerate risk. They are measures "to . . . ensure that households *absorb* risk" (Bryan et al. 2016, 52; emphasis added).

The dynamics and distribution of exposure to financial risk and its absorption are complex. They certainly cannot be read off in any straightforward fashion from established indicators of socioeconomic inequality, including those associated with volumes and quantities of income, especially income in the form of wages. This much was made explicit in the wake of the financial crisis in both the UK and the US: after the crisis, it became clear that not only lower-income households but also middle-income households were overexposed to financial risk (Stockhammer 2012b).[19] This pattern has been shown to be the case outside of the UK and the US as well, that is, outside of what are very often understood to be the geopolitical centers of financialization and financial expansion (see, e.g., Poppe, Lavik, and Borgeraas 2016). This suggests that rather than extending and intensifying preexisting inequalities, the transformations to the capacities of money implicated in the expansion of finance are also connected to the creation of new forms of inequality. These latter include exposure to financial risk, or what might be termed risk positions, that is positions not necessarily driven by volumes and distributions of resources but by what resources might themselves set in motion. What I am outlining here should in no way be taken to mean that the "bads" of financial expansion are felt harder or more by middle-income households and/or women on middle incomes. On the contrary, my point is that in a context where households are dependent on institutions of credit for survival and subsistence, exposure to financial risk or risk bearing—an exposure that has no necessary relationship to income—has become a form of inequality in and of itself, with those who bear more risk being more exposed to any fluctuations or movements in global finance markets.

In this context, it is imperative to locate the exposure to financial risk with which households have become entangled through the necessity of fuelling life via credit-debt in terms of the broad-scale process of the redistribution of risk and protection. While in the Fordist-Keynesian era the state and employers typically shouldered risk and worked toward the social protection of populations through the operation of principles of collective insurance (although these principles were far from universal), in finance-led post-Fordism risks and safeguarding against them—for instance, against the risks of unemployment, illness, retirement, old age—have been redistributed to households (Hacker 2006; Rafferty and Yu 2010; Rose 1996). In this process of redistribution, the expansion of finance has played a critical role (Lazzarato 2009). It is, as I have already set out, precisely through the mechanisms of finance that households now fund those aspects of daily life—housing, education, health, retirement—that the state and employers previously underwrote. It is, however, not simply that through finance households are taking on the costs and risks of funding those aspects of life previously underwritten by the state and employers; for in funding everyday life by means of loans, credit, and mortgages, households also necessarily take on a further risk, namely, exposure to financial risk and the consequences such risk exposure might or might not entail. The fuelling of everyday life and subsistence via finance therefore not only shifts risk, it also generates a topology of exposure to financial risk.

One implication of this broad process of risk shifting and the exposure of households to financial risk is that in our contemporary financialized and austerity-driven moment, any attempt to address justice should focus not simply on redistributing income and other resources but also on the distribution of exposure to financial risk. It is only by way of such a focus, I would suggest, that the apparently contradictory and paradoxical figures of finance-led capitalism may be grasped and understood. This latter would necessarily include the female head of household who speculates on her mid-range but insecure wages, who is locked into a whole lifetime of securitized debt repayment, whose household subsistence is dependent on securitized debt relations, and whose debts—if indexed against income—can never be repaid.

Austerity Reloaded

This prompts me to return to analyses of austerity. It will be recalled that such analyses often stress that austerity involves the entrenchment and extension of existing inequalities. Such lines of argument typically assume that the properties of resources that are built into the making of inequalities have persisted across time. It is, in fact, typically assumed that it is the volume and distribution of resources that are at issue in the making of patterns of inequality. Yet, as my discussion in this chapter has underscored, to understand resources in such a manner—as undifferentiated substances whose distribution and volume literally plot a pattern of inequality—is to overlook how resources themselves may have transformed and to leave the question of the relationship of such transformations to patterns of inequality entirely closed off. There is no doubt that we live in a moment characterized by severe and widening forms of inequality. The analysis I have put forward here, however, suggests that to understand these inequalities requires not assuming in advance how and why resources matter or simply recalling why they mattered in other times. Instead, the very materiality of resources must be a matter of investigation. In any such investigation, the question of what resources can and might do (as well as what they cannot do) must be central. As my analysis of everyday money has illustrated, such an investigation would reveal that it is not only the volume and distribution of resources that may now matter in the making of inequalities but also their capacities to set things in motion.

This transformation of resources should prompt us to pose questions regarding the shifting relationship not only between resources and inequalities but also between resources and justice. Resources and their redistribution have, of course, long been associated with the pursuit of justice. Thus, as I have already highlighted, the UK's second-wave women's movement sought such a redistribution of resources, and especially an equal distribution. In so doing the women's movement assumed that resources such as money were an inequality-remedying material. But such a strategy of redistribution took for granted that resources possessed certain properties: in regard to money it assumed first that money was productive of equivalence and second that it measured. But surely we must ask, if money is now a value and no longer a substance that straightforwardly mediates between things to produce equivalence and commensurability, and if it is also no longer the universal measure of value, where does this leave a strategy of redistributive justice? More specifically, where does this leave a strategy that seeks to redistribute money as a remedy for inequality and a measure of justice? For surely if money no longer commensurates, even its equal distribution cannot achieve or measure either equality or justice.

Prior to the onset of the 2007–8 financial crisis the politics of redistribution came under fire in a rather different set of circumstances. In a clash between feminist critical theory and feminist poststructuralism, the politics of redistribution stood accused of putting in place a problematic distinction between economy and culture as well as excluding forms of inequality and injustice not necessarily directly linked to the uneven distribution of socioeconomic resources (see, e.g., Butler 1998; Swanson 2005). The critique of redistribution I am offering here, however, is of an entirely different order. Rather than constituting a theoretical critique or one based on a politics of inclusion and exclusion (on who or what is counted), the problems I have identified in this chapter relating to redistribution in the age of austerity are grounded in the empirical world: in how transformations to resources may limit the efficacy of a strategy of redistribution for addressing socioeconomic inequalities and for delivering justice. Certainly, there are attempts to rethink the coordinates of a politics of redistribution in the context of the post-Fordist global order (see especially Fraser 2013). Yet such attempts continue to leave the capacities of resources and the relationship of these capacities to inequalities and justice untouched.[20] The implication of my argument here is not only that the politics of redistribution needs to be rethought in the light of transformations to resources, but that these transformations necessarily lead to novel objects that require political attention and action, including but by no means limited to the distribution of financial risks.

In suggesting that the politics of redistribution needs to be rethought in the context of a finance-led mode of accumulation, I am not suggesting that resources do not matter or no longer matter. On the contrary, I am suggesting that transformations to resources and their relationship to inequalities render them an urgent site of inquiry. Yet these inquiries must necessarily take place on territory that is perhaps unfamiliar to those committed to the politics of redistribution, including the dynamics of securitized debt and of finance more generally. In this context, it is vital to acknowledge that austerity is not simply a program of state spending cuts but is part of a set of long-term reforms to the state to which financial expansion is integral.[21] Austerity, in other words, must be understood to be part of—and not an outcome of—the expansion of finance and the enrollment of populations in the economy of debt. This is an economy in which the operation of money as a commodity is core. Austerity must therefore be understood as a political strategy through which the economy of debt and the operations of money as a commodity are being actively expanded and extended. To put it straightforwardly, the cuts to state provisioning and further cuts to (already repressed) wages that austerity entails provoke households to further enroll in the economy of debt by speculating on their repressed incomes. I have suggested further in this chapter that this is an economy that is linked to the enlistment of women's labor in the post-Fordist labor market on a mass scale, an enlistment that has led to women's wages being used as payment streams flowing to finance capital, as well as to the opening out of those wages to the multiplier effects of securitized debt.

My analysis of austerity certainly suggests that while austerity may function as a class-based put option, as Mark Blyth has argued, as a political strategy its dynamics should not only be read in this register. It must also be understood as a strategy that actively extends the economy of debt and the operations of money as a commodity. This is also an economy in which a major transformation to the gender order (and the organization and dynamics of households) is hardwired. In this respect, the changing capacities of money and especially the operation of money as a commodity must be understood not only to tie populations (through necessity) to financial speculation as a mode of accumulation but also to have opened out specific social forms—indeed, a mode of social organization in which everyday practice is speculative in form. The operations of money as a commodity are, in other words, central to the logic of speculation as a rationality.

In identifying the changing capacities of money as central to the tying of populations to the economy of debt as well as to the initiation of distinctive modes of life, this chapter has also necessarily provoked a set of further questions. One of these concerns the question of what exactly wages are in the context of financial expansion, especially how the price of labor is organized and set in this context. A further question concerns the binding of populations to the economy of debt, that is, how exactly populations become attached to the economy of debt and especially the practices of speculation that it necessitates. I will address the subject of wages, and specifically the question of what wages are, head-on in Chapter 4. Meanwhile, in the following chapter I address the binding of the productive capacities of populations to the economy of debt. I will suggest that central to this binding is not only the extension of credit to those previously deemed uncreditworthy or risky and the development of new consumer products, but also the operations of a particular mode of time, a time I term the time of speculation or the speculative time of debt.

CHAPTER 3

The Speculative Time of Debt

In this chapter, my focus returns to the relations between time and money. While in Chapter 1 my exploration of these relations focused on post–Bretton Woods agreement finance markets, especially on the radical temporalization of securities and the significance of this process in regard to the intensification of the capital-yielding capacities of finance, here my attention turns to the temporality of contractual household and personal debt, or debt that is monetary and strictly sanctioned.[1] This chapter will suggest that a focus on the time of contractual household and personal debt—and especially on securitized contractual debt—is essential to understanding both the binding (or attachment) of populations to the economy of debt (or more precisely, to the generation of surplus via financial channels and movements and flows of money) and the expansion of the capacities of populations to shoulder debt, including the capacities of speculation that such debt necessitates. This is so not least because of the modes of practice such debt demands and opens out. By focusing on the time of household and consumer debt, this chapter therefore continues to map the logic of speculation as a rationality, that is, as a historically specific mode of accumulation and social organization. The critical context and background for the interventions this chapter unfolds are two intertwined features of contemporary debt. The first of these is the rise (and rise) in household and personal indebtedness in the Global North, particularly in the form of mortgages and other forms of personal credit-debt, including personal, student, and payday loans—in other words, mass indebtedness. The second is the centrality of debt, especially the income streams that contractual debt entails, to contemporary accumulation strategies, that is, the productivity of debt in the generation of surplus via finance and money.

It is important to note at the outset that the literature on contemporary household and personal debt and especially mass indebtedness is by now expansive and cuts across a number of disciplines, including sociology, cultural anthropology, cultural studies, political science, and political economy (see, e.g., Deville 2015; Graeber 2011; Joseph 2014; Lazzarato 2011, 2015; Soederberg 2014). One motif present in much of this literature is that debt, and especially the debtor-creditor nexus, must be recognized as a constitutive social relation, one that is asymmetrical and imbued with power (see especially Joseph 2014; Lazzarato 2011; Soederberg 2014). Here, then, creditors (and especially institutions of credit such as banks) stand in a structural relation of power with respect to everyday debtors. With debtors needing credit to live, they have no choice but to submit to the contractual demands of their credit agreements. Thus, just as Marx understood workers to be wage slaves, when debt is understood as an asymmetrical social relation, everyday debtors are debt slaves. Debt, then, must be understood as an apparatus of power. But as this chapter will set out, the relations of time and temporality also loom large in the literature on mass debt, on two counts. First, in existing analyses of contemporary debt it is often assumed both explicitly and implicitly that the logic and operations of debt turn on a specific ordering of time, namely, a promise to pay at a time that has not yet arrived. Second, the condition of mass indebtedness is often assumed to have closed down the possibilities and potentialities of time for the indebted, especially possibilities in regard to the future.

This chapter makes a number of significant interventions in regard to existing analyses of mass debt. Against proclamations that debt is destructive of time, especially of the possibilities of the present and the future, I suggest that debt must be understood as generative of time. This is so because the time of debt has taken on specific characteristics in the context of securitization, that is, the process that from the late 1970s onward has served as a bedrock of finance-led accumulation. In the context of securitization, the time of debt, or the promise to pay, has been reconfigured and rewritten. The rewriting of the time of debt is evidenced in two shifts or movements in the schedules of contractual personal and household debt: the movement of such schedules away from a logic of repayment toward a logic of payment, and the movement of these schedules away from a logic of the probable toward a logic of the possible. These shifting logics of debt bind the indebted subject to a time in which pasts, presents, and futures do not stand in a pre-set relation to one another but are open to constant revision. That is, these shifting logics bind the indebted subject to a specific form of time, a time that I term speculative time, which is hardwired to the logics of accumulation via finance and money, and especially to how the process of securitization has opened out novel channels for the harvesting of profit for finance capital from the income streams flowing from households that mass indebtedness necessarily entails. In mapping the time of securitized debt, I will suggest therefore that far from closing down the possibilities of time, especially those of the present and the future, the time of mass indebtedness concerns a particular temporal order, namely, that of speculative time. This temporal order is one that maximizes the productivity of populations in regard to the generation of surplus value from flows of everyday money.

This chapter therefore offers an account of how debt—or more precisely, everyday money flowing from households to service debt—is implicated in transformations to the social and ties the productivity of populations to the generation of surplus value via money. In so doing it departs from understandings of debt as a social relation (a social relation of credit and debt) and posits instead that debt must be understood as implicated in a far more thoroughgoing reconstitution of the social that includes the establishment of specific modes of practice. Understanding how debt operates as such turns on the recognition that what debt is and how it operates have shifted in the context of finance-led accumulation, especially in the context of the securitization of credit debt. It also turns on the recognition that certain key concepts mobilized in existing analyses of debt—particularly the concepts of promise, the possible, and speculation—require rethinking and revising in light of the dynamics of securitized debt.

To lay out this set of interventions, this chapter comprises four parts. First, I address what I term the classical time of debt—the promise to pay—and how contemporary mass indebtedness has been understood to elevate this time to the status of a total social fact. I will consider in particular how the elevation of the promise to pay has been understood to close down the possibilities and potentialities of time, especially the possibilities of the present and the future, since debt renders the present beholden to pre-set futures. Second, notwithstanding the appeal of these understandings I lay out how any analysis concerned with the temporality of debt must necessarily operate in close proximity to its object, namely, to debt. Doing so, I suggest, complicates any claim that mass indebtedness involves the appropriation or loss of time. Taking Jane Guyer's (2007, 2012a, 2012b) analysis as exemplary in this regard, especially her analysis of how debt is defined and characterized by its binding to the calendar, I elaborate how the architectures of debt afford distinctive temporal rhythms, sequences, patterns, and sensations. Third, building on Guyer's analysis, I turn to the calendrics of securitized debt. I map how the schedules of securitized debt as well as calculations of debt-loading are concerned less with the probables of repayment and more with the possibles of payment, especially the possibles of debt service. I elaborate how such schedules and calculations must be understood in terms of changes to what debt is and how it operates, and in particular, how they must be understood in the context of securitization, where profit is yielded by finance capital from the nonchronological and indeterminate movements of speculative time. Finally, in the fourth section, I elaborate on this time and on how schedules of securitized debt bind subjects to that very time. I consider the implications of this for understanding the indebted subject, laying out how this is not a subject without a future or present but one that must constantly adjust to recalibrations of pasts, presents, and futures, as well as to changes in the relations between and across these states. This is a subject whose social attributions are actively translated into distributed financial attributions in the calculus of securitized debt. I highlight, then, how the calculus of securitized debt both works on the social and transforms it, and how this movement must be central to any account of contemporary debt.

Promising to Pay

Debt, it is widely assumed, concerns a specific temporal relation, indeed, is defined by time (see, e.g., Ascher 2016a; Bauman 2010; de Goede 2000; Graeber 2011; Jasarevic 2014; Jeong 2016; Lazzarato 2011; Martin 2002). Specifically, debt concerns a promise to pay[2] at a time that has not yet arrived, namely, in the future, a promise that binds the debtor contractually and legally not only to the terms of that promise but also to that very future. Debt therefore allows deferral in (and of) the present, but at the expense of a contracted-out future, that is, at the expense of a future that is already plotted and mapped, one that is known before it has arrived. Debt, or the promise to pay, therefore operates via a double movement in regard to time: it defers the present but does so by counting on (and counting) the future. As Larisa Jasarevic eloquently describes it, the promise to pay is marked by "suspension and anticipation, by necessary deferral and eager or anxious looking forward" (Jasarevic 2014, 264).

In the context of mass debt and indebtedness across the Global North, where debt has become the key mechanism through which economic and social existence is to be secured, the double temporal movement of the promise to pay has taken on a particular significance,[3] not only because debt is a fact of the present that is impossible to ignore, but as Holly High (2012) argues, because "everything intermingles in it," indeed, has attained or is close to attaining the status of a Maussian total social fact (High 2012, 364). To give just a few examples, wages, health care, education, housing, standards of living, and economic survival are all thoroughly entangled with—and impossible to separate out from—debt and indebtedness. Debt is therefore not only necessary to meet the demands of everyday life, but debt and indebtedness have become key defining features of contemporary existence. This is underscored by how the past thirty-five years have witnessed not only the stagnation of real wages but also the emergence of record levels of household and personal debt and rising debt-to-income ratios (see Figure 3.1). Such increases in debt-to-income ratios are evident particularly (although by no means only) in the US and the UK, where in recent years they have hit historic peaks, particularly for middle- and lower-income households (Stockhammer 2015). In everyday terms such pervasive household and personal debt means not only that indebted

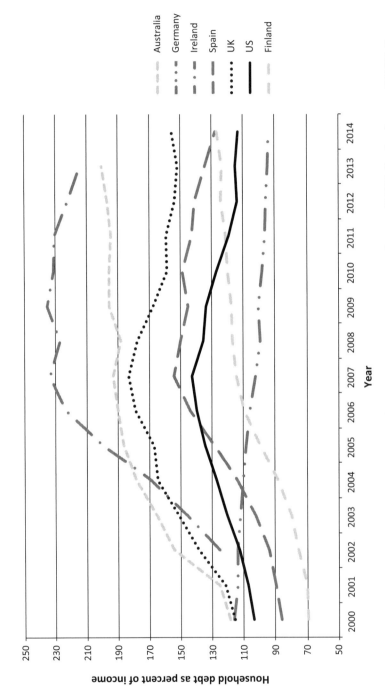

Figure 3.1. Household debt-to-income ratios, selected OECD countries, 2000–2014. Source: OECD Factbook 2014; OECD Factbook 2015–2016.

laboring has become a permanent feature of work and working, but also that whole populations are inescapably entangled with the double temporal movement of the promise to pay. Indeed, the elevation of debt to a total social fact means that the time of society is now the time of debt. In the society of mass debt, the promise to pay is therefore the preeminent mechanism of temporal organization: the pasts, futures, and presents of the debt society are those born of the promise to pay.

For Maurizio Lazzarato (2011), the elevation of the promise to pay to a universal is little short of a disaster. Capital, he contends, has become a Great Creditor, and the asymmetrical creditor-debtor relation has become a constitutive social relation—in fact, *the* social relation. Present-day society is therefore not only a debt society but one in which the dynamics of power and control have necessarily been reworked. This reworking is evident, Lazzarato argues, in how debt society reveals Foucault's (2008) analysis of neoliberalism as a form of postwelfare governmentality to have reached certain limit points (see also Lazzarato 2009). In debt society, becoming an entrepreneur of the self, for example, necessarily involves the debtor-creditor relation, because the subject must take on the financial costs and risks of this endeavor her- or himself. But more than this, the subject must take on the costs and risks of the whole of existence: the whole of life is routed through debt and hence is beholden to institutions of credit. Indeed, debt society demands that the subject—whether waged, unwaged, poor, or displaced—always stand as a "self-guarantor" (Lazzarato 2011, 49), that is, assume the financial risks and costs of existence across whole lifetimes (including the costs and risks of social provisioning that have been externalized by the state and employers). The whole population, Lazzarato argues, must "take charge of everything business and the welfare state 'externalize' onto society, debt first of all" (ibid., 9). As such, the elevation of the promise to pay as a universal (and the emergence of debt as a core technology of power) has not only unfolded the debtor-creditor relation as the constitutive social relation but also produced a specific subject, the "indebted man [*sic*]," who now occupies the entirety of public space and is "at once responsible and guilty for his [*sic*] particular fate" (ibid.).

For Lazzarato the elevation of the promise to pay to a universal is a tragedy on a further count, one that concerns the relations of time. Mass debt, he maintains, amounts to the closing down of time, especially the possibilities that should be afforded by time. This closing down of the potentialities of time takes place not only through the pre-ownership on the part of financial and banking institutions of futures that have not yet arrived, but also through the appropriation of the present and the pre-emption of nonchronological time.[4] Thus, the promise to pay not only ties the indebted to futures that are not and might never be their own, it also renders the present beholden to those pre-possessed and pre-set futures. For Lazzarato the society of debt therefore closes down the possibilities for nonindebted and nonchronological forms of time: it is a society without potentiality and hence without foreseeable rupture. In the society of debt, time as a plane for the creation of new possibilities is therefore foreclosed, and with it the materials for any kind of sociopolitical change. Indeed, Lazzarato suggests, debt society is one lived with a "strange sensation of living . . . without time" (2011, 47). In the society of mass debt, modern-day moneylenders not only appropriate money, they also appropriate time.

Steady Time

While Lazzarato mourns the loss of time in the society of debt, it is important to stress that the time of debt has a complexity that is not entirely captured or contained in ideas of the appropriation and loss of time. Such complexity is made clear in analyses that operate in closer proximity to the dynamics of debt, an excellent example of which is found in Jane Guyer's (2007, 2012a, 2012b) examination of debt and obligation. At first sight this claim may seem puzzling, since Guyer's consideration of debt is nestled in a broader account concerning the "strange evacuation of the temporal frame of the 'near future'" (Guyer 2007, 409). While this evacuation, Guyer maintains, is evident in social and collective doctrines (including economic forecasting and planning), the near future is nonetheless being reinhabited or filled in by what she terms the calendrics of "punctuated" or "dated" time. Guyer identifies debt as one form of dated time, not least because the architectures of modern debt demand regular and continual repayments at fixed points on a calendar. Such architectures, moreover, bind the subject to what Guyer refers to as the "calendrics of repayment" (2012a, 497), or dated schedules of repayments. This binding, in turn, affords a specific temporal rhythm to debt and, I would add, to the indebted subject, namely, one of steadiness. The nexus of repayment thus demands a steady and punctual subject, a subject who can avoid (potentially violent) sanctions by satisfying the demands of repayment on time. This is a subject who yields to and satisfies the temporal rhythms and schedules of the calculus of debt.

Importantly, as both Fiona Allon (2014, 2015a) and Silvia Federici (2014) have elaborated, for the case of personal and household debt, financial institutions and their intermediaries have found a particularly reliable source of such steadiness and punctuality in the female subject. As Federici frames it, financial institutions have captured the energies and inventiveness of women worldwide, particularly the informal tactics of women in regard to economic survival, to both create a reliable source of steadiness in regard to repayment and extend the reach of the architectures of debt. This enrollment of the female subject in the architectures of debt has involved a range of strategies, including experiments with the social fabric of women's everyday lives—for instance, their social networks—to bolster and optimize the disciplines of repayment (Federici 2014).[5] These strategies have also involved, as part of a process of the inclusion of women in access to mortgage and consumer credit from the late 1970s onward,[6] the explicit targeting of women as consumers of financial products or consumers of debt. As Allon (2014) makes clear, this targeting has involved the development of specific financial products together with customized advertising and branding strategies. Such strategies have, moreover, not simply targeted women as the subjects and objects of debt but, as Allon details further, integrated the management and repayment of debt into aspects of everyday life conventionally coded as feminine, especially the home and domestic activities. Such strategies on the part of financial institutions have, in other words, folded the everyday life of households into the operations of finance and have done so by locating and coding the arts and disciplines of repayment as feminine domestic activities—indeed, as a form of domestic labor. Such labor, as Randy Martin has observed, "is to be maintained with round-the-clock vigilance" (Martin 2013, 94). The strategies of financial institutions and banks have therefore opened out the rhythms of the domestic to the calendrics of debt. In terms of the concerns of this chapter, what is of particular significance in regard to these strategies is not only how the female subject has emerged as a preferred subject of the calendrics of repayment, but also the implications this has for transformations to that very subject, particularly in regard to the relations of time.

I will return to this transformation, but before I do so I wish to draw out the implications of Guyer's analysis for the idea that the society of debt is one in which time is closed down, and especially for the idea that such a society is lived with the sensation of living without time. In many respects these implications are straightforward: rather than a simple process of the closing down and/or appropriation of time, Guyer's analysis highlights how debt and indebtedness concerns a specific temporal universe. Hence, her analysis underscores how the society of debt is alive to the temporal rhythms, sequences, patterns, and sensations of repayment structures, repayment plans, and repayment schedules, as well as to the futures and presents such calendrics may unfold. In short, her analysis suggests that the calendrics of debt afford the society of debt not a present emptied out or dispossessed of time, or a society in which time is appropriated by the operations and architectures of debt, but one that opens out a distinct universe organized and defined by the rhythms and sensations of steadiness.

It is worth reflecting further on this form of time, not only on how calendrics afford rhythms of steadiness and punctuality but also on how this is an objective or extensive form of time. Thus, calendar time is a form of time that stands in an exterior relation to subjects, practices, and events, even as it regulates and organizes them and claims them as its own. Such time is therefore one that is experienced by subjects as operating exterior to their own actions and to their own being. As a form of what Barbara Adam (2004b) refers to as time reckoning, the calendar is, in other words, a framing of time that is invariable and unaffected by context, although it orders and arranges the very context that it appears to stand outside. As Adam also makes clear, not inconsequentially, this form of time is intricately entangled with the emergence of sovereignty and the nation-state, not least because calendar time allows for the coordination of actions and events as well as for the regulation and disciplining of subjects. This time is, moreover, front and center to the history of debt: as an extensive form of time through which entities travel and can be measured, calendar time enables the calculation (and accrual) of interest across intervals of time, including the calculation of interest into the future, as well as speculation in regard to such calculations. In short, the extensive time universe of the calendar enables the conversion of time into money (Nowotny 2005), a conversion that is pivotal to the process of accumulation via debt.

The Payment of the Possible

In her focus on calendrics, particularly on dated schedules of repayment and the steadiness such schedules afford, Guyer is surely correct to name the rhythms, sequences, and sensations of repayment as those of the time of debt. These temporal sequences, patterns, and rhythms of repayment have, however, taken on a rather different character in the context of the calculus of financialized debt, or more precisely, in the context of the calculus of securitized debt. Before turning to these sequences and rhythms, it is important to emphasize (as underscored in preceding chapters) that the securitization of debt has served (and continues to serve) as the bedrock of financial expansion. This is especially the case for the securitization of mortgages and other forms of consumer credit. The securitization of mortgage and consumer debt is, in other words, the mainstay of finance-led accumulation (Konings 2010). Developed in the US in the 1970s, securitization exploded in the 1990s and has spread (albeit unevenly) around the globe, with securities now forming a global market (Wainwright 2012). Notwithstanding continuous innovation, and as set out in the Introduction, at its core securitization is a process whereby—via financial and legal instruments—contractual debt (i.e., contracted debt obligation) is pooled, sliced, and transformed into liquid assets that can be iteratively traded on finance markets (Nesvetailova 2015). This process has not only vastly expanded possibilities for the generation of surplus via money for finance capital but has likewise increased the possibilities of mortgage and consumer credit. It has also shifted the nature of mortgage and consumer debt markets away from facilitating markets and toward capital investment markets. This shift has integrated everyday debtors into the workings of finance and led to direct links between debtors and finance capital, especially (as the subprime mortgage made explicit) between debtors and the operations and dynamics of finance markets (Aalbers 2008, 2012). The process of securitization has also been (and continues to be) promoted by the state (in, for instance, the US and the UK) as part of the political project of neoliberalism, not least as a vehicle for promoting and extending private property ownership and expanding the conditions for asset-based welfare (Konings 2010; Poppe et al. 2016).

While these points regarding securitization are well established, what it is vital to stress here is that securitization has also involved a reworking of the schedules of debt, that is, the schedules of repayment. Specifically, securitization has afforded the development of consumer finance and mortgage products whose repayment schedules, rather than being regular, steady, and in sequence, are variable, flexible, and adjustable (Coco 2013; Piskorski and Tchistyi 2010; Scanlon et al. 2008). Repayment schedules may, for example, be sped up, slowed down, suspended, delayed, rescheduled, reset, restarted, reassembled, reorganized, and even reversed. As Langley (2008) has observed in regard to US home mortgages, the securitization of debt, particularly the securitization of mortgages, has led to schedules of mortgage repayment that have broken with previously dominant models in which repayments were made on loans at (relatively) fixed rates at set calendar dates across set periods of time (typically twenty-five or thirty years) and moved progressively, steadily, and gradually toward a fixed point in the future at which point mortgage debt would finally be repaid (see also Gerardi et al. 2010). The products whose repayment schedules broke with such models first appeared as alternatives to the traditional amortized mortgage. They have, however, become so popular and pervasive (in the US and the UK especially) that they can no longer be considered to operate as such (Aalbers 2008, 2012).[7]

In pointing to the changing schedules of debt, I am not attempting to simply suggest that they are now more variable and dispersed, nor am I suggesting that the calendrics of securitized debt have ushered in new forms of individualized discipline on the part of debtors in regard to the promise to pay. I am not suggesting, therefore, that securitization is a technique of individualization. On the contrary, in highlighting the shifting schedules of debt I am interested more broadly in how these changing calendrics are thoroughly entangled with and implicated in transformations to debt itself, especially the dynamics of its productivity in the process of capital accumulation. This entanglement becomes clearer if two further characteristics of the changing schedules of debt are considered.

The first of these is that the variable schedules of securitized debt as well as calculations of debt-loading are not geared toward repayment structured by a future end point of debt clearance but rather toward the servicing of debt, toward *payment* rather than repayment. This is evidenced in a range of developments, especially in interest-only loans and mortgages and in flexible and adjustable loan- and mortgage-payment products that provide options for extended interest-only payment periods, repayment holidays, and extensions to loan terms. Indeed, it is evidenced in the way calculations of household debt-loading and debt schedules hinge on calculations of debt-service ratios by creditors, that is, precisely on the capacity of debtors to *service* rather than repay debt.

The gearing of debt toward capacities to pay rather than to repay is also expressed in how calculations of securitized debt-loading are no longer indexed to wage rates measured across working lives. For the twenty-five- and thirty-year amortized mortgage, debt-loading and schedules of repayment that worked toward the future point of acquittal were statistically calculated with reference to the probables of wage rates across predictable and measurable working lives.[8] Such probables were calculated and mapped from the point of the present, that is, from current wage rates. In the time of repayment, probable futures were therefore unfolded from the knowns of the present. And it is worth recalling here that these futures were mapped, plotted, and charted with respect to the probables associated with the male laboring body. In fact, during the post–Second World War period, mortgages were extended to white male workers in particular, whose wages—guaranteed by the state and unions—functioned as collateral (Federici 2014).

In the calculus of securitized debt, the relationship between debt and income has, however, been rewritten. Wages and income are calculated by brokers of credit not in terms of the probables of repayment but in terms of their possibilities and potentials in regard to debt, especially their possibilities in regard to debt service. The rewriting of this relationship is evidenced in loans and mortgages outrunning working—and lived—lives; in debt and mortgage lending to those both in and out of work—to the waged and the wageless; and in debt-loading that, if indexed to current income, is impossible to repay. The United States' Federal Reserve Board has made this reshaping of the relationship between income and debt explicit. It reports that for the case of home mortgage lending in the US, calculations of possible future incomes have become central to calculations of mortgage debt-loading and debt scheduling (Dynan and Kohn 2007). Indeed, the securitization of mortgages has aimed at precisely such a rewriting of the relationship between mortgage borrowing and income, that is, to enable borrowing to be indexed to possible future rather than current incomes (Gerardi et al. 2010).[9] Significantly, rather than by way of calculations of the probable, predicted, and projected from the present into the future, the calculus of securitized debt hinges on calculations of the possible, and especially of possible futures.[10] In this calculus, futures do not unfold from the known present, but the present is remediated by futures that have not yet and might never arrive. As one financial economist has framed it, securitized mortgages "allow borrowing-constrained households to transfer resources from the future to the present" (Coco 2013, 1664). And here it is important to stress that these are futures that have not yet and might not ever take place.

In its emphasis on possible futures, the calculus of securitized debt may be understood to form part of what Louise Amoore (2013) refers to as the contemporary politics of possibility, a politics marked in its change in emphasis from the statistical calculation of probability to the algorithmic arraying of possibilities such that they can be acted upon. Amoore shows how the change in emphasis from probability to possibility is at the heart of a reconfiguration of state authority, which has taken place, she argues, via the enlistment of the calculative techniques associated with economic life in the operations of the state, especially those techniques and capacities associated with private consulting, risk management, software, and biometrics engineering.[11] The enlisting of these techniques has activated a mode of governance and modality of power that act upon possible projected futures, and in doing so authorize the preemption of possible emergent events, including the preemption of threats yet to come (see also Amoore and de Goede 2008; Massumi 2007, 2015).[12] By embracing such techniques, state authority and sovereign decision have come to operate less through actions on future knowns calculated with reference to the past and present and more through actions on future unknowns calculated with reference to the possible. Sovereign power has therefore been refocused on what may emerge (Massumi 2015).

In the context of the emergence of this modality of power, Amoore stresses that it is important to recognize that calculations of the possible and the probable are by no means necessarily discrete. The emergence of the politics of the possible should not, therefore, be understood as a simple retreat from probabilistic forms of calculative practice, not least because probabilistic calculation often involves what Amoore terms the speculative (Amoore 2013, 44), that is, possibilistic or speculative modes of calculation.[13] It is precisely the speculative dimensions of calculation that the algorithmic techniques employed and activated by the state both authorize and enhance.[14] In the practices and operations of contemporary sovereign power, the speculative yet already present elements of such calculations have therefore multiplied, "[taking] flight as imaginable, if not strictly calculable, possibilities" (ibid., 10).

With its emphasis on possible futures that have not yet and might not ever arrive, together with its move away from tracking probable futures forward from the knowns of the present, the calculus of securitized debt should clearly be understood as constituting part of this broader shift in calculative practice that Amoore locates as central to the emergence of the politics of possibility. In this sense, the calculus of securitized debt should not be taken to stand outside the shifts in governance and operations of power that she lays out. The calculus of securitized debt should, in other words, be understood precisely as a technique that resonates with this new modality of power—as part of a moving complex "governing emergent, uncertain, possible futures" (ibid., 5).

Yet while it is important to locate the calculus of securitized debt within this complex, it is also important not to reduce this calculus—

including its variable schedules of payment and the pasts, presents, and futures it unfolds—to an issue of shifts in modes of calculative practice alone. Instead, it should also be understood to be connected to changes to accumulation via debt, that is, to changes in what debt is and how it operates. Specifically, it should be understood to be connected to how, in the context of securitization, the productivity of debt lies not simply in the accumulation of profit on debt and indebtedness across time, especially in interest accrued on debt across pre-set blocks of time, but in the accumulation of profit from trading on debt itself, especially on the contracted income streams that debt necessarily entails. This includes the accumulation of profit from trading on losses and defaults in regard to debt and bets on those losses and defaults. The shift toward calculations and measurements of the possible should be understood, in other words, in terms of how the process of securitization—involving the breakdown of debt into its constituent attributes and the bundling, pricing, and trading of these attributes in risk-rated tranches (Bryan and Rafferty 2007, 2010)—has enabled profit to be accumulated from contractual debt in novel ways. Thus, rather than being yielded primarily through interest over relatively fixed periods of time or by events moving in and through time, the process of securitization has positioned debt itself as a source of profit, allowing profit channels to be created in regard to experiments with debt. Profit may be yielded for finance capital, for example, from credit defaults or credit events, debt restructures, credit event auctions, credit event restructures, credit default swaps, credit forwards, credit futures, and even credit backwards.

The productivity of debt in the age of securitization and the significance of securitized debt in the process of capital accumulation are well documented (see, e.g., Bryan and Rafferty 2011; Cooper 2010). But what is critical in terms of my concerns in this chapter is the temporality of accumulation via securitization, and especially the shift in the relationship between time and debt that securitization unfolds. When profits accrued on debt and other financial objects primarily via interest, the time of debt—including the rate of profit—was (relatively) predictable and steady, or at the very least, profits accrued in and through time. In the time of securitized debt—where profits are yielded from unpredictable and contingent events, such as credit events and future events that have not yet arrived and even past events that have not yet taken place—far from moving forward from a fixed point in the present toward probable futures, the time of debt is speculative in form.

The Time of Speculation

In proposing that the time of debt is speculative in form, I mean a great deal more than that time itself forms part of experiments with debt, that is, that time itself has become a speculative proposition. While, as elaborated in Chapter 1, this latter—especially in the context of the floating of interest rates—is demonstrably the case (Zaloom 2009), nonetheless by "the time of speculation" I am not simply referring to a form of time that is limited to the financial practice of trading—including trades on time—in anticipation of gains in the future. That is, I am not simply referring to how bets on temporal relationships may yield profits in the future. I am not, therefore, pointing to a process of the commodification of time. Nor am I referring to the temporality of the speculative form of capital documented and disparaged by Marx (1981 [1894]) as "fictitious capital." Marx described this form of capital as comprising the circulation and exchange of promissory notes and other financial instruments and securities, such as titles, as if they were money. He understood this form of capital to be speculative because its value lay not in real income but in the expectation of a future return. For Marx, this capital was fictitious in that he understood it to neither represent nor be anchored in any real capital, be that money supply or business transactions. As such, he understood the value of securities to be an illusion.

In the context of the recent financial crisis and ongoing financial expansion, Marx's analysis of fictitious capital has enjoyed something of a renaissance, not least because of the role he attributed to this form of capital in crises of accumulation (see, e.g., Chesnais 2014). But Marx's insistence on the fictitious character of such capital belies how contemporary securities operate not as if they are money or capital but as a form of money and as a form of capital. As Bryan and Rafferty (2006, 2007, 2011, 2012) have made explicit, financial instruments such as derivatives have distinctive money-like capacities. These include the commensurability (or conversion) function derivatives as a system perform in regard to different forms of assets across time and space. It also includes their transferability (or liquidity), a transferability rendered possible by derivatives being unencumbered by the ownership of any underlying assets. In this liquidity, derivatives embody "money-like attributes" (Bryan and Rafferty 2012, 99). In addition, as explained in Chapter 2, in their capacity to set things in motion derivatives blur conventional distinctions between money and capital, with derivatives operating as "money with commodity characteristics" (Bryan and Rafferty 2007, 153). Understood in these terms, far from being fictitious, contemporary securities are both real money and real capital. In suggesting that the time of debt is speculative in form I am not, therefore, proposing that this time is the time of speculation as outlined by Marx, that is, the expectation and anticipation of returns on fictitious forms of capital adrift from real capital and real value.

It is also important to make clear that in suggesting that the time of debt is speculative in form, I am not referring to the broader idea present in some analyses of debt that mass indebtedness has led to an explosion of counting on the future, an explosion bolstered by a range of formal and informal technologies that make such a counting possible (see, e.g., Adams et al. 2009; Jasarevic 2014). I am, then, not simply proposing that the time of mass debt is one in which there is an intensification in counting on and anticipating the promise of the future; on the contrary, I am drawing on the notion of speculative time developed in recent social and cultural theory (especially in feminist theory) that, through engagements with strands of pragmatist philosophy, has proposed understandings of time that aim to secure alternative stances toward the future (see, e.g., Barad 2010; Coleman 2010, 2014, 2016; Grosz 2000, 2004, 2010; Sewell 2005; van der Tuin 2015). Critically, from the point of view of my concerns here, such stances do not tie the forthcoming to the promise of the new.

In such understandings, time is not a thing that simply passes or that contains and orders events, nor is it something that moves in one direction or another, proceeding, for example, chronologically, progressively, or sequentially, with the past standing behind the present and the future unfolding from the now. Speculative time is a time in which pasts, presents, and futures stand not in a predetermined or pre-set relation to each other but are in a continuous state of movement, transformation, and unfolding. It is this form of time that belongs to the time of securitized debt. Thus, in the time of securitized debt, futures may remediate not only the present but also the past; the present and its relation to the past and the future may be reset in one action (via, e.g., index rolling); pasts and presents can be forwarded and futures and presents backwarded. It is, moreover, along the flows of these nonchronological pasts, presents, and futures, including their reordering and resetting and even their suspension, that channels for profit are yielded. In short, in the time of securitized debt, the time of profit lies in the nonchronological and indeterminate movements of speculative time.

It is precisely against this background of speculative time and especially of the productivity of this time in regard to the process of accumulation via debt that the shifting schedules of personal and household debt—which may be sped up, slowed down, delayed, reorganized, or reversed, and which are geared toward payment and the possible—must be understood. For these are schedules that are continuous with those of the indeterminate speculative time of securitized debt, and as such must be understood as schedules that bind the subject to that very time. In this context, Guyer's notion of the "calendrics of repayment" might be usefully supplemented and even replaced by the "speculative calendrics of payment," a calendrics that binds the subject not to the extensive time of the calendar but to the indeterminate movements of the time of speculation.

What is significant in regard to this binding is that it does not condemn the subject to a life without time or a life in which the possibilities of nonchronological time are preempted. Nor does it tie the subject to the classical time of debt, that is, a time where the present is continuously suspended and deferred in anticipation of a better future. While such assumptions are rife in analyses of the consequences of mass debt, they fail to appreciate or take into account the dynamics of securitized debt. As my analysis in this chapter has underscored, rather than emptying out, suspending, or preempting time, or heralding an extension and intensification of the classical time of the time of debt, the time of securitized debt is one of intense activity in regard to time, a time in which presents, pasts, and futures and crucially their relations to each other are open to a constant state of revision: they may be drawn and redrawn, assembled and disassembled, set and reset. The speculative subject bound to the time of securitized debt is not a subject who mourns the loss of time or does not feel time, nor is this a subject without a present or a future or without temporal orientation. On the contrary, this is a subject who must stand ready to adjust to recalibrations of pasts, presents, and futures, as well as to changes in the relations between and across these states. Far from being dispossessed of time, the subject who is bound to the speculative time of securitized debt has *too much* time, albeit not too much of the steady time of the calendar but of the eventful and nonchronological temporal frames that comprise the time of securitized debt.

The speculative time of debt must therefore be understood to open out (and demand) specific modes of practice that center on adjustment to the nonchronological and indeterminate flows of speculative time, that is, that center on the capacity to adjust to potential changes to the flow of time. Such modes of practice raise significant challenges for social theory, especially social theory concerned with the temporal dimensions of practice. As elaborated in Chapter 1, Bourdieu, for example, insists that practice is temporalization, because the future (the forthcoming) is always inscribed in the present. The calendrics of securitized debt, however, afford modes of practice that break from this formulation, not least modes of practice oriented both to futures and to pasts and presents whose relations to each other may potentially be reset. The calendrics of securitized debt therefore inscribe the present with speculative time. At play, then, is not practice as temporalization as Bourdieu understands it but what might be termed practice as speculation, a mode of practice that both binds the subject to the calendrics of securitized debt and maximizes the capacities of populations in regard to the payment of the possible across whole lifetimes. Thus, in mastering the slowing down, speeding up, stretching out, compressing, suspending, and resetting of (as well as defaulting on) schedules of securitized debt, populations expand opportunities for finance capital to generate surplus on those very adjustments and the nonchronological flows of money that such adjustments afford.

Rewriting the Social

In concluding this chapter, I want to return to one of the preferred subjects of securitized debt, especially of household and personal debt, namely, the female subject. If the analysis I have proposed in this chapter holds—if the time of securitized debt is the time of speculation and if the schedules of that debt bind the subject to this very time—then one of its implications is that this preferred subject and object of securitized debt may not be a steady but a speculative female subject. That is, one of the implications is that the time of securitized debt has afforded not a female subject who offers a source of reliability and steadiness in terms of the disciplines of repayment, but an indebted and thereby necessarily speculative female subject who offers a source of potential in terms of the payment of the possible. It might be proposed, then, that it is such potential that finance capital seeks to enroll into the architectures of securitized debt.

In this context, however, it is vital to recognize one further feature of securitization, namely, how this process involves not only the pooling and slicing of the attributes of contractual debt (and in particular, the income streams that such debt comprises) and the transformation of these attributes into liquid assets that can be traded, but also the pooling, slicing, and transformation of the social attributes of the people who are contractually bound to such debts. Thus, as part of the process of securitization, the social attributions of the holders of debt contracts—such as gender, age, race, education, and health—are classified and ranked in terms of financial risk or risk exposures and are distributed to different classes of security (Bryan and Rafferty 2014; Martin 2002). In turn, these exposures are bundled and rebundled to form part of the asset-backed securities (such as mortgage-backed securities) that are traded on finance markets. The process of securitization therefore involves a rewriting of the social life of people in terms of the financial life of securities, with social attributions being rewritten as exposures to financial risk that are integral to the life of securities themselves. The process of securitization therefore involves what might be understood as a double movement in regard to the social: securitization both works on the social and transforms it, turning social attributions into financial attributes, including as profit-producing exposures to financial risk.

It is in this process of the translation of social attributions into financial attributes that are part of (and not separate from) securities that the issue of how and why the female subject has emerged as a preferred object and subject of securitized debt must be tracked and traced. After all, in the rewriting of the categories of gender as financial attributes (e.g., as points along a continuum of financial risk), the social life of many women (especially middle- and lower-income women) is being rewritten as the life of securitized debt, that is, in terms of the nonchronological and indeterminate movements of securitized debt. At issue in the process of securitization is therefore not only the opening out of nonchronological speculative time and the binding of subjects to this time but also a broader rewriting of the social in terms of the very logic of the securitization.

This process of rewriting is vital for any critical account of debt. It is especially important for any aspiring sociology of debt. This is not only because—as laid out in Chapter 2 in regard to income and financial risk exposure—social and financial attributions do not map onto each other in any straightforward fashion (i.e., financial attributes cannot be read off from social attributions), but also because this movement concerns an active modulation of the social field through the calculus of securitized debt. Indeed, the modulation of the social that securitization involves should surely be located as exemplary of the operations of what Gilles Deleuze (1992) has termed control society. This is a society open to continuous processes of disassembly and reassembly (i.e., to processes of modulation) that has replaced a society ordered and confined through discipline (operating, e.g., via sites such as workplaces and schools). In working on and transforming the social, and in particular, in transforming social attributions into financial attributes (that are neither equivalents nor reducible to each other), the calculus of securitized debt precisely concerns processes of disassembly and reassembly paradigmatic of control society. Moreover, the calculus of securitized debt concerns a mode of control that operates not through an external discipline (e.g., the external discipline of the clock) functioning in discrete sites that contain and enclose, but through the active enrollment of populations in the indeterminate and nonchronological movements of flows of money (including the multiplier effects of debt), an enrollment that opens out the productive capacities of populations in regard to such flows. Understood in this way, the calculus of securitized debt should be identified as a key mechanism through which a shift from disciplinary to control society is effected.

This modulation of the social that the calculus of securitized debt involves should be at the very center of any sociology of debt and any account that seeks to understand the significance of debt for the lived present. Yet recognizing that the calculus of securitized debt is involved in such a modulation raises particular challenges for sociologists, not least because this modulation does not operate by way of a logic of embeddedness. That is, the efficacy and force of the calculus of securitized debt does not gain traction by becoming embedded in social relations—for instance, by feeding off and reinforcing existing social divisions, hierarchies, and classificatory systems. Indeed, the calculus of securitized debt has no respect for previously established hierarchies of borrowing and creditworthiness (including those based on social attributions). Instead, this calculus operates by way of an expansionary logic, seeking the enrollment of whole populations in the payment of the possible. More than this, in transforming social attributions into financial attributes, the calculus of securitized debt transforms the cartographies of the social into a spectrum of financial attributes that are hardwired to the movements of securitized debt. In this context, it must be recognized that a sociology of contractual debt cannot be arrived at by analyzing the operations of debt and indebtedness in terms of the cartographies of the social that the calculus of securitized debt rewrites. Instead, a sociology of debt must confront the topologies of financial attributes that securitization unfolds. A sociology of contractual debt is yielded, then, not from asking how debt is social but by tracking how the social is actively being rewritten by the calculus of securitized debt. In this sense, the calculus of securitized debt and the modulation of the social that it entails add further fuel to the claims presented in Chapter 1 that the embeddedness school of economic sociology (associated with Granovetter, Polanyi, and Bourdieu) has reached certain limit points: rather than being nestled or embedded in the social, the calculus of securitized debt actively rewrites the social it acts upon.

CHAPTER 4

Wages and the Problem of Value

So far in this book I have focused on a number of features of the reconfiguration and expansion of finance from the 1970s onward. These have included the vast increase in the profitability of finance (including the capital-yielding capacities of securities and other financial instruments); the associated process of securitization (especially the securitization of credit); the extension of creditworthiness to populations previously deemed risky and/or uncreditworthy; austerity as a permanent political reality; and debt as a necessary condition of life. In so doing I have unfolded a number of lines of intervention regarding the time of money, that is, a time in which a logic of speculation is at the heart of capital accumulation strategies and guides the dynamics of social formation. These interventions have included the following propositions: (1) that in post–Bretton Woods finance markets, trade in money is not a matter of trading the future at the expense of the present but rather concerns a shifting relationship between time and money, in particular a radical temporalization of securities such that channels for profit lie in movements of time; (2) that austerity should be understood not as a program of cuts provoked by the financial crisis but as a political strategy through which the economy of debt is being actively expanded and extended, further enrolling the productivity of populations in the generation of surplus value via the movements and flows of money; (3) that rather than standing still, the capacities of everyday money must be understood to have been restructured in the context of long-term financial expansion; (4) that rather than being an issue of volume, it is what money might put in motion that is critical for economic survival; and (5) that the operations of money as a commodity are linked to the restructuring not only of class relations but of the social more broadly, and that these forms of restructuring concern the development of modes of everyday practice that are speculative in form. I have also argued that such modes of practice are not anticipatory but concern adaptation to indeterminate flows of time required by the schedules of securitized debt, schedules that maximize the potential for the payment of the possible, payments that are integral to the generation of surplus via the movements and flows of money.

In the previous chapter, I indicated that the shift to the payment of the possible that securitization has involved concerns a reworking of the relationship between debt and income, especially between debt and wages. So in calculations of debt-loading, wages are counted and measured by brokers of credit not in terms of the probables of repayment but in terms of their possibilities and potentials in regard to debt, and especially in re-gard to debt service, that is, payment streams. One effect of this calculus is the increase in debt-to-income ratios also outlined in the previous chapter, as well as extensions of credit to those previously deemed uncreditworthy, including the intermittently employed, the unemployed, and the jobless. In Chapter 2, I also indicated how in a context of long-term political strat-egies of structural reform, wages are increasingly repressed, and that in order to finance everyday life, households must leverage and speculate on their repressed, stagnant, and contingent wages to access securitized debt from banks and other financial institutions. In other words, households must attempt to finance everyday life by exposing their repressed wages to the multiplier effects of securitized debt. I suggested that this raises a series of important questions about wages, including what, if their quantum can-not finance life, wages are in the context of financial expansion, and espe-cially how the price of labor is organized and set in this context.

In this chapter, I address these questions about wages head-on. I am concerned with a number of interrelated characteristics and problems with wages in the context of financial expansion, some of which I have already mentioned: an increasing disconnect between wages paid and the labor performed and exchanged for such wages; the stagnation and repression of real wages; indebted laboring; and the existence of a pervasive gap between what labor earns and what it needs to spend. These have been noted in numerous analyses and commentaries and have been connected, albeit sometimes sketchily, to a range of processes, including the broad process of financialization, ubiquitous precariousness, new forms of the extraction of surplus, attacks on social reproduction, the dismantling of the social wage, and a generalized intensification of the power of capital vis-à-vis labor. In turn, and as I will elaborate in this chapter, various strategies have been proposed to address the problem of wages, strategies that attempt in different ways to reconnect wages to labor and/or to the costs of social reproduction, that is, to the reproduction of life, including the reproduction of labor power. In the midst of increasing insecurity about the reproduction of life, such strategies seek to reconnect wages with the creation of value, particularly value constituted by laboring activities. In so doing, such strategies assume not only that laboring activities are a key source of value but that such value should be expressed in the abstract via money, and especially via wages paid in the money form. Thus, such strategies seek to anchor value expressed in the money form in labor or to reconnect such value with labor.

Notwithstanding the precarious nature of both labor and the reproduction of life in the contemporary finance-led post-Fordist present—a precariousness that Lauren Berlant (2010) has argued now links all workers affectively with subproletarian populations at the level of insecurity—I will suggest that such attempts to address the problem of wages tend to sideline broader transformations to the capacities of money. These transformations have rendered money, including money paid in the form of wages, an unstable and unpredictable measure of any value that may or may not be constituted via labor. Indeed, these transformations have rendered money a substance that does not and cannot represent or capture the value of other things in any straightforward fashion. In turn, these transformations demand a focus not on what wages should measure and comprise but on what they can or might do, that is, on their potentiality. In this regard I will suggest that we can find in Georg Simmel's *The Philosophy of Money* (2004 [1907]) important points of orientation, not least his critique of what

he termed labour money and his emphasis on money not as a singular object with fixed properties but as a complex, in-process, multidimensional
surface (Frisby 2004a). Through this emphasis on the work of Simmel, especially on his analysis of money, in this chapter I therefore add weight to
the claim heard recently in the social sciences that Simmel's vitalist social
theory has increasing relevance for the contemporary world, especially for
the socioeconomic formations and processes associated with finance-led
post-Fordist capitalist accumulation (Dodd 2012, 2014; Harrington and
Kemple 2012; Lash 2007, 2010).

Wages and Rethinking Money

At first glance, the focus on wages in this chapter and in a book broadly
concerned with transformations to money in the context of the expansion of finance may appear slightly out of place. For when it comes to
money, isn't the important action taking place elsewhere? Aren't the sites
and processes that demand and invite serious attention to transformations
to money and its operations far removed from money paid in the form of
wages? Certainly, a burgeoning literature on money implies that everyday
wages operate at some distance from the exciting and significant action
as far as money is concerned, suggesting instead that attention should be
focused not only on derivatives, securitization, and practices of speculation
but also on the operations of digital currencies, technologies, and infrastructures of payment and borrowing, as well as on money as information
(see, e.g., Aitken 2015; Bjerg 2016; Maurer 2015). This literature can easily
give the impression that such developments have created the most pressing issues in regard to money today, issues such as how payment systems
and the records of transactionality they afford are reworking the contours
of persons and publics (Maurer and Swartz 2015), as well as enhancing
opportunities for institutions of credit to deepen their relationships with
indebted populations (Tiessen 2015). In addition, such developments are
often located as opening out new political possibilities in regard to money.
Digital currencies such as Bitcoin, for example, have been taken to have
the potential to expose the forms of risk and violence associated with state-
authorized credit money (Bjerg 2016). In such registers, not only does

money paid in the form of wages appear remote from these developments, but the wage as a site of inquiry appears anachronistic, operating as it does not at the interface between populations and banks (and other institutions of credit money) but at that between employers and laboring populations. Indeed, a focus on the wage appears to call up a social formation that has been usurped by the rise of finance capital, which is interested primarily not in the extraction of surplus from labor power (i.e., in the exploitation of labor power) but in the generation of surplus from money.

But a focus on the wage could be read as not only calling up a mode of social formation that is out of time with the present but also shoring up and reinscribing a problematic privileging of the wage and of wage labor that feminist and postcolonial scholars, among others, have fought to deprivilege and decenter (see, e.g., Federici 2012; Haraway 1991; Spivak 1978). At issue for these scholars was how attention to wage labor concerned a focus on the already enfranchised and how such a focus excluded forms of work—and particularly socially reproductive work—that made wage labor possible. In this context, one might rightly wonder if a renewed focus on wages and wage labor would serve as a device to both refocus on the enfranchised and exclude the multiple forms of work and labor that fall outside of this rubric and are, or at least were, entangled with the very conditions of possibility of waged work. One might also observe that a focus on waged work might skew the realities of the present. As Donatella Alessandrini (2014) has documented, the role of wage labor in productive processes is declining. Additionally, wagelessness is not only expanding worldwide but becoming increasingly institutionalized in the context of the increasing precariousness of work (Denning 2010; Federici 2012).

Taken together, these points firmly caution against a focus on wages and wage labor, and do so especially if one takes seriously the view that the generation of surplus in finance-led post-Fordist accumulation processes is removed and disconnected from wage labor and that money and finance have trumped work and labor as the main loci of societal control. My interest in wages in this chapter, however, is not driven by a concern to downplay these features of finance-driven post-Fordist economies, nor is it motivated by a concern to restore wage labor to a privileged position in analyses of the dynamics of contemporary capitalism. Even if one were compelled by this latter agenda, the radical and ongoing restructuring of labor under conditions of finance-led post-Fordism, including the dismantling of sociotechnical devices such as those implicated in the family wage that secured the privileging and privilege of certain forms of wage labor, would make any such attempt imprudent and ultimately unproductive. Rather than driven by such concerns or motivations, my interest in wages is in how they serve as a site for understanding transformations to money, and especially transformations in the relationship between money and labor.

In proposing that wages serve as such a site, I again join other recent calls to understand transformations to money—particularly those connected to the process of financialization—as transformations present not simply in particular specialist, differentiated, or autonomous spaces such as finance markets, or in particular forms of money, but present in mundane, everyday money and in routine, everyday spaces. As I will elaborate in this chapter, rather than being separate from the features associated with financial expansion (or with financialization), the operations and logics of wages are continuous with them. Indeed, I will illustrate how the ordering, logics, and operations of wages in the era of finance-led post-Fordism increasingly resemble—and are continuous with—new forms of money born of financialization, including the operations and dynamics of the financial derivative.[1] I suggest, therefore, that wages in the era of finance-led post-Fordism are not divided from such forms of money but share a common rationality. It is precisely this rationality that provides wages with their in-motion and postrepresentational qualities and demands that wages paid in the form of money be rethought, a rethinking that necessarily involves a replotting of the relationship between wages and labor power. Recognition of this common rationality also provides some much-needed explanatory purchase on key features of wages in finance-led post-Fordist capitalism, which for the purposes of this chapter are of significance and hence require mapping.

What Are Post-Fordist Wages?

One feature of wages in finance-led post-Fordism particularly stands out, namely, wage stagnation and repression. While often taken to be entangled with the financial crisis and its aftermath, especially with the roll-out of

austerity programs, which include wage freezes and wage cuts, wage stagnation and declines in wage rates within finance-led post-Fordism have a
history that is by no means coterminous with the crisis and the social and
economic turbulence it unleashed (Wisman 2013). Instead, wage stagnation and repression are permanent features of finance-led post-Fordism
and as such should be understood as part of what defines this era.

This permanence has been stressed by David Harvey across his recent
writings (Harvey 2004, 2007, 2010), especially in his identification of a
politics of wage repression as endemic to the logic and functioning of post-
Fordist accumulation. Harvey elaborates how such a politics of repression,
especially for the US and the UK, has been in play from the 1970s onward,
as real wages and household incomes have been stagnating and weakening.
Harvey documents how, aside from a brief period in the 1990s, real wages
have continued to follow this pattern. This tendency is, however, by no
means specific to the paradigmatically low-wage economies of the US and
the UK. Wage stagnation, as well as declines in real wages and wage shares
for labor over the past twenty-five to thirty years, has been experienced in
different forms across most OECD countries and also, albeit rather more
unevenly, across emerging capitalist economies (Stockhammer 2012b,
2013; Vidal 2013). Indeed, wage repression has been and continues to be
a central strategy of accumulation in emergent capitalist economies. And
as is by now well documented, the broad post-Fordist politics of wage repression has taken place at the same time as a vast accumulation of wealth,
especially the accumulation of wealth via finance (Krippner 2005), the
intensification of wealth-based (and especially asset-based) inequalities
(Piketty 2014), and increasing labor productivity (International Labour
Organization 2013).

For writers such as Harvey, the pattern of wage stagnation from the
1970s onward and declines in real wages and wages share must be located
in the context of the disassembly of the Fordist-Keynesian social contract (including the social wage), a sustained attack on labor (especially
organized labor and its political institutions), and the consolidation and
concentration of the power of capital. In short, the wage repression paradigmatic of finance-led post-Fordist accumulation must be understood in
terms of a major shift and recalibration of the balance of power between

capital and labor in favor of capital, a capital now unleashed from the regulatory restraints and equilibrium-seeking devices and requirements of Fordism. Wages in the era of finance-led post-Fordism are, however, not only characterized by wage repression; alongside stagnation and declines, wages are also characterized by volatility and unpredictability (Farrell and Greig 2017; Hacker 2006; Pew Charitable Trusts 2017).[2] In addition, a gap has opened up between what labor earns and what it needs to spend. Indeed, as discussed in Chapters 2 and 3, wages paid to labor increasingly fail to cover the costs of social reproduction—that is, the everyday activities of maintaining life—amounting to a pervasive crisis of livelihood (Lansley 2011) or what is sometimes also referred to as a crisis of or assault on social reproduction (Bakker 2007; Fraser 2013; Leonard and Fraser 2016).[3] This assault has been compounded by ongoing reforms to the welfare state, including the withdrawal of the state from the key forms of social provisioning with which it has been associated historically, especially in the post–Second World War Fordist-Keynesian era: a withdrawal from health and care provisions, education, housing, social insurance, and other forms of welfare protection. This withdrawal has, moreover, intensified and accelerated through the politics of austerity. Even those forms of social provision with which the state remains entangled are sites of intense transformation. Reforms to social provisions for unemployment, for example, have located unemployment as a site for the restructuring of labor, especially for the extraction of surplus from labor outside of the wage labor relation and the rewriting of labor in terms of the unpredictable event.

These ongoing reforms to the state have not only contributed to the restructuring of labor but have also meant that services previously provided by the state are now increasingly purchased on privatized markets. This compulsion toward privatized provisioning and the dismantling of Keynesian collective insurance has created further cost pressures on individuals and households, amounting to the effective off-loading and privatization of the costs and risks of social reproduction from the state (as well as employers) onto individuals and households (Roberts 2013). This ongoing process of off-loading, together with falling real wages, has contributed to the gap between what labor earns and what it needs to spend. It has also contributed to the precarious nature of the reproduction of life paradigmatic of finance-led post-Fordism, a precariousness that points to a major transformation—indeed, to the decomposition—of the wage relation.

In regard to this decomposition, it is worth recalling the paradigmatic account of wages and the wage labor relation in capitalism, namely, that provided by Marx. Marx challenged the view that wages are the sum of money paid for a particular labor time or output of labor and hence took issue with the idea that the wage labor relation simply involves the buying or selling of labor for money. This, he emphasized, "is merely the appearance" (1979 [1891], 19). Instead, for Marx, wages must be understood as the exchange of labor power as a commodity for money. Thus, in *Wage Labour and Capital* he asks rhetorically: What are wages? He responds: "[W]ages are . . . a special name for the price of labour power," which he describes as a "peculiar commodity" (ibid.). For Marx, the peculiarity of labor power is that it is embodied. He writes: "[L]abour power has no other repository than human flesh and blood" (ibid.). Labor power is therefore a commodity that its possessor, the waged worker, sells to the capitalist. Marx proceeds to ask: "[W]hy does he [*sic*] sell it?" He responds that the worker does so "in order to live," to "secure the necessary means of subsistence" (ibid., 20). The worker therefore puts labor power into action precisely to secure the means to sustain and reproduce life.

Marx recognized, however, that the sustainability and reproduction of life through the exchange of labor power for money was in no way a given.[4] Indeed, he documented how it was only after persistent struggles between workers and capitalists, including struggles over the working day, as well as the intervention of the law and the state that a reproductive wage—and a space of social reproduction (Federici 2012)—began to emerge.[5] While acknowledging that a reproductive wage was by no means a lived reality in industrial capitalism, Marx argued nonetheless that the price of the cost of the existence and reproduction of the worker should constitute what he termed the wage minimum (Marx 1979 [1891], 27). The ideal of the reproductive wage is one with which the workers movement has been strongly aligned historically, and it came close to being realized for certain male workers under the conditions of Fordism through the family wage. Such workers exchanged their labor power for wages set at levels assumed to enable the support of dependents—crucially including a housewife—who daily performed the work of the social reproduction of labor power. For this Fordist moment, Marx's observation that a refusal on the part of the worker to sell labor power is tantamount to "renouncing his [*sic*] own existence" (ibid., 22) has a particular significance: not only because the Fordist worker had his labor power maintained and reproduced, but also because a range of sociolegal rights attached to the family wage afforded the worker both economic and social, legal, and political existence.

The history of the wage relation within capitalism, especially the near realization of the ideal of the reproductive wage for certain male workers under Fordism, is instructive here, not least because it lays bare the decomposition of the wage labor relation in finance-led post-Fordism. While Fordist workers sold labor power to secure the costs of existence and the reproduction of their labor, post-Fordist workers have no guarantee that wages secured for the exchange of labor power will or can have such an effect. And while a refusal of the sale of labor power for Fordist workers amounted to a refusal of particular forms of existence, including sociolegal existence, for post-Fordist workers social existence is by no means certain when they do sell their labor power.[6] Indeed, the decomposition of the wage labor relation raises the question of what exactly wages are in finance-led post-Fordism. If wages are no guarantee of subsistence and social existence, how are they to be defined and understood? Does Marx's definition of wages as the exchange of labor power (as a commodity) for money still hold? Can the dynamics of wages in the era of financial expansion be understood in terms of the relationship between money and labor power, and specifically their exchange? I will return to this issue, as well as to the related question of what wages are in finance-led post-Fordism, but first it is vital to address an issue on which I have so far been silent, namely, indebted laboring.

Indebted Wages

So far in this chapter I have elaborated the decomposition of the wage relation in finance-led post-Fordism, evidenced in a pervasive gap between what labor earns and what it needs to spend and in how wages no longer meet the costs of subsistence, social reproduction, and even social existence.

I have further indicated how a complex set of ongoing processes is at play in regard to this decomposition, including long-term strategies of wage repression and ongoing reforms to the state. But also implicated are dramatic and ongoing reforms to the labor market, which include the dismantling of Fordist collective wage agreements and the disassembly of employment contracts linking the exchange of labor power for wages to various forms of social protection and sociolegal rights. Also included are the emergence of precarious work as a generalized condition and new forms of employment contracts and working agreements that not only are divested of any form of social protection but that also concern forms of work, and crucially, wages that are uncertain and unpredictable. Emblematic here are zero-hour contracts, that is, contracts that set out no specific working times or wages and demand a permanent state of work-readiness, as well as forms of working contracts and work agreements that operate outside established frameworks of employment rights and labor law. In the EU, for example, "trash" service contracts and "agreements on work performed outside of the employment relationship" have been explicitly designed to bypass EU directives regulating fixed-term and part-time work (Lang et al. 2013).

It is clear that the breakdown of the wage labor relation in finance-led post-Fordism is not a singular process but involves multiple economic, legal, and political actors. It is also clear that one key outcome of this decomposition, namely, the gap between what labor earns and what it needs to spend—including on privatized forms of social provisioning—has been and continues to be compensated for by debt. Thus, as set out in Chapter 3, the past thirty-five years have witnessed the emergence of record levels of household debt and rising debt-to-income ratios. This is particularly evident in the US and the UK,[7] where the highest debt-to-income ratios are clustered in low- to middle-income households (Barba and Pivetti 2009; Montgomerie 2009). Indeed, debt service as a share of household income has hit historic peaks (Stockhammer 2015). It is worth recalling here, as set out in previous chapters, that this not only represents an intensification and expansion in the quantum of debt but that this debt has taken a highly specific form, namely, that of securitized debt. Thus, household debt in the form of mortgages, student loans, credit, and payday loans has taken the form of securitized loans and credit, that is, of contractual debt transformed via financial instruments into assets and traded on fast-moving and roving finance markets (Bryan et al. 2009; Lapavitsas 2009, 2011). Workers, therefore, have not simply become indebted to fill the gap between wages earned and necessary spending, but in so doing have become entangled in the operations of finance markets, including the exposure to risk that such entanglement entails.

In accounts of increasing household debt, the rising debt-to-income ratios and extensions to debt financing[8] that such indebtedness has entailed are very often understood in terms of the maintenance and expansion of consumer demand—especially for housing and consumer goods, as well as education and medical services—in the context of wage stagnation and repression.[9] In accounts of finance-led post-Fordism, increases in indebtedness are therefore frequently understood as having served and continuing to serve to fuel the consumer demand required by the expansionist logic of capitalist accumulation. While this line of reasoning has a certain functionalist appeal, it ignores at least two important issues. The first of these is the productivity—including the unpredictability—of contractual debt itself, which is central to the process of accumulation via securitized debt. The second is wages, and specifically how the emphasis on the creation of indebted consumer demand as a solution to stagnant wages has sidelined an interrogation of transformations to the wage labor relation. Indeed, in accounts of indebtedness and financialization—and despite the fact that increases in indebtedness are continuously and iteratively measured and reported via increasing debt-to-income ratios, that is, with reference to the expansion of debt relative to wages—attention has focused overwhelmingly on the expansion of debt (including the creation of the indebted consumer-subject) rather than on what these shifting ratios might mean in terms of wages and transformations to the wage labor relation in finance-led post-Fordism.

Even when wages are tackled in accounts of indebtedness and the broad process of financial expansion, a similar problem is encountered, namely, that potential transformations to wages and the wage labor relation are not confronted directly. It has been observed, for example, that in recent decades new forms of the extraction of profit have emerged in regard to wages and salaries. Costas Lapavitsas (2009, 2011) has elaborated how, under conditions of financial expansion and pervasive indebtedness, profits are extracted from the personal wages and incomes of workers by banks and other financial institutions rather than only from surplus value obtained from the exploitation of labor power. This has taken place via the extraction of profit in the form of interest accruing on various forms of securitized credit debt. He observes further that this form of profit extraction presupposes the involvement of workers in the mechanisms of finance "in order to meet elementary needs, such as housing, education, [and] health" (Lapavitsas 2009, 129). It is only under such conditions, he suggests, that financial institutions can extract profits from wages. But while Lapavitsas makes these critical observations, his focus is nonetheless on what happens to wages once the exchange for labor power is complete, and in particular, on how wages that have already been paid become entangled with the mechanisms and operations of finance. His analysis thus implies that wages become entangled with finance outside the zone of the exchange of labor power for money—indeed, that this exchange (however decomposed the wage labor relation might be) is removed and separate from the operations and mechanisms of finance. Lapavitsas' analysis therefore leaves intact, or at least unexamined, the assumption that wages comprise the exchange of labor power for money, albeit that those wages may be stagnant, declining, or intermittent and that the wage labor relation is both decomposed and desocialized, that is, decollectivized.

Clearly, writers such as Lapavitsas are concerned with how finance-led post-Fordism has involved the opening out of a range of novel sites for the extraction of surplus, as well as with the connections between such forms of extraction and processes of accumulation by dispossession (Harvey 2004). I do not wish to downplay the significance of such processes. Nonetheless, in terms of my concerns in this chapter, what is significant in this account is not only the assumptions regarding what wages comprise but also how wages are positioned by Lapavitsas in regard to value. This positioning is made explicit in his reflections on the subprime mortgage and financial crises:

> The roots of the disaster . . . are now easier to see. The ultimate bearers
> of mortgages in the USA were workers, often of the poorest means. Real

wages had not risen significantly throughout the bubble even for workers on higher incomes. Thus, the source of value that would ultimately
validate both mortgages and mortgage-backed assets was pathetically weak.
On this precarious basis, the financial system had built an enormous super-
structure of debt, critically undermining its own liquidity and solvency.
(Lapavitsas 2009, 137–38)

Of importance here is Lapavitsas' identification of wages, that is, the exchange of labor for money, as *the* source of value—indeed, his identification of the labor exchanged for wages not only as a key source of value but
as that value which is, and should be, expressed in the abstract through
money, that is, by wages. It is of importance, in other words, to note
Lapavitsas' positioning of money paid for the exchange of labor as a measure of value, and in particular as a measure of value produced by labor,
although the politics of wage repression has ensured that the measurement
of that value by money is now damaged and compromised. His analysis
therefore implies not only that it is politically efficacious and necessary
to prevent debt being built on the basis of weak and repressed wages, but
also that the value produced by labor should somehow be better captured,
measured, and represented in and by wages—that is, in and by money.

Reconnecting Labor to Value

I will return to this account of the relationship between wages, labor, and
value, but for now I wish to stress that Lapavitsas is not alone in understanding that stagnant and repressed wages create a problem of value in
today's financialized reality, or to posit—whether implicitly or explicitly—
that money, and specifically wages, should better capture and represent
the value created by labor. This latter sentiment forms the impetus behind
various campaigns, movements, and other forms of coordinated action that
seek to redress collapsed wages and the decomposition and desocialization
of the wage labor relation by reconfiguring the relationship between wages
and labor. Many such campaigns are well known, including demands for
the resetting and/or ratcheting up of minimum wages, living wage movements, fair wage campaigns, and decent pay and decent work campaigns

(see, e.g., Dullien et al. 2011; Pollin and Luce 1998; Wills and Linneker 2014), as well as campaigns for the revival of wage-coordinating mechanisms. In the UK, for example, the Trades Union Congress (TUC) has campaigned for new wages councils to guarantee "not just a minimum wage, not just [a] living wage but a fair wage, and fair shares of the wealth workers help create" (Trades Union Congress 2013). Indeed, the TUC has argued for a wages-led recovery from the ongoing fallout from the financial crisis and the recession that followed, as well as for wage-led growth, a strategy that involves increasing the wage share for workers (Lansley and Reed 2013).

While these campaigns and many of their key goals are by no means novel and have important lineages,[10] what is new are the highly complex and fluid labor market conditions they find themselves operating within: where subcontracted employment along complex supply chains is standard; where there is constant pressure on wages and conditions of work (where, e.g., repetitive tendering processes place wages in perpetual states of externalized competition); where there are no channels for wage bargaining or negotiation; where there is no obvious or straightforward employer-employee relationship; and where parties to employment contracts may be unclear (Wills 2009). While these campaigns and movements operate within such conditions and often have ostensibly differentiated aims (tackling low pay, dismantling wage inequality, confronting in-work poverty, raising standards of living and household subsistence levels, among others), nonetheless they are united in locating wages, especially their resetting and recalibration, as central to these aims. What is of particular interest here is that many of these campaigns seek to halt the process of stagnating and declining real wages, especially the process of the decoupling of wages from the value created by labor (including outputs, rates of productivity, and profits), by reconnecting wages to that value.

This pursuit is made explicit not only in calls such as those from the TUC that wages should be set at a level that indexes and references the economic value workers help create, but also in calls to develop globally coordinated policies that "promote a close connection between the growth of labor productivity and the growth of workers' compensation" (International Labour Organization 2013, 62). While at face value such demands concern measures to deal with stagnating and declining wages, they should not necessarily be understood in such a straightforward fashion. In calling for wages to be reconnected to the value created by labor and be anchored in that value, these campaigns are also making demands about money, especially that money do certain things. Specifically, they demand that money, and in particular money paid in wages, should act as a measure of the value that labor creates and represent that value. In short, in demanding a recalibration of wages, such calls amount to demands for the reconfiguration of money.

In the context of wage repression and stagnation and the cutting loose of wages from productivity it is, however, not only such campaigns that seek to re-anchor money in the value that labor creates and demand that money both measure and represent this value. These aims are also found in alternative currency and credit systems designed precisely toward these ends. Paradigmatic here are person-to-person time banking schemes where the units of currency are time dollars or time credits. Such schemes make use of time dollars as a unit of account and coordination for the exchange of labor and services in specific settings. In such schemes, the unit of currency is therefore quite literally anchored in labor, specifically labor measured in units of time. In such schemes, one time dollar typically represents and measures one hour of labor; once earned, it can either be spent to purchase one hour of labor or saved in a time bank. As this implies, there are localized infrastructures built around the exchange and circulation of such dollars, including both time banks and exchange services.

While interest in such alternative currencies has grown considerably in the context of current economic turbulence, they are by no means coterminous with it but have important connections to the schemes and ideas of utopian socialism (Cooper 2014). Peter North has located the postfinancial crisis wave of interest in alternative currencies in the countercultural environmental movements of the 1960s and notes how such movements gave rise to networks of people "wanting to exchange skills . . . without using capitalist money but valuing an hour of each other's labor equally. They used notes denominated not in dollars or pounds but in hours of labor" (North 2007, xii). While North traces these lineages, he is by no means utopian in his assessment of this alternative form of money. Indeed, present-day time-dollar schemes have been critiqued for the propertied forms of life and personhood they assume (Cooper 2014), as well as for their entanglement with contemporary communitarian sentiments and neocommunitarian policy agendas. The UK's Conservative–Liberal Democrat coalition government (2010–15) made this entanglement explicit in their employment of time banking and time banks as devices for fostering Big Society voluntarism in the context of the roll-out of postcrisis austerity measures (Slocock 2013).

Although these alternative currency schemes are far from unproblematic—and in the current moment are entangled with sets of policy measures connected to the ongoing reform of the welfare state and the rolling back of state-sponsored forms of social reproduction—what is significant nonetheless about such schemes is that they attempt to reinvent the foundational value of labor as the fundamental value underlying all exchange through the design of a form of money whose value is directly tied to that labor. Understood in this way—as attempts at reinventing foundational value—the entanglement of such alternative currencies with neocommunitarian postcrisis policy agendas is hardly coincidental, not least because, as Melinda Cooper (2012, 2017) makes clear, present-day capitalist accumulation contains a double movement that is both transgressive and foundational, and in which the dynamic between the two is neither dialectical nor progressive. Understood in this register, the search for foundations—including those in money and in labor—should be comprehended as immanent to (not outside of) the dynamics of finance-led post-Fordism.[11] While for Cooper such an understanding (and critique) of the search for foundations is to be found in Marx's analysis of the dynamics of capital accumulation, we can also find a critique of the search for foundational value in other branches of social theory. In regard to attempts to anchor money in the foundational value of labor, the figure of Simmel looms large, especially because of his critique of what he termed labour money.

Discussing blueprints for the reform of money that sought to secure the money equivalence of labor—that is, the expression of the "pure and immediate unity of labour in a symbol that functions as a means of exchange and measurement, that functions as money" (Simmel 2004 [1907], 410)—Simmel declared such schemes technically possible but ultimately flawed. For Simmel such "labour money" schemes were flawed because of the composition and dynamics of labor. Specifically, he proposed that different forms of labor are not interchangeable, since they produce qualitatively differentiated forms of value that are neither equivalent nor convertible into equivalents. As such, he argued that labor cannot provide a common measure of value in which money can be anchored or that money can easily represent. Indeed, for Simmel any attempt to anchor money in the value of labor would lead to a situation "more threatening to the differentiation and personal creation of life's contents than money as it already exists!" (ibid., 428). Labor money produces such a threat, since while attempting to tackle the abstraction of money by bringing it "closer to personal existence," it nonetheless requires that "*the* personal value . . . become the standard of value" (ibid.; emphasis in original). In so doing, labor money demands that the personal values toward which it attempts to bring money closer themselves become unified, abstract, fungible, and universal. Labor money, therefore, not only stumbles on its presumptions regarding labor but also misfires, because it "forgets" that money anchored in labor will still need to "possess the qualities of all money" (ibid.).

Simmel's assessment of labor money has itself been the subject of critique, not least for its failure to come to grips with Marx's labor theory of value and in particular for collapsing the distinction between use and exchange value in regard to labor power (Frisby 2004b; Spivak 1985). Yet it is clear that Simmel was opposed to any attempt to reform money, including money in the form of wages, through anchoring it to any fundamental form of value. Following Simmel's line of thought, we would therefore arrive at a critique of any attempt to anchor money in the value produced by labor, including contemporary labor money schemes such as time banking and blueprints for dealing with wage stagnation and repression by reconnecting wages with and realigning them to the productivity of labor. For Simmel such schemes and blueprints would be flawed not only because of the threat they pose to the differentiation of life but also because money is not tied to any one kind or type of value. Indeed, he argued that the importance of money lies not in the fact that it represents, measures, or has (or should have) equivalence with one source of value, but that it is "clothed in [a] plurality of values" (Simmel 2004 [1907], 428). Although this formulation of money has left him open to accusations of relativism from sociologists and naivety from economists, it nonetheless finds extraordinary resonance with the operations of money today. Specifically, Simmel's insistence that money is not necessarily anchored in the value of other things and that the dynamics of money are not necessarily tied to the representation or measurement of objects external to its own coordinates—indeed, that money should be analyzed as a thing in and of itself—finds resonance with material transformations to the capacities of money in the context of financial expansion.

Money in Motion

I discussed these transformations to the capacities of money in Chapter 2, but for the purposes of the present chapter it is important to recall certain features of these transformations here. The first is the rise of money not simply as a mediator, medium, or means of exchange but as an object of exchange in its own right. In financial markets, for example, money does not simply act as the medium and measure of exchange for assets but is in and of itself an object of exchange. I therefore stressed in Chapter 2 that one feature of financial expansion is the pervasive operation of money as a commodity or product. But I also emphasized that money as a product is not straightforward, and that it is not the case that money in a singular form or in its totality has simply become commodified. I pointed instead to how financial expansion has involved more and more monetary forms with novel attributes and capacities, and how for Bryan and Rafferty (2006, 2007, 2010) the financial derivative is paradigmatic in this regard. While derivatives are commonly understood as instruments that derive (and trade) value from underlying entities such as commodities, goods, and other assets, Bryan and Rafferty call for a radical revision of this understanding, not least because in derivative trading there is a separation between the underlying asset and derivatives, with derivatives operating as commodities in their own right. The organizing feature of the derivative is therefore "the separation of the contract from its underlier" (Poovey 2015, 154), with derivative trading comprising trading in the constantly morphing relationships between, across, and within other financial instruments. In this context Bryan and Rafferty suggest that derivatives must be understood to constitute a new form of money, which is made clear in the very opera-tions of these so-called instruments. Derivatives deconstruct any particular form of money into its various constituent attributes and commodify them, both individually and in a range of combinations, by pricing and trading them. Derivatives may, for example, take a debt contract—with particular payment demands, a particular interest rate, over a particular period of time—and break it down into these attributes (or risk exposures) and trade them individually or in bundles of attributes. In so doing, derivatives trans-form conventional money forms into spaces of possibility—a set of capaci-ties that might set things in motion. Moreover, this very transformative capacity itself can be traded. It is this capacity of transformation—of what derivatives might set in motion—together with the fact that this capacity can itself be traded, that Bryan and Rafferty insist constitutes derivatives as a new form of money. In the context of financial expansion, then, it is not simply that money is no longer a straightforward medium of exchange and is now a product, but also, as the case of derivatives demonstrates explicitly, that what money can do and what it might do have shifted.

Another important aspect of the transformation of money discussed in Chapter 2 is that in no longer functioning only as a medium or means of exchange, money loses its measurement function, especially its func-tion as the measure or standard of value and of equivalence. That is, in becoming a commodity, money can no longer commensurate, or act as a general measure of equivalence: it has become a value in itself rather than a measure of value. As such, money no longer functions in any clear or direct sense as an equivalence-producing instrument. That money has lost its measurement function is evident in a range of developments, including not only volatility in the previously hegemonic measure of value, namely, the US dollar, but also broader developments such as the so-called crisis or loss of measure in finance-led post-Fordism, as well as the search for value in singularity, uncertainty, and inequivalence (Karpik 2010). In becoming a commodity or value in and of itself, not only has money lost its privileged position as the universal arbiter and measure of value, but as a consequence the value of money as a value is now itself uncertain and unpredictable. And even as derivatives perform the work of "anchoring" the global finan-cial system (Bryan and Rafferty 2006), they do so not by recuperating or providing a new source of fundamental value but instead by turning the very contestability of fundamental value into a tradable commodity.

These transformations to money have all manner of implications for the issues raised so far in this chapter; here I will highlight only two. First of all, they position Simmel's social theory—especially his understanding of money not simply as an abstract mediator between things that both commensurates and produces and measures equivalence, but as a thing in itself—as having particular purchase and traction for the in-motion capacities of money. Specifically, Simmel's insistence that money is clothed in a plurality of values and does not act as a measure of or represent other things finds extraordinary resonance in a context where money is a value or when money is a commodity whose dynamics and value are not anchored in differentiated and externalized things. That is, it finds renewed relevance when money is a nonrepresentational and in-motion surface whose coordinates are not held in place by external anchors. It finds traction in the case of derivatives, for example, where rather than being rooted in an underlying asset or set of assets, value is created by the operations and dynamics of derivatives themselves, that is, in what the operations and capacities of derivatives set in motion. As this suggests, the increasing relevance and purchase of Simmel's social theory for money in today's financialized reality is firmly based in the empirical world—in substantive transformations to money and its dynamics. In turn, these transformations demand that previous objections to his understanding of money (and to his more general social metaphysics) require revision, particularly the objection that his understanding of the dynamics of money rests on a relativism in regard to the question of value. Indeed, in the context of ongoing global economic uncertainty, as well as concerns regarding the future of money, the renewed relevance of Simmel's social theory is increasingly recognized (see, e.g., Dodd 2012; Harrington and Kemple 2012; Lash 2007). This chapter therefore adds weight to this recognition, specifically in regard to the shifting capacities of money.

The second issue for which the transformation of money has important implications is the question and problem of the wage in finance-led post-Fordism. At face value, the realities of the exchange of labor for wages may seem sharply differentiated from the dynamics of nonrepresentational forms of money such as the derivative, especially in a context of precariousness, wage repression, and indebted labor. Yet a focus on the question of what wages do—that is, on what they set in motion, rather than (*pace* Marx) what they are (or should be)—suggests that these forms of money are not necessarily divided. Indeed, such a focus suggests that wages are organized in a manner that cannot easily be separated from nonrepresentational forms of money, not least because their value lies in what they might set in motion. To begin to think about what wages do, it is instructive to return to the issue highlighted by Lapavitsas regarding wages, in particular his observation that under conditions of financial expansion and mass indebtedness, profits are increasingly mined out of wages by financial institutions in the form of interest accruing on various forms of securitized credit debt. While the extraction of profit via such means is undoubtedly at play under these conditions, Lapavitsas fails to appreciate a central defining feature of these arrangements: specifically, that when indebted workers put their wages to work in securitized loans, mortgages, bills, and credit, they are necessarily putting money to work as a value. They are trading wages to access what that money might set in motion, trading money whose properties and capacities are not already set and given but exist as an as yet unrealized potential. When workers put their wages to work in securitized loans and credit, they are therefore trading wages not as a medium of exchange or measure of value but as a value in and of itself whose productive force might—though not necessarily—be put to work to set things in motion.

While the subprime mortgage crisis indicated that what wages might set in motion is far from unproblematic, what this trade implies nonetheless is a restructuring of the wage form in finance-led post-Fordism. As we have seen, for Marx wages comprised money paid in exchange for labor. Yet in finance-led post-Fordism, wages are framed less as a form of remuneration or compensation for the exchange of labor power and more as the right to access trade in the unrealized potential of money, that is, the right to access what money might put in motion. This framing is made explicit in the emergence of employment contracts that compensate workers with financial assets (such as shares) whose value lies in the as yet unrealized potentiality of those assets. Importantly, such contracts often demand that employees waive certain labor rights, including those relating to unfair dismissal and redundancy (Lang et al. 2013). In such contracts, not only is compensation for the exchange of labor explicitly formalized as access to money as an unpredictable value, but also evident is the commodification of labor rights, which in effect become tradable by agreement. Of significance here, therefore, is not only how such contracts make explicit a shift in the capacities of money paid as "wages," but also how those same contracts highlight that this shift relates to changing forms of employment agreements—to the very sociolegal conditions of work and working.

Critically, such contracts also outline the contours of the ideal worker in finance-led post-Fordism. This is a worker who actively compensates for repressed wages by putting money in motion, by becoming an asset-owning and interest-earning investor-subject.[12] This subject stands in contrast to the ideal worker of Fordism, who earned not financial assets and the potentialities of those assets but income, and who sought by various means to enhance the exchange value of her or his labor power through the accumulation of embodied capacities and resources. While it might be tempting to assume that a worker who compensates for repressed wages by speculating on those repressed and stagnant wages and becoming an asset-owning investor-subject is one whose contours have emerged relatively recently, it is worth pointing to national agreements forged in moments usually located as outside of, and even antithetical to, the logics of financial expansion, which laid down the very conditions of possibility for the emergence of this worker. In the case of Australia, for example, Elizabeth Humphrys and Damien Cahill (2017) have documented how such conditions were put in place during a period of Labor government (1983–96) by way of a series of policy measures forging an agreement (or social contract) with organized labor, an agreement formally known as The Accord. Focusing on wages, working conditions, and living standards, Humphrys and Cahill make clear that the reforms associated with The Accord are usually considered as both interventionist and progressive, and are also commonly understood as a repudiation of the kinds of reforms taking place contemporaneously in the UK and the US. Nonetheless, this set of policy measures forged an agreement between the state and organized labor for workers to compensate for static real wages growth with extended access to superannuation schemes for the whole workforce. While for Humphrys and Cahill the significance of The Accord lies in how it shows the active role of labor within the development of the political program of neoliberalism, what is of significance for this chapter and this book is how it concerned an institutionalized agreement to wage stagnation and provided compensation for such stagnation with access to financial assets, to what money might put in motion. The Accord had at its core the very contours of the ideal worker of finance-led post-Fordism that I am seeking to delineate in this chapter, with organized labor effectively bargaining away rights to claim increases in wages in return for access to financial assets. In this context, it is important to note—as Humphrys and Cahill do—that these agreements took place alongside the floating of the Australian dollar and the so-called deregulation or liberalization of finance, a set of policy measures that expanded the operations of finance.

Employment compensated not by wages but by the potentialities of financial assets makes explicit not only the contours of the ideal worker in the context of financial expansion but also the reworking of wages I am seeking to underscore in this chapter, namely, that in finance-led post-Fordism the most significant question is what wages can *do* rather than what they comprise. But such employment also underscores how current attempts to tie wages to labor power, and especially to re-anchor wages in the value that labor creates, may be counterproductive, not only because such attempts involve a problematic search for fundamental value but also because they bracket how the capacities of wages themselves have shifted. Specifically (as is also the case for the financial derivative), when wages are a value they can neither represent nor measure the value of other things, since their value is not pre-set but is constituted in motion by dynamics internal to themselves. It might be proposed, therefore, that contemporary attempts to anchor money in labor are problematic not because they flatten out qualitative differences in labor, as Simmel might suggest, but because such attempts fail to acknowledge that when wages operate as a value—as an in-motion and complex surface—this work of re-anchoring is difficult, if not impossible, to achieve. Indeed, it might be suggested that just as derivatives are separated out from any underlying asset or set of assets, wages must be understood as separated out from labor power. Rather than being a measure or an index of such labor, or even as the price of labor, the dynamics of wages operate independently from those of labor power.

Within Fordism the (albeit limited and problematic) measurement function that wages performed for the value of the labor of some workers was, of course, the outcome of particular institutional arrangements as well as specific social struggles. And within finance-led post-Fordism it should be recognized that the separating out of the dynamics of wages (specifically the operations of wages as a value) and those of labor are also the outcome of a range of complex institutional and policy arrangements, including the operations of working agreements and working contracts, as well as agreements such as The Accord forged between the state and labor. But once this has been recognized, then some of the key features of wages that I have outlined in this chapter, including the increasing disconnect between wages and the costs of social reproduction, as well as stagnant and declining wages in the face of rising labor productivity, can be grasped.

The Politics of Asset-Based Wages

In concluding this chapter, I wish to address the implications of the analysis I have laid out here for a politics of the wage in the context of financial expansion. If, as I have argued, such wages are arranged as a commodity whose dynamics concern not the price of labor but access to what money might or might not put in motion, a politics focused on "correcting" the decomposition of the wage labor relation through demands that wages better capture and represent the value created by labor may be understood both as bracketing the changing capacities of wages and as being misplaced. Indeed, according to my analysis a politics of wages in the context of financial expansion should focus squarely on what such wages are, namely, money, and more particularly, an access point to what money can do. As part of his analysis of indebtedness and indebted society, Lazzarato (2011) has argued that a key fault line lies precisely in money, especially between those who have access to money and those who do not. My analysis suggests that this formulation is in need of some refinement: specifically, that a key fault line lies not simply in access to money but between those who have access to what money might set in motion and those who do not. What, then, would a relevant politics geared to addressing this fault line look like? Should it not precisely engage its very ground, namely, financial assets, their access and distribution? Shouldn't a politics of the wage directed toward socioeconomic change in the time of money abandon attempts to realign wages with labor and instead focus on demands for access to money as an asset? Instead of endeavoring to undermine the ideal of the asset-owning and interest-earning investor worker-subject through attempts to reinstate the fiction of the commodity-owning free laborer, why not embrace this ideal and develop an ambitious set of goals for this worker-subject?

In proposing such a politics, I am drawing on the work of Michel Feher (2009),[13] especially his argument regarding the replacement of the free laborer by the speculative subject, that is, a subject who does not *own* (or make claims to own) human capital but *is* human capital. Feher asks what a radical politics for this subject would look like. He suggests that, much as the workers movement adopted the figure of the free laborer, critics ought to adopt the notion of human capital and push it to its limits, "allow[ing] it to express aspirations and demands that its neoliberal promoters had neither intended nor foreseen" (Feher 2009, 25). This is precisely the kind of politics I am proposing for wages in the time of money, namely, a politics that embraces asset-based wages and attempts to challenge them from within. So, if the ideal worker is an asset-owning and interest-earning subject who long since traded away the right to claims to wage increases and the indexing of those wages to labor power for access to financial assets, why not demand the rights and conditions that would allow all workers— and all aspiring workers—to put money in motion? Could such tactics serve as a point of departure for political change in regard to the wage in the time of money? How would the state and employers respond to such demands?

The proposition for such a politics is by definition speculative. However, what I am suggesting is that such a politics may offer a more relevant and pertinent mode of engagement with wages when they are arranged as a commodity whose dynamics involve access to what money might or might not put in motion. But while speculative, such a politics might also serve as a corrective to the considerable nostalgia—a nostalgia evidenced in the various campaigns and schemes this chapter has charted—that so many progressives and progressive labor organizations continue to attach to the figure of the worker who makes claims to own various forms of capital and whose labor power is exchanged for wages. It is, I would suggest, only by directly confronting the reworked relationship between labor and wages (or more precisely, between labor and money) that such nostalgia can be challenged and a space opened out for a new politics of wages and of the worker who must speculate on those wages as money across whole lives and lifetimes.

CHAPTER 5

Out of Work

One of the central arguments of this book is that the expansion and reconfiguration of finance from the 1970s onward has involved not only an intensification of the productivity in finance in terms of the generation of surplus from the movements and flows of money, but also the emergence of distinctive social forms. These forms are concerned not with equilibrium states or stasis but with disequilibrium and asymmetry. I have pointed, for example, to a postprobabilistic reworking of the relationship between credit-debt and wages such that credit-debt outruns working and lived lives and if indexed against income can never be repaid; a nonchronological temporal universe that binds everyday practices to the indeterminate movements of money; and modes of practice that are attuned not to the reproduction of labor but to the optimization of the possibles of payment. While for many social theorists such disequilibrium states are cause for alarm and a sign of a dysfunctional and degenerating social order, I have stressed that they constitute the very social fabric of the time of money, not least because they afford modes of practice and activate capacities that attune populations to the logic of speculation.

In this chapter, I turn to a further instance of the activation of such capacities, and especially to how a logic of speculation guides and organizes the composition and organization of labor. My interest in labor is certainly not to recuperate its status as the foundational or fundamental value

underlying exchange. Instead it is in how, in the time of money, labor has
been restructured in terms of the unpredictable event. The restructuring
of the probables of Fordist wage labor into a range of contingencies has
been made explicit by a number of writers, as have the sociolegal devices,
infrastructures, and practices that have enabled this reworking (see, e.g.,
Cooper 2012; Peck and Theodore 2012; Rafferty and Yu 2010). The latter
include zero hours and other forms of employment contracting that have
uncertainty and the shouldering of risk at their very core. They also include outsourcing and subcontracting chains, contingent work strategies,
tendering and procurement practices, and employment policy regimes that
seek to optimize the working capacities and employability of whole populations, as well as to maximize such capacities across whole lifetimes. Also
at issue are a range of sociotechnical devices and institutional mechanisms
that have transformed the certainties of the Fordist wage into the necessarily unknowns of what money might put in motion. Such devices, practices,
and infrastructures must be recognized as central to the transformation of
the Fordist into the post-Fordist labor market and the establishment, as
Melinda Cooper (2012) has framed it, of contingency not as a marginal or
peripheral principle in the organization and realities of wage labor but as a
necessity and a standard.

In this chapter I situate—perhaps at first sight paradoxically—the labor
of the unemployed in these terms. I am concerned with that labor which
is the subject and object of regimes of activation, that is, of a range of
techniques ostensibly designed to enhance the employability of the unemployed and underemployed through the activation and enhancement
of laboring capacities. Sometimes referred to as workfare or welfare-to-
work policy, activation regimes became embedded across OECD countries
beginning in the 1990s through a complex and still ongoing set of policy
exchanges and transfers. Activation has been located as a key postwelfarist
policy that has supported the functioning of post-Fordist labor markets
through the provisioning of a supply of cheap and flexible labor (see especially Peck 2001). It has also been understood as comprising a set of techniques for the formatting of risk-bearing postwelfarist subjects (see, e.g.,
Triantafillou 2011, 2012), as well as for disciplining and punishing the poor
and/or an abandoned underclass (Streeck 2014; Wacquant 2009, 2010).

In this chapter I suggest that what remains absent from these debates is the recognition of how regimes of activation serve to restructure labor, opening out the capacities of workers in regard to events that have not yet and might never take place. I set out how this restructuring is eroding the long-lived historical distinction between employment and unemployment by positioning unemployed workers—like their contingently employed counterparts—as always needing to adapt and adjust to the possible. But more than this, I suggest that in their command that the wageless and jobless adapt to the possible, activation regimes open the productive capacities of the unemployed out to the logic of speculation through binding unemployed populations to the indeterminacy of speculative time. I thus situate activation regimes not as a policy analogue to post-Fordist flexible labor markets but as an analogue to the creation of surplus via the indeterminate movements and flows of money.

Many contemporary social scientists might be tempted to take the processes this chapter charts, especially the making productive of unemployment, as being exemplary of economization, that is, the broad-scale process of the folding of the economy into society. This process has been located as central to transformations to the economy-society relation in the context of neoliberalism or the rise of market society (see, e.g., Brown 2015; Çalişkan and Callon 2009, 2010; Foucault 2008),[1] and has been understood to include the movement of laboring activities away from the enclosures of the formally productive sphere and their dispersal across the social body (see, e.g., Chicchi 2010; Lazzarato 1996). I suggest, however, that economization is less an issue of a benign dispersal of laboring activities across the social body and/or the harvesting of value from activities within the social body, and more one of the activation of the capacities of the wageless—especially of would-be waged workers—in regard to the demands of the logic of speculation. Indeed, I suggest that what is missing from the debates on economization is a recognition that a logic of speculation centered on the creation of surplus from the flows and movements of money has replaced a logic of extraction centered on the mining of surplus from the human laboring body.

There is, however, a further dimension to my interest in unemployment, underemployment, and wagelessness in this chapter: how, in the post–financial crisis era, rising unemployment levels across the US and Europe were understood (and for the EU area continue to be understood) to evidence the disruptive qualities of the generation of surplus via finance for the social order. This is the case—so the story goes—not only because of the inevitable crises that the excessive generation of surplus from finance inescapably contains but also because those very crises threaten to return us to previous states of existence, especially to undesirable states, both real and imagined. My interest in such accounts lies in how they explicitly situate financial expansion and the generation of surplus via money and finance as degenerate in regard to the social order and as especially reprobate in regard to the ordering of time. In this chapter I show how the assumption of this degeneracy is entirely mistaken, not only because the time of money has unfolded a specific time universe and specific social and economic forms but also because, unlike their historical counterparts, the labor of the contemporary unemployed and jobless is the subject and object of the logic of speculation. I shall address first the claims that financial expansion threatens a return to previous states of existence.

Turning Back Time

Following the financial crisis, a range of voices claimed that the global financial crisis and subsequent recession evidenced not only an excessive trade on the future at the cost of the present but also the return of previous deleterious states. Rises in rates of unemployment, for example, prompted the drawing of a wave of parallels between the post–financial crisis era and the Great Depression, not least because of their shared backgrounds in financial turbulence (Haywood 2010; Livingston 2011; Reinhart and Rogoff 2009). In a *New York Times* opinion piece in 2009, for example, the American Keynesian economist Paul Krugman warned that prevailing economic and social conditions in the US looked "an awful lot like the beginning of a second Great Depression" (Krugman 2009a). According to Krugman's diagnosis at the time, these conditions included plummeting manufacturing activity, rising unemployment, a freeze in consumer and business spending, and a massive slowdown in bank lending. In *The Return of Depression Economics and the Crisis of 2008*, Krugman (2009b) fleshed out the apparent parallels and continuities with the Great Depression. He suggested that what he termed depression economics—that is, "the kinds of problems that characterized much of the world economy in the 1930s but have not been seen since"—had "staged a stunning comeback" (ibid., 181). He went on: "[F]ifteen years ago hardly anybody thought that modern nations would be forced to endure bone-crushing recessions for fear of currency speculators, and that major advanced nations would find themselves persistently unable to generate enough spending to keep their workers and factories employed" (ibid.).

Krugman was certainly not alone in his understanding that the conditions and socioeconomic problems of the 1930s had returned in the post–financial crisis era. In a 2010 interview the then chief economist of the IMF, Olivier Blanchard, remarked that "unemployment [following the financial crisis] remains high, particularly in countries such as the United States and Spain. Long-term unemployment is alarmingly high: in the U.S., for instance, half of the unemployed have been out of work for over six months, something we have not seen since the Great Depression" (International Monetary Fund Survey 2010). Indeed, in the years immediately following the financial crisis, rates and durations of unemployment were consistently compared to those of the Great Depression, with the latter serving as an affective benchmark or index of the devastation the financial crisis had unfolded, together with the dangers of the generation of surplus via money and finance.[2] In testimony to the US Congress in 2010 on long-term unemployment, Harvard labor economist Lawrence F. Katz noted that "labor market conditions have deteriorated dramatically since . . . late 2007 making this the severest labor market downturn since the Great Depression of the 1930s" (Katz 2010, 2); while in 2013, economist William K. Black assessed joblessness in the Eurozone to be running at "rates higher than the best estimates of European unemployment during the Great Depression" (Black 2013).[3] The ongoing unemployment crisis in the Eurozone continues to be indexed and referenced to the Great Depression. Describing this crisis, and especially increases in long-term joblessness (i.e., increases in enduring unemployment), a journalist for *The Telegraph* recently pronounced that "[t]he problem is not new. Similar forces gripped the US during the Great Depression" (Khan 2015).

Notwithstanding any similarities in unemployment rates and out-of-work durations, it is clear that the prevailing social and economic conditions of both the immediate period after the 2007–8 financial crisis and the ongoing post–financial crisis era did not and do not parallel those of the late 1930s. The kinds of institutional transformations—including to banking and monetary policy—that enabled the expansion of finance from the 1970s onward and have become further entrenched in the post–financial crisis era, for example, were simply not present before and after the Wall Street crash; neither was a mode of financial expansion that pervaded everyday life. Present-day securitization, for example, could hardly have been imagined, let alone lived, in early to mid-twentieth-century industrial capitalism—nor, for that matter, could social forms organized and ordered by a logic of speculation. Understood in this way, claims that the conditions and problems of the 1930s have returned in the post–financial crisis era clearly fall short of the mark in regard to matters of historical specificity, especially in regard to the expansion and transformation of money and finance. Such claims should, in other words, be understood as bypassing what in 1979 Stuart Hall termed a conjunctural analysis of the present, an analysis that demands that the present be understood not as a series of repeats of history but in terms of the specifics of a concrete moment.[4] While Hall was concerned with developing such an analysis for the then-emergent economic, social, cultural, and political features of Thatcherism as well as for combatting what he saw as economistic interpretations of the "swing to the Right" (Hall 1979, 14), it is clear that a conjunctural mode of analysis has not lost its relevance, not least for combatting claims that the problems of the 1930s have returned in the post–financial crisis era.[5]

While it is imperative to stress the significance of a conjunctural analysis in and for the time of money, it is also important to register that the idea that the post–financial crisis era is returning us to past states of existence is by no means limited to claims concerning the return of the conditions and problems of the 1930s. In addition to these claims, the post–financial crisis era has also witnessed repeated declarations that the crisis—especially the recession that ensued—risked the return of an exclusionary sexual contract, especially the sexual contract of Fordism, because the post-crisis recession placed women's jobs at risk. In early 2009, for example, the business editor of the UK's *Observer* newspaper, Ruth Sunderland, predicted that, while in previous recessions men had borne the brunt of job losses, the current recession would be the UK's "first fully feminised recession" (Sunderland 2009). Women, she went on, "will suffer the most, jeopardizing their hard-earned financial independence and equality at work" (ibid.). And this is so, she argued, because in the UK women tend to dominate in those sectors that would be hardest hit by the recession, namely, in retail and services. She asked: "[C]ould this downturn reverse the huge economic gains women have made over the past few decades?" (ibid.).

Katherine Rake of the UK's Fawcett Society shared similar concerns, warning that the recession meant that "the advances made by women in the workplace . . . are currently at risk" (Rake 2009a, 2). Women, she argued, "are more directly exposed to the impact of this recession as employees than they were in the recessions of the 1990s or 1980s" (ibid.) because women and men were entering the recession on unequal footing. She claimed that although there have been major increases in women's employment, "the nature of women's employment still remains markedly different from men's. . . . [T]heir experiences of employment are shaped by motherhood and other caring duties, concentration in particular sectors of the economy and the traditional undervaluation of women's jobs" (ibid., 4). Women's working patterns, she went on, "make them, on the majority of counts, more economically vulnerable than men from the outset" (ibid.). In a further commentary in *The Guardian*, she declared:

> This recession must not be used as an excuse to send women back to the kitchen. The enormous strides that women have made in workplace equality must be protected during tough times and we cannot afford to lose women's vital skills as we seek a route to recovery. Women are now looking to the Government to send out a strong signal to business that it will not compromise on women's rights. (Rake 2009b)

Sunderland and Rake were not alone in expressing such fears at what was then the start of the postcrisis recession. At this time a range of agencies and organizations commissioned research that attempted to map, measure, and predict the gendered contours of the unfolding recession.[6] This body of research typically assembled and put to use a range of indicators and measures to chart these contours, including employment and unemployment rates, redundancy rates by economic sector, economic inactivity rates, take-up rates of unemployment benefits, and distributions of workforce jobs. In addition, the techniques of econometric forecasting were employed in attempts to predict the future shape of the recessionary trends in regard to men's and women's relative economic outlooks.

Yet while researchers went about the business of assembling their various indicators and measures to produce their analyses and forecasts, what was striking was that very little attention was paid to questions of what exactly was being measured, of how things were being measured, and of what the various indicators tracking the contours of the recession were assumed to be indicating. Instead, these things tended to be taken for granted. While many of the research reports relating to these efforts certainly stressed that the current recession departed from previous recessions in all manner of ways, not least because a large and expanded number of women faced potential job loss, nonetheless it was also striking that many of the instruments used in attempts to measure the effects of the recession for men and women remained the same as those used in previous recessions. Just as in previous recessions, the number of economically active men and women were counted and then compared to numbers in earlier recessionary moments; and just as in previous recessions, unemployment and redundancy rates for men and women were counted, charted, and compared across different time frames.

As the recession became more entrenched and governments devised and unfurled stimulus plans and austerity programs, activities attempting to map and evaluate the impact of the economic downturn for women in particular, but also for men, intensified—not least because, for the case of austerity programs in particular, such measures typically involved cuts to public spending. As set out in Chapter 2, such cuts were and still are widely assumed to have deleterious effects for women because of the latter's concentration in public sector employment, a concentration constituted by the massive expansion of women's employment prior to the global financial crisis. In the UK, for example, a 2011 Trades Union Congress (TUC) research report recorded that "the proportion of women employed in the public sector has risen at three times the rate of men over the last decade" (TUC 2011). Together with this, however, the report recorded the women's unemployment rate in the UK to be at a twenty-three-year high. This situation would, the TUC warned, "only deteriorate as job cuts in . . . health, education, local government and the civil service continue to mount" (ibid.). Indeed, and within this report, the then TUC general secretary Brendan Barber cautioned:

> The rising number of women in work has been a great success story of the last decade, but as childcare and child benefits are cut, vital services including education and health are pared back and women's job losses mount, we risk moving backwards and reducing, rather than improving, women's opportunities in the workplace. (Barber, in TUC 2011)

He went on: "The TUC is calling on the Government to do far more to boost investment in the private sector, and to think again about its spending cuts. Our economy simply can't afford to lose a decade of social progress" (ibid.). Thus, much as at the onset of the recession, a differential positioning of women and men in the economy was assumed to mean that women were particularly vulnerable in terms of job losses. As the recession rolled out, this vulnerability was understood to intensify, not only in terms of potential job losses but also in the form of cuts to a range of state and quasi-state services. Such cuts were assumed to mean that there would be increasing demands on women to perform unpaid caring work, demands that militate against employment and employability. Moreover, just as initially the recession had been understood as threatening to return us to a previous state of existence, this return was assumed to be ever closer to actualization as the economic downturn marched on.

Again, many echoed such fears. A report commissioned by Northern Ireland's Women's Resource and Development Agency (WRDA) highlighted how cutting public sector employment "predominantly means cutting women's jobs as it is they who make up the majority of the public service workforce" (WRDA 2011, 8). Just as the TUC feared that the actions of governments threaten to turn back time, so too did the WRDA:

> Under cover of the recession, welfare support is being slashed along with incentives that encourage women into work and towards economic au-

Figure 5.1. Fawcett Society, 2011. Used with permission.

tonomy. The model of society being held up for women is: go back to the home, pick up the unpaid caring role that we, the governments, cannot cover and we will focus on incentivising your husband to support you. (WRDA 2011, 8)

Reflecting on the findings of this report, Lynn Carvill of the WRDA claimed that Northern Ireland is "returning to the 1950s when a woman's place was in the home" (Carvill, in BBC News 2011). Women, she continued, "are less well positioned than men to weather the crisis. . . . [G]government responses to the crisis mean we are in danger of turning the clock back in terms of women's equal economic participation. The [government's] proposed . . . reforms will remove women's economic autonomy" (ibid.). In a political campaign launched in late 2011 protesting the UK government's austerity measures, the Fawcett Society voiced similar fears. Organized around the theme of "Don't Turn Back Time," the campaign included a call for a day of action in which protestors were encouraged to adopt 1950s-style clothing. The Fawcett Society advised: "[D]ress up to send the message that women don't want to be catapulted back to the levels of inequality of yesteryear."

Rethinking Unemployment

What is clear in these reports, analyses, forecasts, conjectures, and campaigns is that the financial crisis and ensuing recession were ascribed enormous social and political powers. These included but were by no means limited to the power of disassembling the present and returning us to an undesirable past (i.e., the power of creating an anachronistic present); the power of undoing social progress; the power of blunting the force of political movements; and the power of delaying the fulfillment of sociopolitical dreams. But while not explicitly stated, such reports and campaigns also claimed much more than these powers for the ongoing recession. For example, in the claim that the recession was returning women to the kitchen, the home, economic dependency, and unpaid domestic and caring roles, these reports and their authors were implicitly declaring that the global financial crisis and subsequent recession had somehow pushed a mode of capitalist accumulation based on the generation of surplus via money and finance—along with its associated institutional and infrastructural arrangements and arrangements of life—entirely to one side and begun a return to a socioeconomic formation that seeks and requires equilibrium states, especially equilibrium in regard to the work of production and social reproduction. More precisely, these reports and campaigns were by default claiming that the post–financial crisis era is reinstating or has the power to reinstate an economic and social formation in which the work of production (and the extraction of surplus value from that labor) is underpinned, mediated by, and requires unpaid socially reproductive activities performed in the private sphere. The authors and their reports were, in other words, declaring a return of arrangements of labor and life associated with Fordism, arrangements organized by and founded on a sexual contract that limited many women's social, economic, and political rights, including their right to lay claim to property in the person.

Inasmuch as any moment cannot be perfectly mimicked and reproduced in time (Butler 1993), such a return to a historically specific mode of socioeconomic organization—whether desired or not—is clearly impossible. But while the philosophy of time teaches that a return to any past is unattainable, nonetheless, in the immediate post–financial crisis period, a narrative of such a return framed debate, research agendas, political interventions, and political imaginations. As such, it is worth thinking through exactly how and why such a narrative is not only philosophically but also sociologically problematic. It is worth, in particular, thinking through the immediate and ongoing post–financial crisis moment not as one that repeated or is repeating history but in conjunctural terms. The issues here are multiple, but two stand out from the reports and campaigns as demanding immediate attention, both of which concern unemployment and joblessness.

First, the reports and campaigns assume that if women are not in paid work, they will necessarily be carers, wives, and mothers. Leaving aside the assumption that all women are partnered, heterosexual, and parenting, as well as the further assumption that when women are in paid employment they do not also perform caring and/or domestic labor, what is striking about these accounts is that women occupy only two, mutually exclusive positions: they are either in paid employment or in the home as subjects without political right to property in the person. Yet surely, given the rewriting of the relations among capital, labor, and the state in finance-led post-Fordism, especially the unfolding of a post-Fordist sexual contract, this understanding must be questioned. In regard to social reproduction, for example, not only—as outlined in Chapter 2—has the provisioning of this labor undergone radical transformation in the context of finance-led post-Fordism (and is increasingly politicized as it is provided by commercial services), but the home is increasingly geared to (and organized by) a logic of speculation, such that it has been rewritten not as a site for the reproduction of labor power but for the production of the possible in regard to flows of money.

The second (and related) issue that stands out from these reports is that in assuming that women are either in employment or in the home as subjects without the political right to property in the person, they do not consider women as occupying the state of being unemployed. In this assumption, these reports again suggest a return to a Fordist-Keynesian social formation in which women's labor was positioned as a reserve for capital, one in which (through the operations of social security laws) many women, especially those defined as dependents, were denied unemployment status, including the rights associated with unemployment such as the right to access unemployment benefits (see, e.g., Fox Piven 2011; Morris 1990; O'Connor et al. 1999). This is an extraordinary omission given the now undisputed reliance of capitalism on women's labor: the massive incorporation of women's labor into the labor market and the system-wide changes that have driven this incorporation. It is, in other words, an extraordinary omission, given how women's labor no longer operates as a reserve for capital (if it ever did so cleanly or decisively [see, e.g., Ferguson 2003; Walby 1984]) but is central to capital's own valorization, and in particular, for the valorization of finance capital through putting wages in motion. It is also extraordinary given the significance of the putting in motion of women's (repressed and contingent) wages to the survival and sustainability of households both pre- and postrecession. Given this latter, it is clear that if any meaningful sociological assessment of the post–financial crisis recession is to take place, it is vital not only to consider the changing conditions of women's employment—of the incorporation of women's labor into the labor market on a mass scale—but also to open out the conditions of women's unemployment for critical investigation. Such a procedure should necessarily involve putting aside long-lived assumptions regarding the place and role of joblessness for women in capitalist accumulation—for instance, the assumption that women who are not in employment constitute a reserve of labor who stand ready for exploitation but who nonetheless perform the unpaid work of social reproduction in the household—and instead involve asking a series of open questions regarding the changing relationship between unemployment and finance-driven accumulation processes. For if in finance-led post-Fordism the labor of women is no longer positioned as a reserve and/or as that which serves to reproduce and sustain labor power in the household but stands as a site of potential and possibility in regard to flows of money, then surely this implies a transformation in the conditions of joblessness, including a transformation in how joblessness might be sensed and lived.

In the context of the massive incorporation of women's labor into the labor market and especially into the wage labor imperative, such questions have, however, received little attention. Indeed, prior to the post–financial crisis recession, and as suggested by the discussion in Chapter 2, attention was focused on the ways in which employment had changed for women and how, in turn, such transformations were integral to shifts in accumulation processes, including changes to employment policy regimes. In retrospect, what stands out from this body of work is that very little attention was paid to the issues of unemployment, joblessness, and wagelessness. In fact, what stands out especially is an assumption that transformations to women's labor, including the frontier status ascribed to that labor by both capital and the state, were evident in wage labor—in employment and waged work—however contingent and unpredictable that employment might have been. In many ways, this assumption was not surprising, given the rapid expansion of women's paid employment, or more precisely, that employment growth in the time of money has been largely an issue of the incorporation of women into the wage labor imperative. Nor was it surprising given how rights and access to employment and wages had served as a key feminist goal of the Fordist-Keynesian era. Yet while much attention was paid to women's wage labor, what often went unnoticed was the ways in which unemployment and joblessness were also changing, a transformation that is significant in regard to questions concerning the character and place not only of women's labor but of labor more generally in finance-led post-Fordism, both before and after the financial crisis and the subsequent recession. Thus, transformations to unemployment and joblessness are of considerable significance for understanding the character and place of labor in and for the time of money.

Regimes of Activation

The landscape of unemployment and joblessness during the time of the expansion of finance has one especially outstanding feature, namely, the take-up and intensification of a range of labor market activation policies across Europe, North America, and Australasia from the mid-1990s onward, as well as the promotion and coordination of these policies through a range of transnational agencies and organizations, including the OECD, the IMF, and the World Bank. During the time of the expansion of finance, activation policies have, then, been supported and promoted by key post–Washington consensus institutions. Such policies are ostensibly designed to facilitate reentry into employment for the unemployed and/or underemployed by means of a range of devices and techniques, including the application of unemployment benefit conditions whereby receipt of benefits is conditional on participation in a range of activities: mandatory training, job placement programs, job coaching, counseling, job-searching, and unpaid laboring activities, among others. Activation measures and techniques also include the application of time limits on unemployment benefits and the enforcement of work availability. According to the OECD (2014b), such measures aim "to enforce work-availability and mutual obligation requirements, meaning that benefit recipients are expected to engage in active job search and improve their employability, in exchange for receiving efficient employment services and benefit payment"; while for the World Bank, activation measures aim to "incentivize job search and job finding, productive participation in society, and becoming and remaining self-sufficient and less dependent on public support" (Immervol 2012, 1).

Activation strategies are not entirely novel (see, e.g., Banoli 2010). What is new, however, is the "centrality of activation to modern welfare states" (Kenworthy 2010). It is vital to register that such strategies are, however, not simply characteristics of modern welfare states but have been and continue to be central to their transformation (i.e., their reform). Activation and workfare strategies and the regimes of conditionality they involve have served as a centerpiece in the transformation of the welfare state from an institution whose foremost rationality is one of the maintenance and protection of lives, most notably the protection, maintenance, and reproduction of the laboring capacities of national populations (particularly the capacities of the male laboring body), to an institution whose rationality is one of contingent, provisional, and uncertain support (Cooper 2008; Povinelli 2011). Such support is, moreover, dependent on the fulfillment of an ever-shifting set of conditions associated with work-readiness and working in exchange for state benefits. The reform of the welfare state has therefore transformed the universal social rights of welfarism into a set of obligations and compulsions, especially obligations to work (Bertram 2015; Cooper 2012; Gilbert 2002; Peck 2001).

This transformation should be understood to have morphed Esping-Andersen's (1990) three worlds of postwar welfare capitalism into a continuous workfare state,[7] including the previously much lauded (and often fetishized) social democratic Nordic model (Kananen 2012, 2014). Indeed, despite local variations in activation policies they are united in their transformation of the rights of welfare into the constantly shifting obligations of workfare. These transformations are postnational in character and should be understood as part of the broad political project of the neoliberal reform of capitalist states (Jessop 2002a, 2002b; Samers 2011). This project has relied in part on the coordination of political action through transnational agencies and a complex and still unfolding process of policy transfer and exchange.[8] To give just two examples, in the 1990s, workfare policy transfers took place between the US, Canada, and the UK (Peck and Theodore 2001), while the Finnish state—one previously coded as socially democratic—is currently experimenting with aspects of the UK's (The Work Programme) and Australia's (Job Active) models in its latest round of workfare reforms. It is clear that there is now a complex and thoroughly entrenched postnational infrastructure for the promotion, transfer, roll-out, and continuous morphing of activation policy, even though, paradoxically, such policies are delivered in increasingly devolved contexts. It is also clear that activation is so embedded that it is a mainstay of capitalist states and at present the conditions and obligations associated with access to out-of-work benefits are tightening and intensifying.

To engage with activation policies necessitates not only an understanding of the transformation of the welfare state into the workfare state—that is, of the residualization of welfare and the enforcement of work (Peck 2001)—but also the transformation of the state-economy relation. In particular, it necessitates an understanding of the shift from a state-economy relation concerned not with securing the conditions of possibility for capitalist accumulation driven and ordered by the logic of Fordism, but with the conditions of possibility for capitalist accumulation driven and ordered by the logic of finance-led post-Fordism. This shift is evidenced in employment policy. From the mid- to late 1970s onward, across advanced liberal states (states that embraced neoliberal governance as a political strategy), there was a move away from the full (male) employment ideals of Keynesianism to the embrace of Schumpeterian policies aimed at securing employability and enhancing the competitiveness of open economies (Jessop 2002a). Concerning this shift, two issues are critical for the concerns of this chapter. First is the move away from a focus on demand (including the role of the state in ensuring the demand for labor or securing full male employment) toward a focus on labor supply, especially a self-organizing and flexible supply of labor. In this supply-side universe, unemployment is located and understood not as a problem of demand that the state should work to amend but as a problem of competitiveness, especially the competitiveness of labor (Triantafillou 2011).

The second issue, as indicated in Chapter 2, is that while the full employment policies of Keynesianism in practice almost always concerned the employment of men (and assumed that the vitality of this labor force was assured by the protections of the welfare state, including by the state-backed socially reproductive labor of women), the embrace of nonequilibrium Schumpeterian employment policies has exposed whole populations to the command to work and to employability in the name of enhancing the competitiveness of economies. This has meant that those previously exempted and protected from work and working have been (albeit unevenly and messily) exposed to the demand to work. The paternalistic protections afforded to many women by welfare states, have, for example, been progressively removed and replaced with the demand (and the necessity) that they either work or become work ready. Indeed, women who do not work, especially women with dependent children, along with out-of-work youth, mature-aged job-seekers, the long-term unemployed, and indigenous populations, are subjects of intense scrutiny in activation regimes, including intensified activation measures and conditionalities. They are also regularly the subjects of experiments in activation measures. Understood as problems in need of attention within the classificatory schemes of activation regimes, these groups are consistently taken as being in urgent need of enhancement of their work-readiness and employability.

What is apparent in the shift to Schumpeterian employment policies is that they have been critical in the fade-out of Fordist social formations, including those through which labor power was organized as a substance to be replenished on a daily basis. Indeed, as set out in Chapter 2, one of the key mechanisms that kept this arrangement in place in the Fordist-Keynesian era, namely, the family wage, has been thoroughly dismantled, and the ideals of the male breadwinner and female dependency have been replaced by adult worker models (Cooper 2012; Deeming 2014; Lewis 2001) that assume that all adults should be working, or if not in work then actively seeking work. Such policy models are properly located as part of the Schumpeterian drive through which whole populations have been opened out to the command to work. As such, the massive incorporation of women into the labor market and the wage labor imperative detailed earlier in this book should be understood in these terms, that is, in terms of the establishing of a state-economy relation concerned with the competitiveness of labor, including competitiveness in regard to the wage (or the price of labor).

It is also apparent that with their mandates of employability, work-readiness, and working activity, activation measures are part of the management and regulation of labor by Schumpeterian means. Indeed, one of the most influential and powerful analyses of activation characterizes activation and workfare reform precisely in such terms. Developed by Jamie Peck in particular (Peck 2001; see also Peck and Theodore 2001), in this mode of analysis activation schemes, especially the regimes of conditionality and the mandatory work activities they involve (including commands that oblige those enrolled in activation schemes to accept any form of paid labor or risk losing state benefits), are understood as providing a supply of free and/or cheap labor to fuel low-paid and highly contingent jobs. Thus, activation schemes operate as a labor-supply mechanism for the bottommost rungs of highly flexible labor markets (see also Krinsky 2007; Wacquant 2010). It is important to add that such provisioning serves not only as a labor-supply mechanism but also as one that operates to persistently undercut the price of labor (and hence should be noted as one route through which wages have been exposed to perpetual competition).[9]

What is vital to understand in regard to activation regimes, then, is how they serve as an institutional pillar of the regulation of labor and labor markets in finance-led post-Fordism. Activation regimes not only open out the capacities of whole populations to the imperative to work but in so doing provide the very kind of labor—cheap, flexible, and compliant—on which the post-Fordist labor market depends. As a policy orthodoxy operative throughout the period of the expansion of finance, activation regimes have also contributed to the stagnation and repression of wages as well as to the broad-scale transformation of the probables of Fordist wage labor (including the probables of the wage itself) into a range of contingencies.

The Sexual Politics of Activation

But should activation regimes be understood primarily as providing a supply of cheap and flexible labor to contingent labor markets? Frances Fox Piven (2011) has questioned the easy functionalism of this argument. She suggests that the post–financial crisis recession and subsequent drop in demand even for cheap labor, together with long-term increases in in-work poverty, reveal there to be far more at stake in activation regimes than issues of labor supply alone. What became obvious in the recessionary postcrisis moment, she suggests, is how work-enforced welfare is a strategy of "impoverishment and insult" (Fox Piven 2011, 110). This strategy, more-

over, is one that is aimed particularly at out-of-work women and especially minority women, those who are defined precisely as problems in the
classificatory schemes of activation regimes. Activation, or work-enforced
welfare, should be understood, she argues, in terms of the expansion of the
imperative of wage labor to incorporate women. Activation regimes (and
the broader project of the structural reform of the welfare state) operate,
then, not only to provide a supply of labor to contingent jobs but to subject
those who are now included in the imperative of wage labor to punitive
work-based disciplines, benefits sanctioning, and mandatory low-paid or
unpaid contingent work. Evidenced in the explosion of activation schemes
and measures targeted at women, including the "noisy application of wage
work imperatives to the mothers of young children" (ibid., 115), at issue
in welfare reform is the incorporation of all women into the regulatory
disciplines of post-Fordist labor and the creation of an impoverished yet
incorporated class of women who exist in a constant churn of mandatory
low-waged contingent work and work-enforced welfare.

What is critical about Fox Piven's argument is that it draws attention to
how the project of welfare reform in which activation plays a central part
has at its core a distinctive sexual politics—indeed, that along with youth,
indigenous populations, the long-term unemployed, and the over-fifties,
activation regimes target out-of-work women and especially (although
certainly not only) women with dependent children. They do so precisely
to incorporate these populations into the imperative of wage labor. The
sexual politics of such welfare reform is downplayed or buried in the idea
that activation operates as a simple policy counterpart to flexible labor
markets. But even if activation operates in such terms, its schemes and the
punitive measures it contains are targeted at particular populations. These
politics, moreover, are also downplayed and sidelined in a further mode of
analysis of activation prevalent within the critical social sciences, where the
techniques of activation are understood as serving to format postwelfarist
subjects and especially to configure risk-bearing, entrepreneurial subjects
who take on the problem of unemployment as their very own (see, e.g.,
Dean 1995; Triantafillou 2011, 2012; Walters 2000). The expansion of finance has already stretched this mode of analysis to certain limit points,
not least because it has placed money, finance, and debt at the very core of

the entrepreneurial project (Lazzarato 2009, 2011). But what is also clear is that in their generalist claims regarding postwelfarist governmentality, such analyses always erase the sexual politics operating at the center of the reform of welfare states, especially the sexual politics of postwelfarist activation regimes.

Understanding that welfare reform has taken place alongside the expansion of finance and that this reform has at its core a distinctive sexual politics involving the incorporation of all women into the imperative of post-Fordist wage labor has a number of implications for the claims detailed earlier in this chapter that the post–financial crisis recession heralded the return of the figure of the politically dispossessed woman whose labor is not incorporated into wage labor. One implication is that this position clearly fails to register that the incorporation of women into the labor market has gone hand in hand with the structural reform of welfare states and in particular the emergence of women as specific subjects and objects of workfare. Thus, in contrast to that sector of women who were paternalistically protected by the Keynesian welfare state and who could not, owing to their assigned status as dependents, formally claim unemployment status, by far the majority of women in workfare states, if they are not in paid work, are now formally designated as job-seekers and are subject to the demands and regulations associated with that status. In this context, the idea that out-of-work women replace wage labor with unpaid housework and caring labor in a domestic setting is clearly out of time with the present. Just as was the case prior to the financial crisis, in the post–financial crisis recession and the continuing post–financial crisis era, out-of-work women who are unable to survive through independent means (i.e., private wealth) are subject to the commands of workfare, that is, to the command that they will work either for wages and/or for state benefits.

What is distinctive about the post–financial crisis era, however, is that the targeting of women, especially of lone mothers with dependent children, by activation regimes is intensifying. Resting on the established transformation of lone mothers from subjects in need of paternalistic assistance and protection into job-seekers, this intensification includes tougher penalties for noncompliance with the conditions of workfare schemes; the application of more stringent benefit payment conditions; a progressive and ongoing lowering of child-age conditionality thresholds at which lone parents (who almost invariably are women) are compelled to seek work; and experiments with the lives of women with dependent children. This latter includes experiments with new forms of conditionality and sanctioning relating not only to work and working activities but also to behavioral change, especially in regard to mothering practices (Deeming 2016; Kowalewska 2015; Taylor et al. 2016; Whitworth and Griggs 2013). In seeking such change, workfare measures act as powerful devices through which distinctions are made between good and bad mothers and the regulation of mothering and sexuality takes place. In this sense workfare states are by no means unique: these forms of regulation connect with a longer history of the policing and disciplining of poor women enacted by welfare states (Abramovitz 1996; Wilson 1977). In a series of interventions concerning welfare reforms in the US, Anna Marie Smith (2002, 2007, 2008) has argued that the regulations at play in reformed workfare states are nonetheless distinctive in being more intensive than those operating in the pre–welfare reform era. Moreover, they involve a specific logic not present in the Fordist-Keynesian era. At issue, Smith argues, is a logic of the "transformation of the collective obligation to support poor mothers and their children into a private familial debt" (Smith 2002, 212). It is clear that, together with a new politics of familialism (Cooper 2012, 2017), this logic is at work in the intensification of the targeting of lone mothers in activation regimes. Indeed, through the operation of tighter forms of benefit conditions and intensifications in obligations to work, the operations of this transformation are laid bare. While such intensifications have been taken to be specific to the post–financial crisis era, as an outcome of the adoption of austerity measures (see, e.g., MacLeavy 2011), the escalation of the transformation of collective obligation into private familial debt should properly be understood as symptomatic of how the ongoing and long-term project of welfare reform has always had sexual politics at its core.

This is a politics that inheres around the opening out of the working capacities of women who previously came under the paternalistic protections of the welfare state. It is also one that concerns the creation of a class of poor, contingent female workers who fuel the bottom rungs of the post-Fordist labor market, workers who constantly churn between working for benefits and/or working for wages that do not pay enough to live. As a consequence, these workers must by necessity enter into relations of indebtedness in order to survive. Indeed, Susanne Soederberg has suggested that the deadly cocktail of workfare, contingent labor, and the expansion of finance means that workfare states should properly be understood as debtfare states, not least because for the class of contingent workers it creates, credit is necessarily relied upon "to augment and/or replace the living wage or the government benefit cheque" (Soederberg 2014, 3). In this analysis Soederberg recognizes—as I have done throughout this book— how the axis of value creation has shifted from the extraction of surplus from human labor to money and its operations. Indeed, she recognizes that through regimes of activation the state is implicated in creating the conditions for the entanglement of a class of contingent workers it has fashioned with the operations of money, debt, and finance. Activation, then, does not just produce a feminized class of contingent workers but a class of workers who must by necessity put their wages and/or state benefits in motion in order to live. In this respect activation might be understood to operate as a policy analogue not only to the post-Fordist labor market but to the generation of surplus via movements and flows of money. Activation regimes should, in other words, be considered as part of (and not separate from) the institutional and infrastructural arrangements that have expanded the possibilities and capacities of populations to shoulder credit debt.

Eventful Unemployment

It is not only in the creation of a class of contingent workers who must put their wages and/or state benefits in motion in order to live that regimes of activation are linked to the logic of speculation. This is also present in a reworking and rewriting of the very labor that is the subject and object of activation, a rewriting that turns on demands that unemployed workers carry out all manner of activities. As already mentioned, these activities include not only mandatory unpaid work but also training activities, work experience placements, active job searches and job-search reporting, counseling sessions, intensive interviews, and the drawing up of individual action plans. In their demands for these activities, the techniques and devices of activation have rendered the condition of unemployment a highly active state—indeed, as a condition that pulls against the historical positioning (and experience) of unemployment as a state of inactivity and especially of being out of work. Here it is essential to register that, as Michael Denning (2010) has elaborated, the concept of unemployment and its definition as being out of work emerged in the late nineteenth century, as part of the process of normalization of a market for (wage) labor.[10] The emergence of the notion of unemployment and the identification of being out of work or unoccupied as a specific condition, namely, being unemployed, was, therefore central to both the establishment and stabilization of a labor market and the normalization of employment and wage labor. It was also central to the establishment of the modern state's power in regard to the management and administration of unemployed (and employed) populations. Against this background it is clear that through the command that the unemployed participate in all manner of activities—including mandatory unpaid work—regimes of activation are reworking the relationship between unemployment and employment in such a way that, rather than being opposing states, they exist along the same continuous plane. In this way, the commands of activation have rendered unemployment an activity that is continuous with work and working, albeit without a wage. In this context, it is important to appreciate that the infrastructures of activation are now so embedded and elaborated that markets have emerged for the unpaid labor of the unemployed (Adkins 2017).

It is not only by reference to the late nineteenth century, however, that a reworking of the materiality of unemployment through regimes of activation can be identified. This reworking or rewriting is also made explicit through a consideration of sociological studies of unemployment, especially those that took place across the twentieth century. In *Marienthal*, the classic Great Depression–era study of unemployment first published in English in 1971, Marie Jahoda and her colleagues not only established unemployment as a proper object of sociological study but also elaborated the specificity of the experience of unemployment in regard to the relations of time. *Marienthal* described the "paralyzing effects of unemployment" (Jahoda et al. 1971, 5), effects that were understood to turn on the collapse of the future as a horizon of hope and possibility. In describing the dispositions of unemployed households, Jahoda and her colleagues elaborated the most usual disposition as one of "drifting along, indifferently and without expectations, accepting a situation that cannot be changed. With it goes a relatively calm general mood, and even sporadically recurring moments of serenity and joy. But the future, even in the shape of plans, has no longer any place in the thoughts or even dreams of these families" (Jahoda et al. 1971, 52–53). *Marienthal* thus underscored that unemployment concerned a particular experience of time, one whereby, while order may be maintained in the present, "all relationship to the future" is lost (ibid., 57). The loss of relationship to the future, moreover, was recorded in this study as being felt especially by unemployed men. Besides key events and reference points, unemployed men were, for example, unable to recall in interviews how they spent the day. Beyond the issue of job loss, then, *Marienthal* specified that unemployment concerned a particular experience of time, namely, an experience of empty time.

While the *Marienthal* study took place prior to the formation of modern capitalist welfare as well as workfare states, its key motif—that unemployment concerns a distinctive experience of time—has been a recurrent theme across post–Second World War sociological studies of unemployment, as well as within social theory. Indeed, this understanding of unemployment, especially that unemployment concerns empty or dead time, is orthodox within the discipline of sociology (Burnett 1994; Cole 2007; Fleck 1971). Bourdieu (2000 [1997]), for example, posited that unemployment concerns alterations to the experience of time. The unemployed, he argued, experience time as purposeless and meaningless, as dead time. Indeed, for Bourdieu the unemployed have "no future" because they are excluded from the objective conditions of the labor market (schedules, timetables, deadlines, targets, and so on) that would allow for the practical making of time. Bourdieu, like Jahoda, understood unemployment to concern a distinct experience of time and elaborated this distinctiveness by comparing the temporal experience of unemployment to that of employment. Outside of social theory, an understanding of unemployment as an altered experience of time is also in play within empirical sociological studies. One such study has detailed the experience of unemployment as one of "a 'limbo' of 'doing nothing'" (Boland 2015, 12)—indeed, of unemployment as "void, limbo, cold storage, suspended animation or liminality" (ibid., 24) and of "perpetual . . . waiting" (ibid., 30).

At present, however, such understandings of unemployment as dead time or a time of waiting are incongruous with the demands placed on the unemployed, especially demands that they activate themselves and their labor through participation in all manner of work and work-like activities. Indeed, such understandings are anachronistic at a time when unemployment has been transformed into an activity: where unemployment does not involve "drifting" or "doing nothing" but is a highly active and lively state. Certainly some sociologists are aware that the experience of unemployment is by no means fixed. Zygmunt Bauman, for example, discussing unemployment in the welfare state era, referred to the unemployed as a reserve army of labor who "waited" but were sustained through this waiting by means of the provisions of the welfare state. In the context of the reform of welfare states, however, he observed that the positioning of the unemployed has shifted: no longer a waiting—but maintained—reserve army of labor for capital, they have been abandoned and actively recast as failures, especially as failed and flawed consumers. This latter leaves them "without a useful social function—actual or potential" (Bauman 1998, 2; see also Bauman 2010). While Bauman certainly understood that the experience and positioning of unemployment vis-à-vis capital is not a historical universal, what he nevertheless failed to grasp is how in the post–welfarist era, activation regimes are tied into the inclusion of whole populations in the wage labor imperative and the rewriting of unemployment as a state of busyness and activity.[11] Indeed, what his account misunderstood is how, with its demands for work and work-like activities, activation has rendered unemployment antithetical to a state of uselessness or inactivity: it has rendered it a highly active and work-full state.

The busyness of contemporary unemployment is recorded in the following abridged account of unemployed life in contemporary London:

> I'm looking to become a trainee electrician, but it's really hard to find anything. I ring companies, email them, anything, but, so far, I've had no luck. I went on an IT course last year, but it really didn't help me out like they said it would. . . . But earlier this year I passed a construction course with JTL

[a training provider for the building and engineering sector]. Every morn-
ing, I spend time with Tomorrow's People [an employment charity working
with marginalized adults and young people] volunteering. I hope this will
help my CV and show I've got a bit of experience. In the afternoons, I
spend my time looking for trainee schemes or a part-time job. . . . Having
experience is more important than having the right qualifications, it seems.
But even though I would work for free with an electrician to get experience
they can't do this unless I've been through a trainee scheme first. . . . I'm
applying for a part-time job at Waitrose [supermarket] at the moment so I
can hopefully show employers that I can work hard. (Kingsley et al. 2011)

From this account[12] it is clear that contemporary unemployment is not
a site of inactivity, drift, or doing nothing but one of intense activity. In
this transformation of unemployment from a state of inactivity into one of
activity, what is critical is the erosion of the historical distinction between
unemployment and employment. This is far more than a matter of the
employed and the unemployed both becoming active and engaged in work
activities; it also involves the ways in which, within regimes of activation,

Figure 5.2.   Queue at a London job center for the Battlefront Campaign, 2011.
Photograph: Leon Neal / AFP / Getty Images. Used with permission.

the unemployed—like their contingently employed counterparts—must stand restlessly available and ready for work that might not ever arrive as well as adapt to events that take place in unpredictable ways.

For the jobless and wageless, this adaptation includes adjustment to the ever-changing and endlessly morphing demands of activation regimes, especially those associated with work readiness. As I have already suggested, one feature of activation regimes in advanced liberal states is that the policies governing their shape and form are constantly mutating.[13] Such mutations are a matter not only of the intensification of conditionalities but also of the extensification of the commands of activation, especially commands to work; recent reforms to activation in Australia and the UK, for example, have expanded and extended the work conditionalities attached to the receipt of job-seeker benefits. But alongside adaptation to constantly shifting conditionalities and especially to expanding commands to work, unemployed populations must also adapt and adjust to the unpredictability of the work and work-related activities they are mandated to undertake—indeed, to work and work-related activities that are characterized by their very unpredictability. Without forewarning or notice, the demands of work-readiness may shift, with unemployed populations needing to respond instantly to new commands to become active: attendance at a training scheme, for example, may abruptly be replaced by a command to participate in a work placement scheme; an interview at a welfare agency may suddenly be cancelled and replaced with a command to attend a job-search session at a job service provider; a volunteer placement may unexpectedly be changed to a mandatory work activity; or the hours required in a mandatory work activity may suddenly be altered. Often communicated by electronic means (e.g., via automated text message or email), such commands require immediate accommodation and action. Indeed, if the unemployed fail to adjust and respond to such unexpected and unpredictable commands, they may face fiscal sanctions, including the suspension of job-seeker benefit payments.

While such shifting and unpredictable commands are sometimes attributed to the chaotic and disorderly character of the ongoing reform of welfare states (see, e.g., Bach 2016; Struyven and Steurs 2005), to understand them in this way is to overlook how such unpredictability demands a specific orientation to work and working activities—how the wageless and jobless enrolled in activation regimes must adapt to work and working organized as a set of possible events, a set of "things that happen in unpredictable ways" (Zarifian, in Lazzarato 2004, 192). It is important to draw attention to two points in this regard. First, by virtue of the command that they constantly adapt to unpredictability—to a range of possibles in regard to work commands—the wageless and jobless find themselves positioned in regard to work and working in the exact same way as their contingently employed (albeit waged) counterparts. Just as the contingently employed must typically respond to the demands of unpredictable work—for instance, to abrupt changes to work schedules or to surges or slumps in demand for the services they provide—with such unpredictability itself being secured through employment contracting (e.g., via on-call, just-in-time, or zero-hours contracts), the out-of-work must likewise respond to the demands of unpredictable work commands as a condition of benefit payment. It is thus clear that activation regimes do far more than serve as a source of cheap and/or free labor for post-Fordist labor markets; they also serve as a site for the restructuring of labor, and especially for the rewriting of this labor in terms of the unpredictable event. Activation therefore enlarges the capacities of the jobless and wageless in regard to the possible, that is, to events that have not yet and might not ever take place.

The second point in regard to the unpredictability around work and working that operates at the core of activation or welfare-to-work regimes is that in their command that the jobless and wageless adapt to the possible, activation regimes open out the capacities of the jobless to the logic of speculation, and especially to indeterminate movements of speculative time. Thus, through the necessity for constant adjustments and adaptations to the unpredictable, the practices of the out-of-work are tuned and bound not to the probable—that is, to events that are predictable and knowable and unfold in time—but to the indeterminacy of the possible. It is, as set out in Chapter 3, precisely such indeterminacy that marks the specificity of speculative time. In attuning the capacities of the jobless and wageless to such time—in demanding endless adaption to the possible—activation regimes should be understood as a critical site in and through which the productive capacities of the unemployed are being actively enrolled in the logic of speculation, that is, in and through which the everyday practices of job-less populations are being tied to the indeterminate movements of specula-tive time—a site in which everyday practice is speculative in form. At play in activation regimes is therefore not only the creation a class of contingent workers who must by necessity put their wages and/or state benefits in mo-tion, but also the activation of the capacities of jobless and wageless popula-tions to adopt and adapt to the very indeterminacy of speculative time—to the movements of time through and in which finance capital yields profits.

In this context, it is important to recall that activation regimes target jobless and wageless women (especially women with dependent children), youth (especially young men), the long-term unemployed, the over-fifties, and indigenous populations. Activation regimes must then be understood as operating to expand the capacities and practices specifically of these jobless and wageless populations in regard to the logic of speculation and especially to the movements of speculative time. In this regard, we en-counter the operations of the logic of speculation as a rationality head-on: it is not just the employed, the waged, and the salaried who are subject to its commands but whole populations, including the wageless, the unem-ployed, and the jobless. Just as Marx observed that there was no "outside" to the extractive logic of industrial capitalism, in the time of speculation whole populations must enter into its logic in order to secure economic and social existence, that is, into a temporal universe in which actions and practices are organized in such a way as to maximize productive capacities. These productive capacities, however, are not geared toward the extrac-tion of surplus from the human laboring body but toward the creation of surplus from the indeterminate movements and flows of money. In this respect it can be proposed that activation regimes operate as a policy ana-logue to a mode of accumulation based on the generation of surplus via finance and money.

In closing this chapter, it is important to highlight that many of the developments mapped herein—including the making productive of ac-tivities outside of the formal labor market and the erosion of the histori-cal distinction between unemployment and employment—could well be thought of as part of the process of the economization of the social, or the folding of the economy into society. As outlined in the introduction to this chapter, a number of writers have located the process of economization as central to the transformations of the economy-society relation that lie at the very heart of the process of neoliberalization, especially of the capitalization or making productive of the social that is entailed in the political project of neoliberalism (see especially Brown 2015; Foucault 2008). The process of economization has, for example, been located as central to the process of market-making across areas of life previously classified as being outside the competitive market order (see, e.g., Çalişkan and Callon 2009, 2010). For a certain strand of post-Marxist thinkers (see, e.g., Chicchi 2010; Hardt and Negri 2001; Lazzarato 1996), the process of economization, or the making productive of the social, has been understood to comprise the movement of laboring and value-producing activities away from the enclosures of the formally productive sphere and their dispersal across the social body. Along this line of thought, value is understood to be increasingly harvested from mundane but nevertheless value-producing activities of actors in society, that is, from the whole of life. These activities—or sources of free labor—include engagements with social media and everyday transactions with institutions such as health-care providers and local governments. While the opening out of the productive capacities of the wageless and jobless suggests that activation regimes could easily be situated as techniques or devices of economization, particularly inasmuch as they enlarge a source of free labor, the dynamics of regimes of activation set out in this chapter make clear that to view activation (or workfare) in such a manner would be to entirely negate how activation regimes expand the productive capacities of the wageless in regard to the demands of the logic of speculation, especially capacities in regard to the indeterminate flows and movements of speculative time. Indeed, the analysis offered in this chapter and across this book suggests that in their focus on free labor and the harvesting of value from activities outside of the formal labor market, post-Marxist understandings of the process of economization are out of time with the present, and especially out of time with how a logic of extraction that governs both economy and society has been replaced—albeit untidily and unevenly—by a logic of speculation.

Conclusion

In this book I have shown how a logic of speculation is replacing a logic of extraction in regard to both capitalist accumulation strategies and the dynamics of social organization, such that it has emerged as a pervasive rationality. Across five case studies—post–Bretton Woods finance markets, austerity programs, household and personal debt, wages, and state-led activation (or workfare) programs central to the ongoing reform of welfare states—I have outlined the operations and dynamics of this speculative rationality. These dynamics turn on unpredictability and indeterminacy and are expressed in the generation of surplus from indeterminate flows and movements of money as well as in modes of everyday practice that are attuned to continued adjustments to the flow of time, including to the indeterminacy of the possible. I have suggested that the opening out of such modes of practice—through the expansion of finance, the securitization of credit, shifts in the coordinates of money, the repression and stagnation of wages, the everyday necessity of debt, the operations of contingent contracting, shifts in the schedules of household and personal debt (especially toward schedules of securitized debt), and transformations in the state regulation of labor—have maximized the capacities of populations in regard to the generation of surplus via flows and movements of money. Not only do such modes of practice work toward maximizing the possible in regard to payment (especially payments flowing from households to finance markets), but they also bind populations to the very time through and in which surplus is created via the operations of financial instruments—what I have termed speculative time.

In the Introduction, I laid out how, in his ground-breaking essay "Time, Work-Discipline and Industrial Capitalism," E. P. Thompson (1967) suggested that at the heart of the enrollment of populations and their productive capacities in industrial capitalism was a specific time universe. At the center of this universe was the sociotechnical device of the mechanical clock, which organized people and their actions in such a way as to maximize their productive capacities, especially their laboring capacities. I have suggested that in the time of money, where surplus is generated primarily through movements and flows of money, a specific time universe is also present—not the standardizing, homogenizing, and equilibrium-seeking universe of the mechanical clock but the nonsynchronous, indeterminate, and unpredictable universe of speculative time. This time organizes people, their practices, and their actions so as to maximize their capacities in regard to the generation of surplus via the indeterminate movements and flows of money. It demands continuous adaptation to the possible, particularly—although not only—in regard to money. While the time of the mechanical clock expanded the laboring capacities of populations and bound people to a mode of production and accumulation centered on the direct extraction of surplus from the human body, in the time of money a speculative time universe binds people and their actions to a mode of accumulation centered on the creation of surplus from money.

The binding of people and their actions to this mode of accumulation has yielded specific forms of life—indeed, much of this book has been concerned with mapping these forms of life and their specific characteristics and contours. They include labor that is organized in terms of the unpredictable event; reformed "welfare" systems that act as policy analogues to the creation of surplus via the indeterminate movements and flows of money; households geared not to the reproduction of labor but to the payment of the possible; a sexual contract organized not in terms of exclusionary equilibrium states (such as the equilibrium states sought paradigmatically in the Fordist-Keynesian era between the activities of production and those of social reproduction) but in terms of the inclusionary disequilibrium states of the logic of speculation; and a topography of inequalities whose map is not plotted by the volumes, distributions, and quanta of income but by what money puts in motion, including the risk exposures that putting money in motion necessary entails.

In mapping these forms of life as well as their dynamics, I have sought to give substance to the claim that the operations of money and finance do not stand discretely outside of society. In so doing, I have also thoroughly problematized claims that are ubiquitous across the social sciences, namely, that the operations of money and finance have somehow transgressed their ascribed place and role. While much recent scholarship on money and finance is fuelled by such sentiments, especially scholarship that calls for a re-regulation or disciplining of finance and financial institutions, I have stressed that to pursue such normative agendas is to thoroughly misunderstand the finance-society relationship. It leads scholars, in particular, to systematically downplay the centrality of money and finance in the operations of the social, and especially to downplay how this centrality is long-term in character. To pursue such normative agendas is also, as I set out in Chapter 1, to misunderstand how the expansion of finance is thoroughly institutionally based. Moreover, the pursuit of such agendas leaves no room to explore—as I have done throughout this book—how the expansion of finance and the penetration of the operations of finance and money into society have fundamentally shifted the fabric and dynamics of the social. Indeed, instead of asking how the operations of money and finance are implicated in the operations of the social, scholars pursuing such normative agendas, fuelled by the idea that finance has "transgressed the boundaries of its proper role and place in society" (Cooper and Konings 2015, 239), assume that the expansion of finance will only ever distort, disfigure, and deform the social. Thus, the expansion of finance has been taken to be destructive of the future, to interfere with the proper flow of time, and to threaten to return us to previous, unenlightened eras.

Working against such normative assumptions, I have argued that instead of distorting or disfiguring the social, the expansion of finance is implicated in a broad-scale and wide-ranging rewriting of the social—indeed, that this expansion has afforded a particular rationality, namely, the logic of speculation, in which whole populations are enrolled. This rationality is at the heart of contemporary capitalist accumulation strategies, directs the dynamics of social formation, and has yielded specific social forms. I have stressed, however, that this rewriting of the social can only be accurately grasped if the dynamics of financial expansion itself are properly understood, including not only the institutional and regulatory contours of financial expansion but also innovations in finance that have reworked the relationship between money and time and vastly expanded the capacities of finance in regard to surplus generation. I have mapped how these shifts involve transformations to everyday money and alterations to the schedules of everyday debt. I have also laid out how these shifts are implicated in both the translation of social attributions into financial attributions and the unfolding of maps of inequality that have distributions of exposure to financial risk at their core.

In stressing that the expansion of finance rewrites the social and that to understand this rewriting requires taking the operations of money and finance seriously, I have outlined how this rewriting raises particular challenges to certain orthodoxies in the social sciences, such as the embeddedness school of economic sociology associated with writers such as Granovetter, Polanyi, and Bourdieu. In relation to this school, I have argued that the expansion of finance marks certain limit points to its ongoing relevance, not least because, rather than functioning and gaining traction through a nesting or embedding of finance and money in the social, the architectures and operations of finance actively rewrite the social that they work upon, by such means as the calculus of securitized debt. The analysis set out in this book, however, raises challenges not only to orthodox positions within the social sciences; I have also suggested that more recent analyses of money and finance fall short precisely because they black-box the latter, and in particular, assume that their operations have remained largely unaltered across time. A lack of attention to the process of the securitization of debt, or the assumption that relations of indebtedness have remained historically unchanged, has, for example, led to erroneous claims that increases in indebtedness have led to the universalization of the promise to pay—indeed, to the claim that the promise to pay has been elevated to the status of *the* constitutive social relation. It has also led to erroneous claims that the quantum of personal and household debt serves as a proxy or representative measure of the levels of power and control that institutions of credit now exert over indebted citizenries, such that indebted citizens are now thoroughly beholden to such institutions.

Throughout this book, however, I have stressed that such assumptions are at odds with how contemporary debt operates. They are especially at odds with how—through the securitization of credit, and especially the operations of the calculus of securitized debt—the schedules and architectures of everyday debt have been rearranged in terms of the payment of the possible. In this context, it is not the quantum of debt and the burden of repayment that bind populations ever more closely to the control of institutions of credit but postprobabilistic schedules of payment, together with the payment streams flowing from households. Such schedules—operating for the waged, the employed, the unwaged, the jobless, the underemployed, and the unemployed—have not only rewritten the relationship between household and personal debt and income but tie populations across whole lifetimes to the movements of speculative time, a time in which the relationships between the past, present, and future are not fixed but open to constant adjustment. Contemporary debt, then, does not destroy time by tying populations to futures that can never be their own but opens out a universe in which they are tied to the indeterminate movements of speculative time. This is a time through and in which the productivity of populations is maximized via the flows and movements of money.

A lack of attention to the operations of post–Bretton Woods money and finance on the part of social scientists has led, then, to some spurious claims being made about the social implications of the post-1970s expansion of finance. But while driven by a lack of attention to the operations and dynamics of money and finance, such claims are also an outcome of the reliance on a tradition of social thought that Bruno Latour (2005) has termed the "sociology of the social." This is a tradition with roots in the mid- to late nineteenth century, a tradition that imagines the social as a field of the quantum of substances, equilibrium states, stasis, and seamless reproduction. In this imaginary, the disequilibrium states of the time of money—including debt that outstrips working and lived lives, cuts in spending that provoke more debt, wages that do not cover the costs of life, and the endless drive toward the limitlessness of the possible—can only ever be understood as signs of a social that is disintegrating and/or in crisis. I would suggest that it is for this reason—that is, because of an adherence to some of the core principles of the sociology of the social tradition within the contemporary social sciences—that the expansion of finance has led to so many declarations of crises of various kinds, from crises of time through crises of measure to crises of social reproduction. It is also for this reason that so many social scientists are unable or unwilling to recognize the productivity of money, debt, and finance in regard to the social, that is, to recognize how the operations of money, finance, and debt are now central to the dynamics of social formation.

There is a further issue that this book has tracked concerning this lack of recognition of the productivity of money, finance, and debt in regard to social formation. I refer here to the ongoing identification of money and finance as immaterial or superstructural phenomena, as objects that are only properly ordered and functional for society when they are grounded and anchored in other things. I have tracked how this line of thought is, for example, at play in analyses of the 2007–8 financial crisis, especially in those that identify the crisis of liquidity as an outcome of the trade in so-called fictitious capital, in speculative trades on anticipated gains in the future that are cut loose from "real" material commodities and hence from real value and whose value is, consequently, a dangerous fiction. I have also tracked this line of thought in analyses that propose that the problem of repressed and stagnant wages can only be redressed when wages are regrounded in, and reattached to, the foundational value of labor. I have challenged such forms of analysis not least because they fail to take into account the restructuring of money, debt, and finance in the time of money. They ignore the intense productivity of finance in regard to surplus generation and the contestability of value, especially the role of finance itself in expanding such contestability and transforming it into a tradable commodity. Thus, throughout this book I have suggested that value creation should be understood to lie in the indeterminate movements and flows of money, and especially in what money can or might put in motion. I include here the (repressed) wages paid for labor (which itself is structured as a contingent event) that workers must necessarily put in motion in order to live. I have stressed, then, that in the time of money, rather than being anchored in any external value, form, or substance (including the foundational value of labor), wages are themselves structured as an in-motion surface whose value lies not in what they measure or represent but in their potential to put things in motion.

The restructuring of the relationship between wages and labor in the time of money that I have underscored in this book also dramatically highlights a further problematic aspect of the idea that money and finance are somehow immaterial or superstructural phenomena, namely, the systematic downplaying of how whole populations are enrolled in the logic of speculation—moreover, by institutional and regulatory means. Indeed, the idea that money, debt, and finance are immaterial and not grounded in material production or material value violently erases how the whole of life— including the lives and households not only of the waged and the employed but also the jobless and the wageless—is ordered and organized by the logic of speculation. The idea that money, debt, and finance are immaterial fails, then, to recognize that their very operations are at the heart of the organization of social life—indeed, fails to recognize the operation of speculation as a rationality.

While in the context of the interventions I have laid out in this book the problems with the idea that money, debt, and finance are immaterial and/or superstructural phenomena may seem somewhat obvious, it is important not to underestimate the hold that this mindset has had and continues to exert on analyses of financial expansion, even on analyses that do not appear to subscribe overtly to a reading of that expansion in such terms. For example, in a recent interview discussing the significance of the debt economy to the political project of neoliberalism, Maurizio Lazzarato commented:

> With the end of the gold standard declared by Nixon, the year 1971 represents the outset of th[e] history [of neoliberalism and of the debt economy]. In a certain way, money got completely dematerialized through this process, that is to say that it "became debt." From then on, money lost its bases in both labour in particular and the social world in general. Being reduced to debt, money now mainly constitutes a phenomenon dependent upon writing operations. This appears as the important tipping point: we observed the deterritorialization of money. By virtue of losing any roots in

> commodity or in another social substance, money became infinitely mobile
> and mobilized. It thereby turned into a political apparatus ("dispositif").
> (Lazzarato, in Charbonneau and Hansen 2014, 1043)

Putting aside the problems associated with the reduction of money to debt
that are at play here, what is of interest is how Lazzarato both subscribes
to a substance model of the social and takes processes detailed by this book
as central to the expansion of finance to have amounted to a dematerialization and desocialization of money.

The problems with this understanding are legion. They include a failure to recognize how in the context of financial expansion money itself
has emerged as a pervasive commodity (although one that is by no means
singular). They also include a failure to register that in the context of the
expansion of finance, while money may have been disarticulated from measures of value relating to labor, in the Fordist-Keynesian era these measures were themselves the outcome of specific institutional arrangements,
such as nationally coordinated wage-setting mechanisms and family wage
agreements. In the Fordist-Keynesian era, there was, then, no inevitability
that labor acted as a measure of value and that value was rooted in labor:
it was the outcome of specific institutional arrangements—and moreover, it was the case only for certain sectors of the workforce, in particular
male workers. And just as the relationship between labor and value was the
outcome of particular institutional arrangements in the Fordist-Keynesian
era, so too is the disarticulation of labor and value in the time of money,
along with the emergence of money, especially wages, as an asset form on
which workers must speculate in order to live. Thus, I have mapped how,
in the time of money, strategies of wage repression, contingent contracting, and forms of wage bargaining centering on what money can or might
do have worked toward these ends. I have also mapped how the reconfiguration of the relationship between labor and money, especially the emergence of wages as a speculative, nonrepresentational surface that must be
put in motion, is intrinsic to the shifting architectures of finance and debt,
including the emergence of a calculus of securitized debt involving the
extension of credit to whole populations and a postprobabilistic reworking
of the relationship between income and debt.

Critically, and contra Lazzarrato, the emergence of such everyday forms of money as a nonrepresentational surface that must be put in motion and practices that ensure that the productive capacities of populations are maximized toward such speculative activities is neither immaterial nor does it operate outside of the coordinates of the social world. In fact, they are the outcome of specific institutional and regulatory arrangements, including the architectures of finance, post-Keynesian or post-Fordist employment and growth strategies, and the ongoing reform of welfare states. The emergence of these forms of money is, moreover, implicated in the emergence of the paradigmatic characteristics of life in the time of money, including households that, geared toward the payment of the possible, act as frontiers for continued financial expansion and innovation; a sexual contract that positions women as not only necessary but critical agents of such expansion and innovation; and work and working arrangements (for both the waged and the wageless) that are ordered in terms of the contingent event.

It is, then, altogether inaccurate to locate the expansion of finance in the post-Keynesian or post-Fordist era as involving processes of the dematerialization and desocialization of money. Certainly the coordinates of money have shifted, particularly in regard to its relationship with time, but a money that is on the move should not be equated with one that has dematerialized. The relationship money has with the social has also shifted, but its disassociation from specific social substances or commodities (and especially from the substance of labor power) has not rendered money any less connected to the social world. On the contrary, the productivity of whole populations is attuned and bound to the generation of surplus from the flows and movements of money, and is so via everyday practices. Indeed, at issue is a rationality that is constitutive in regard not only to everyday social practices and social actions but also to social forms, including the organization of work and labor, households, and workfare or debtfare states. Rather than being cut loose from the social, money could, then, not be any *more* social, precisely because of (and not despite) the productivity of money as a nonrepresentational, in-motion, and speculative surface.

There is one issue on which Lazzarato is, however, assuredly correct and that is the entanglement of what he terms the debt economy but what I have specified as a logic of speculation—whose subjects and objects are far broader than debt and the indebted alone—in the political project of neoliberalism. It is no coincidence that the genealogy of financial expansion from the late 1970s onward and the rise of neoliberalism as a hegemonic political practice coincide. In this book, while I have not focused explicitly on the relationship between the logic of speculation and the political project of neoliberalism, the cases I have set out make it clear nonetheless that the two are indelibly connected. From the implication of the calculus of securitized debt in the installment of asset-based welfare, through the connections between austerity-based provocations to more household and personal debt and further rounds of the restructuring of the state, to the involvement of activation regimes that demand work and work-based activities organized as possible events in the transformation of the collective obligations of welfare states into private debts, it is clear that the logic of speculation does not stand separate from the political project of neoliberalism but is thoroughly entangled with it. More broadly, it is also clear from the cases I have laid out in this book that the expansion of finance is contributing to the transformation of collective (albeit far from universal) social rights of post–Second World War welfare-state capitalism into a set of private obligations that are to be met via practices of speculation.

For many writers the relationship between the expansion of finance and neoliberalism is self-evident and clear-cut. For example, it is taken that financial expansion, especially the growth of indebtedness this has involved, has enlarged and intensified technologies of discipline that are central to the political project of neoliberalism (see, e.g., Di Feliciantonio 2016; Mahmud 2013, 2015). Here, the risk-bearing and investor stance toward life that indebtedness necessarily commands is understood to be constitutive of the reworking of the economy-society relation that neoliberalism entails, not least by placing an investor stance at the very heart of the social—indeed, by reforming all forms of such conduct in such terms. According to this understanding, debt is unmistakably a technology of neoliberalism. As this book has emphasized, however, the expansion and dynamics of finance cannot be reduced to increases in the weight of debt that populations bear. To do so is to erase not only the material transformations to money and the dynamics and operations of debt itself that the expansion of finance has involved, but also the social forms that the expansion of finance has yielded. The dynamics of the latter in regard to populations, moreover, cannot be reduced to the disciplines of an undifferentiated and universalizing debt but instead concern speculative practices in regard to a money that is on the move.

In suggesting that the expansion and operations of finance cannot be reduced to the neoliberal governance of populations disciplined by debt, I am not denying the implication and entanglement of the expansion of finance in the hegemony of neoliberalism. Rather, I am suggesting that to reduce money and finance to debt and in turn to reduce debt to an instrument of neoliberal governance is to seriously sidestep the rewriting of the social that the expansion of finance has involved. Indeed, financial expansion has operated less through techniques of discipline and more through the activation and expansion of the capacities and productivity of populations in regard to flows and movements of money, a process that is both transformative and generative in regard to the social. It is, however, precisely the productivity of populations in regard to the flows and movements of money that is central to understanding the nexus between financial expansion and neoliberalism, not least because of the critical role that neoliberal policies and regulatory structures have played and continue to play in the maximization of this productivity. From employment strategies that have placed whole populations under the command to work, through welfare reforms and activation regimes that simultaneously transform collective forms of insurance into private debts and command that the wageless and jobless continuously adapt to the possible, to austerity policies that provoke more household and personal debt and further speculative practices in regard to income streams, especially in regard to (stagnant and repressed) wages, neoliberal policy regimes operate to expand and multiply the productivity of populations in regard to the generation of surplus from the flows and movements of money.

Just as the policies and regulatory structures of the Fordist or Keynesian state worked to manage populations in order to maximize the laboring capacities of male workers—including through the backing of socially reproductive labor performed by women in the household—with the aim of securing the conditions and vitality of a mode of accumulation centered on the extraction of surplus from labor, the policies and regulatory structures of the postnational neoliberal state work to maximize the productive capacities of populations. At issue in the latter, however, are not the laboring capacities (especially the labor power of the male body) but the speculative capacities of whole populations in regard to the generation of surplus from money. While in the time of money the lines between political interventions and the expansion and operations of finance are very often blurred and inseparable (Mirowski 2013), it is nonetheless evident that neoliberalism as a political practice operates to secure the conditions of possibility for a mode of capitalist accumulation driven and ordered by the logic of speculation. Clearly, then, neoliberal governance does not operate outside of or against the logic of speculation but actively actualizes and extends its operations (Konings 2018). Indeed, it is clear that, in the time of money, crossing the threshold into life is to enter an existence that is to be secured and lived not through the exchange of labor in return for a wage but by putting money in motion—a life that is ordered by the logic of speculation.

Notes

The Time of Money: An Introduction

1. Other writers have also drawn attention to the significance of time universes, especially of abstract clock time, in the organization and maximization of productive activities, as well as, more broadly, in the governance of society as a whole. Noting the centrality of abstract time in the exploitation of labor, Moishe Postone has highlighted "the tyranny of [such] time" in capitalist societies (Postone 1993, 214). This tyranny takes place not least because in capitalist society abstract labor time is transformed into a social norm that "stands above and determines, individual action" (ibid.). Extending into all areas of life, abstract labor time—measured in constant, continuous, and interchangeable units of hours, minutes, and seconds—serves, therefore, as an absolute measure of events and actions (and of labor and production in particular).

2. These tendencies are especially apparent in the analyses of heterodox economists. For an excellent exegesis of such analyses, see Sotiropoulos, Milios, and Lapatsioras 2013.

3. On the notion of coproduction, see also Offe 1985.

4. Economic geographers have observed that financial expansion from the 1970s onward has transformed space—indeed, that modern-day finance spatializes. Pryke (2017), for example, has argued that financial expansion has involved the making of new connections between markets and territories, as well as between and across different assets, because of the connective capabilities of modern finance.

5. It is important to make explicit that in understanding debt and indebtedness as a surround to life in this book I am not associating the debtor, the indebted, or indebtedness with the poor and the marginalized. While this association is common in many analyses of contemporary debt, I stress here how whole populations have been enrolled in the shouldering of more personal and household debt and in the creation of surplus via the movements and flows of money. It is only by grasping the latter that the embedding of money, debt, and finance in everyday life and the dynamics of finance-led growth can be understood.

6. This body of work includes analyses that focus on shifting aesthetic forms. La Berge (2014b), for example, has demonstrated how, from the 1980s onward, the logics of contemporary finance have circulated in and structured aesthetic genres,

and in particular, have yielded what she identifies as a new aesthetic-economic form: financial form. Alongside a broad set of changes to finance taking place from the late 1970s onward that made banking personal or everyday (via developments such as personal banking and personal finance), La Berge notes that financial form (circulating in novels and films) has worked toward domesticating and personalizing finance. At the same time this aesthetic form ameliorates the tensions between domestication and the apparently abstract character of finance. In highlighting the operations of financial form, La Berge's key intervention is that the predominance of the generation of surplus via financial channels has heralded a new relationship between finance and cultural production. While the interventions I set out in this book regarding the operations of the logic of speculation do not concern aesthetic forms, nonetheless the set of changes to finance from the late 1970s onward central to La Berge's analysis are also critical to this book. These changes are outlined in Chapter 1.

7. The concept of financialization is used ubiquitously across a range of social science literatures to refer to a number of processes; it is most often called upon to refer to an acceleration of finance-led accumulation (see, e.g., Christophers 2015; van der Zwan 2014). Throughout this book, rather than resting on a vague notion of financialization, my analysis proceeds by way of a recognition that we have witnessed, from the late 1970s onward, a major reconfiguration of finance (Konings 2010). The features of this reconfiguration are set out in Chapter 1.

Chapter 1: Money on the Move

1. For details of the ongoing campaigns and actions of this precarious movement, see www.juventudsinfuturo.net.

2. But see Brenkman 2002 and Power 2009 for critiques of Edelman's analysis of reproductive futurism, especially for a conflation of social reproduction and sexual reproduction.

3. Piketty records widening socioeconomic inequality based on distributions of private wealth and the declining significance of the wage and other forms of occupationally based remuneration in the dynamics and formation of inequalities. He therefore charts the increasing significance of inherited wealth as well as stocks of capital (including income-yielding assets) in the formation of patterns of inequality. Piketty understands this pattern, taking hold from the 1970s onward across OECD countries, to be symptomatic of the emergence of what he terms a wealth or patrimonial society, in which the rate of return on capital outstrips the rate of economic growth (income and output). He writes: "[T]he general evolution is clear: bubbles aside, what we are witnessing is a strong comeback of private capital in the rich countries since 1970, or, to put it another way, the emergence of a new patrimonial capitalism" (Piketty 2014, 125). It is important to observe that this "strong comeback" of private capital is coterminous with the developments I track across the chapters of this book.

4. Even accounts extolling the virtues of finance-led capitalism and financial

expansion warn against an excessive trade on the future. Writing in the *Financial Times*, Peter Fisher, a former undersecretary of the US Treasury, has, for example, argued that the virtue of finance-led capitalism is that "we can convert our future income into current investment and consumption while creating savings vehicles for others" (Fisher 2015). He warns, however, that borrowing too much from the future has its risks: "[W]e might incur debt greater than our ability to repay and undermine the value of financial assets." He continues: "[T]he inter-temporal trade-off of borrowing from the future might make us better off both now and in the future but there is no guarantee."

5. See also Esposito 2011.

6. De-futurization, or the use of the future in the present, Esposito maintains, has taken place in a context where finance markets have progressively given up on external reference points (such as external forms of regulation) and are increasingly self-referential. Indeed, she argues for a program of re-regulation to interrupt and disrupt such self-referentiality and to anchor the dynamics of finance markets outside of themselves. Such an approach, however, sidesteps how the operations of contemporary financial markets are themselves institutionally anchored. As Martijn Konings (2010) has suggested, arguments for the re-regulation of finance markets as an antidote to financial excesses and instability rest on fundamental misunderstandings of financial expansion, in particular an erroneous assumption that the dynamics of contemporary finance markets are a simple outcome of state deregulation, that is, a subordination of state authority to the forces of finance markets. Such an assumption, Konings makes clear, downplays how the growth of financial markets has involved a "process whereby new organizational linkages were forged and particular relations of institutional control were constructed and consolidated" (ibid., 5). Fundamentally, Konings argues, financial expansion must be understood as a process of institutionalization (ibid.; see also Konings 2014).

7. Jens Beckert (2016) has also recently drawn attention to the significance of Bourdieu's analysis of time. While my interest in the latter is with how it problematizes the idea that life is increasingly anticipatory, Beckert's interest forms part of a more general project to elaborate a sociology that is able to attend to the dynamism of capitalist economies. He maintains that the latter can be achieved through a focus on the openness of futures. His project, then, is one of making time and temporal orientation a cornerstone of the discipline of sociology. Rather than seeking to build a general account of the dynamism of capitalist economies by way of attention to time, however, in this book I am endeavoring to understand how a specific temporal universe, that of speculation, is central to the generation of surplus via money and to the dynamics of a particular mode of social organization. I am, in other words, concerned with the specificities of finance-led capitalism.

8. Bourdieu (2000 [1997]) elaborates how the inscription of the future in the immediate present is not a given of practice in the case of the unemployed. The latter, he suggests, often exist with "no future," or to be more precise, experience time as purposeless and meaningless. Without employment, the unemployed are deprived of

an objective universe (deadlines, timetables, production rates, targets, etc.) that orients and stimulates protensive practical action. For Bourdieu, the chronically unemployed therefore have "no future" because they are excluded from the objective conditions that would allow for the practical making of time. Unemployment—including Bourdieu's understanding of the experience of unemployment—forms the substantive focus of Chapter 5.

9. Bourdieu explicitly conceives of the economy as a field, that is, as an autonomous structured space of positions, differentiated from other fields by virtue of the fact that it has its own properties.

10. The social embeddedness school of economic sociology proposes that economic practices and events should be understood as being embedded in social relations rather than taking place in the abstract. Bourdieu explicitly acknowledges his debt to this school when he argues that just as Polanyi (2001) observed to be the case for national markets, the "global market" is a political creation, that is, a product of "a more or less self-consciously concerted policy" (Bourdieu 2005 [2000], 225). Such policy, Bourdieu goes on, was implemented by a set of agents and institutions and concerned the application of rules deliberately crafted for specific ends—specifically, trade liberalization—involving the "elimination of all national regulations restricting companies and their investments" (ibid.). Bourdieu's debt to the social embeddedness school is also registered in his acknowledgment (again, following Polanyi) that economic practice should be conceived of as a "total social fact" (ibid., 2).

11. For Bourdieu, understanding economic action in terms of a philosophy of agents, action, time, and the social world restores economics (especially neoclassical economics) to "its true vocation as a historical science" (Bourdieu 2005 [2000], 216), that is, as a discipline whose epistemological and ontological assumptions are highly contingent. As I will go on to discuss, Bourdieu's critique of neoclassical economics has become destabilized by a number of developments, not least by the logics of financial expansion.

12. This principle does not necessarily always hold; see, for example, Sennett 2006 for the case of craft labor and McRobbie 2002 for the case of creative labor.

13. This is the case notwithstanding the fact that Bourdieu dedicated a whole volume to the study of the social structures of the economy and that in his later, more polemical work (Bourdieu 1999 [1993], 2003 [2001]) he directly engaged with the political economy of neoliberalism, mounting a sustained critique of what he termed the tyranny of the neoliberal market.

14. In the context of these limits to Bourdieu's social theory, it is of little surprise that aside from markets for normatively defined cultural goods, Bourdieu's social theory is rarely called upon to engage with strictly economic processes and formations.

15. Esposito (2011) argues that while widely reported as unpredicted, the global financial crisis is by no means inexplicable.

16. See Gindin and Panitich 2012, Panitich and Gindin 2005, and Panitich and Konings 2009 on US imperialism in regard to contemporary finance.

17. The 1944 Bretton Woods agreement fixed exchange rates, which were pegged to the US dollar between and across participating members. In turn, the US dollar was tied to the price of gold.

18. Based on extensive ethnographic fieldwork, Zaloom (2006, 2010) describes the experience of trade in such securities as flow experiences. This suggests that the time of securities and the time of securities trading are isomorphic.

19. Nigel Thrift (2008) has suggested that in contemporary capitalism, commodities are generally characterized by such openness. See also Boltanski and Chiapello (2005 [1999]), who argue that commodities have taken on properties of openness and indeterminacy.

20. Liz McFall (2009) refers to this as the "new new economic sociology."

21. See also Konings (2010), who suggests that the embeddedness school, and especially embeddedness-inflected arguments for the re-regulation of finance to effect a re-anchoring and re-embedding in a "real value base" (Huber 2017, 4), fail to take into account how finance operates not in an external relation to everyday life but as fully integrated within it.

Chapter 2: Austere Times

1. That is, the process of private becoming public debt. Zygmunt Bauman (2010) has argued that the bailouts and recapitalizations of banks by the state following the financial crisis evidence "a sort of 'welfare state' for the rich" (Bauman 2010, 23).

2. Quantitative easing (QE)—a process of money creation by central banks ostensibly designed to stimulate economic growth in times of acute financial crisis—has taken place in the post–financial crisis era in the US, the UK, the Eurozone, and Japan. It has also recently been road-tested in Australia by the Australian Reserve Bank. Nick Gane (2015) has argued that alongside austerity, postcrisis QE should form a critical object of sociological inquiry, not only because QE highlights the role of central banks as agents of monetary policy—that is, it highlights a restructuring of state authority and the ascendency of central banks in terms of that authority—but also because QE "impact[s] . . . on the private wealth of different social groups" (Gane 2015, 887–88). Here Gane notes how postcrisis QE in the UK boosted the value of the assets of the wealthy, particularly the assets of the richest 10 percent of households. In this respect, and following Green 2013, Gane suggests that QE in the UK was part of a postcrisis recovery package based on a principle of regressive redistribution.

3. My interest in this roundtable discussion is driven by a concern to identify a number of axioms that have emerged within feminism and beyond in regard to austerity and women. I am not suggesting therefore that the views articulated within the discussion are specific to the individuals concerned.

4. The UK's Fawcett Society is an independent charity that campaigns for

women's rights. Operating within the coordinates of the equality project of liberal feminism, the society's agenda is to promote "gender equality and women's rights at work, at home and in public life" (Fawcett Society 2015).

5. It is important to reiterate that I am taking this roundtable discussion to be paradigmatic of feminist sentiments that have emerged regarding the effects of the crisis and austerity on women.

6. Whereby remedies to injustices constituted by unequally distributed re- sources—especially socioeconomic resources such as property, wealth, and money— are sought through strategies of the redistribution of those very resources (see, e.g., Fraser 1995, 1997, 2013).

7. While a transformation of money was not sought in the demands of the women's liberation movement, feminist utopian fiction produced during this pe- riod did imagine alternative scenarios in regard to money. Societies were imagined operating without money as well as with no currency and with cooperative credit systems. Marge Piercy (in *Woman on The Edge of Time*) and Ursula Le Guin (in *The Dispossessed*) both envisaged societies operating with no money.

8. While Krippner's definition of the production of surplus through financial channels (i.e., of financialization) remains popular, it should be recalled—as noted in the Introduction—that there is no consensus on the definition of financialization either as a concept or a descriptor denoting a particular historical period or process within capitalism (see, e.g., Christophers 2015).

9. A process whereby debt (and other forms of illiquid assets) are transformed into liquid assets and traded on financial markets.

10. Other measures include the sheer volume of daily financial transactions, especially derivative transactions (Epstein 2005; Martin 2013; Stockhammer 2012a; Thompson 2016); the roll-out and expansion of new financial markets (Gutt- mann 2015; Mackenzie 2007); the growth in the market for asset-backed securities (Aquanno 2009); and the increasing inseparability of finance from the dynamics and day-to-day operations of those parts of the economy formally designated as nonfi- nancial, including manufacturing and education (Lazzarato 2011, 2015).

11. The centrality of the household for finance-led capitalism has also recently been acknowledged by Zaloom (2017), who writes: "To understand financial capi- talism more fully, we need to assess the shape of the household" (1).

12. The operation of money as a commodity, or money "unmoored" (Martin 2015), raises the issue of how commensurability and exchangeability are achieved in a context of the creation of surplus via finance and money. In a series of inter- ventions, Bryan and Rafferty (see, e.g., 2006, 2007, 2011) suggest that financial instruments now perform these functions, not least because they render asset values commensurable (see also Sotiropoulos, Milios, and Lapatsioras 2013). In this sense, financial instruments should be understood as having money-like capacities. This is not to suggest that financial instruments are now a source or *the* source of funda- mental value. Instead, they have turned the contestability of value into a tradable commodity (see also Cooper 2010; Martin 2013). As Bryan and Rafferty frame it,

financial instruments such as derivatives turn "the contestability of fundamental value into a tradable commodity—a market benchmark for an unknowable value" (Bryan and Rafferty 2006, 37).

13. For some commentators, the withdrawal of the state from the maintenance of life is understood to be contributing to a crisis in social reproduction, a crisis that itself is also understood as being part of what defines the post-Fordist condition (see, e.g., Bakker 2007; Gill and Bakker 2006; Leonard and Fraser 2016; Roberts 2013, 2015; Thorne 2011; Vosko 2002). At issue here is how the renewal, sustainability, and maintenance of life is not only increasingly privatized but also under threat and increasingly precarious. While our current moment is undoubtedly one in which the maintenance of life is by no means a given, it is important to register, as Silvia Federici (2012, 2013) has cogently argued, that far from being necessarily specific to the current moment, capitalism fosters a permanent crisis in social reproduction. This permanent crisis has not, however, been made explicit or categorical in the Global North until relatively recently. This is so, Federici maintains, because the consequences of this crisis (including the human catastrophes it has caused) have very often been externalized and positioned as effects of other forces and causes. And even as the consequences of this crisis began to become more apparent in the Global North in the 1980s and 1990s in the form of flexible or precarious work, they were often situated as cathartic alternatives to "the regimentation of the 9-to-5 regime, if not anticipations of a workerless society" (Federici 2012, 104–5). Thus, Federici hypothesizes that the crisis of social reproduction is a long-term (although often misrecognized) process. She compels us not only to see that capitalism fosters a permanent crisis in social reproduction but also to understand that this crisis is not incidental but central to the process of capital accumulation: "[T]he destruction of human life on a large scale has been a structural component of capitalism from its inception, as the necessary counterpart of the accumulation of labour power, which is inevitably a violent process" (ibid., 104).

14. Cooper makes clear that by the reinvention of tradition she is not referring to a simple return to the family form of a previous era or a straightforward process of reanimation. Instead, and following Siegel 1996 as well as Hobsbawm 1983, she makes explicit that she is referring to a process of preservation *through* transformation.

15. Jane Elliott (2013) has argued that in the context of the rewriting of the relations among capital, labor, and the state, especially of the state-economy relation, suffering has taken on a specific form, such that agency now operates as a burden or affliction, particularly in a context where subjects are compelled to take action on their own behalf. Elliott terms this form of agency "suffering agency" and argues that it should be understood to operate at the intersection of interest, choice, and agential action. Suffering should be understood, then, in its specificity in finance-led post-Fordism, a specificity that turns on the ways in which domination and agential choice have become intertwined.

16. These specific feeling states have been elaborated particularly clearly by Lauren Berlant (2008, 2010, 2011), who argues that the post-Fordist present is characterized by attachments to objects (especially good-life fantasies) that promise possibilities but simultaneously make the achievement of those possibilities impossible.

17. Claims to intensive mothering, as well as to an entrepreneurial stance toward domestic and mothering activities, are, for example, difficult to make by women who, because of economic necessity, provide caring and other forms of socially reproductive labor to others. The latter group of women are likely to be divided from the former along lines of race and class (see, e.g., Taylor 2016).

18. As Federici argues, the entanglement of women with these relations of dependency and subordination captures the energies and inventiveness of women worldwide. She also makes clear that in regard to household and personal debt, women constitute the preferred subjects of banks and other finance institutions. I will explore this in more detail in Chapter 3.

19. This phenomenon should be understood to be part of the decline in the significance of the wage in terms of the distribution of inequalities (Piketty 2014).

20. Such analyses tend simply to extend the spatial reach of inquiry beyond the nation-state.

21. Financial economists have shown the ways in which austerity is indelibly linked to the pre-crisis securitization or collateralization of government bonds (Gabor and Ban 2016, 2017).

Chapter 3: The Speculative Time of Debt

1. I am therefore not concerned in this chapter with debt that is defined as moral, natural, and unenforceable. This latter form of debt has served (and continues to serve) as a particular object of concern for the discipline of anthropology. On the distinction between debt that is defined as moral and unenforceable and debt that is contractual, monetary, and sanctioned, see Guyer 2012 and High 2012.

2. The significance of the promise to pay in the formation of creditor-debtor relations is made explicit by Marx (1981 [1894]).

3. Federici (2014) notes that while historically associated with the Global South, the mechanisms of debt (especially those associated with personal debt) have been extended to the Global North.

4. See also Beckert, who argues that "mounting debt . . . can . . . 'colonize' the present and block out the future by preventing investment into new imaginaries" (Beckert 2016, 273).

5. Federici (2014) links this strategy on the part of finance institutions to the paradox that some of the world's poorest borrowers are often those with the highest repayment rates.

6. This process has taken place in the context of the liberalization of mortgage and consumer finance markets. Until the 1970s, most women were excluded from access to mortgage and consumer credit (Allon 2014; Roberts 2013).

7. It is also important to stress that alternative mortgage products tend to involve more exposure to risk than traditional mortgages.

8. For accounts of the development and operations of probabilistic models of consumer and mortgage financing in the post–Second World War period in the US, see Ascher 2016a, 2016b; Poon 2009.

9. Notwithstanding the crisis of liquidity in the mortgage-backed securities market in 2007–8, such calculations have continued apace as they are joined to long-term shifts in the operations of mortgage markets (Aalbers 2008, 2012). Indeed, and as an outcome of changes to the operation of mortgage markets, financial economists are now able to map the outcomes of the calculus of securitized debt, particularly shifts in mortgage borrowing based on calculations of possible future incomes (see, e.g., Coco 2013; Gerardi et al. 2010).

10. In a recent set of interventions, Ascher (especially 2016a, 2016b) has argued that while industrial capital generated surplus through labor power, finance capital generates surplus through the acquisition of probability, especially the probability that populations who are (necessarily) entangled in debt will honor promises to repay. It is such probability, Ascher argues, that finance capital puts in motion to generate surplus. In making clear that the probables of repayment have given way to the possibles of payment, the account of the operations and dynamics of securitized debt that I have set out departs from this emphasis on the probable and probability. It is important to stress, however, that probabilistic and possibilistic forms of calculative practice are not necessarily separate from or external to each other but coexist and come into play together (Amoore 2013). Notwithstanding this coexistence, and in tune with the intervention I am laying out here, a range of writers have pointed to how calculations of the possible, especially of possible futures, play a heightened role in the operation of modern power (see, e.g., Clough and Willse 2011; de Goede 2012; Massumi 2015). Indeed, I will go on to elaborate in this chapter that through its emphases on the possible and payment, the calculus of securitized debt not only generates surplus for finance capital but also opens out modes of practice that maximize the productivity of populations in regard to that very surplus.

11. This is not a simple matter of such techniques operating in the service of the state or of sovereign power losing ground to private or market authority. Instead, at issue are novel arrangements of sovereign power "that play out on multiple sites and draw mobile lines between inside and outside" (Amoore 2013, 7; see also Brown 2015; Foucault 2008).

12. Massumi (2007, 2015) shows how such a logic of preemption infuses the present. The US National Security Agency, for example, employs preemptive techniques "orientated toward data mining for signs of threats that have not yet fully emerged" (Massumi 2015, 226); while modern policing strategies such as "kettling" (containment policing) act on potential threats that have not yet taken shape. Preemption, Massumi maintains, "is the most powerful operative logic of the present" (ibid., 209).

13. Amoore tends to associate the speculative with the possible, the incomplete, and the intuitive. She does not, as I do in this book, identify the speculative as a rationality.

14. This point is made particularly clear by Parisi (2013) in her analysis of what she terms the "speculative reason" operating at the heart of algorithmic calculation.

Chapter 4: Wages and the Problem of Value

1. As made clear in Chapter 2, derivatives have been understood to constitute a new form of money (see especially Bryan and Rafferty 2006, 2007, 2010). This understanding of derivatives is, however, by no means uncontroversial (see, e.g., Norfield 2012).

2. Income volatility (which includes income losses and gains) has been found not only to be an endemic feature of everyday life but also (for the case of the US especially) not to be confined to any particular income or demographic group. Such volatile wages require that populations adapt and continuously adjust to unpredictable flows of money in order to survive. Indeed, alongside the schedules of securitized debt, such wages should be understood to expand the productive capacities of populations, especially their adaptive capacities, in regard to indeterminate and unpredictable flows of money. It is noteworthy that fintech companies are developing applications to assist households in the management of the ebb and flow of wages, particularly in the payment of contracted mortgage debt and household bills, in the context of such volatility (Pew Charitable Trusts 2017). Such applications should be understood as infrastructural devices that work not only to ensure that payment streams continue to flow from households to finance capital but also to afford adaptive modes of practice in regard to volatile wages. In short, such devices should be understood as contributing to the expansion of speculative modes of practice in regard to everyday money. I am grateful to Dick Bryan for drawing research on the issue of income volatility to my attention.

3. While a crisis of social reproduction is often posited to be in play in those geopolitical zones in which a Fordist-Keynesian social contract has been undone, it is important to recall Federici's (2012, 2013) incisive point, outlined in Chapter 2, that capitalism fosters a permanent crisis in social reproduction.

4. Marx (1983 [1897]) documented how an unchecked extraction of surplus from workers in mid-nineteenth-century industrial capitalism produced a starving and exhausted proletariat, literally dying from work. He thus documented how the exchange of labor power as a commodity for money guaranteed neither life nor its reproduction.

5. As Federici (2012) documents, it was only at the end of the nineteenth century that the capitalist class began to invest in the reproduction of labor. This investment was, however, "by capital for capital," that is, for the requirements of factory production. Along with other feminist writers, Federici observes that Marx assumed that the reproduction of labor power took place by means of the market and ignored the significance of women, domestic labor, sexuality, and procreation in this process.

6. On the undercutting of social existence, see Butler 2004.

7. Between 1995 and 2007, the debt-to-income ratio rose by 49 percent in the US and 70 percent in the UK (Vidal 2013).

8. Especially extensions to lower-income households and the precariously and intermittently employed.

9. See, for example, Harvey 2010.

10. See, for example, Bennett 2014 on the history of the living wage.

11. Understanding this double movement also puts a rather different spin on the popular idea that present-day capitalism has captured, incorporated, and instrumentalized the spirit of external critique, including the spirit of the feminist and civil rights movements of the 1960s (see, e.g., Boltanski and Chiapello 2005; Fraser 2013). It does so not least by locating such critique as immanent to (and not transgressive of) the dynamics of capitalism.

12. Just as the ideal of the Fordist worker was by no means a lived reality, this ideal is not necessarily lived in finance-led post-Fordism. Nevertheless, there are socioeconomic consequences for those unable to access what money might put in motion.

13. Thanks to Melinda Cooper and Martijn Konings for alerting me to connections between my analysis and Feher's arguments regarding human capital.

Chapter 5: Out of Work

1. Thus, the process of economization has been located as central in the establishment of the market as the mode of rationality for society (as well as for the state).

2. It is worth noting here not only that the post–financial crisis era has been taken to share the same substantive conditions and problems as the Great Depression, but also that explanations of the Wall Street crash and the subsequent recession have been reloaded to make sense of the 2007–8 financial crisis and ensuing economic turbulence. As Duménil and Lévy have said, while no consensus has been reached concerning the roots of the Wall Street crash and the Great Depression, "the same set of . . . explanations are often retaken in the discussion of the ongoing crisis" (Duménil and Lévy 2014, 26). This tendency is especially apparent in the fields of political economy and heterodox economics.

3. In the EU-28, between 2011 and 2013, unemployment steadily increased, reaching a record level of 26.6 million, or a record rate of 11 percent. In May 2015, the unemployment rate for the EU-28 sat at 9.6 percent, and at 11.1 percent for the Euro Area (EA-19). In January 2017, in the EU-28, 19.95 million were recorded as unemployed; the EU-28 unemployment rate was 8.1 percent, with 9.6 percent for the Euro Area (Eurostat 2017).

4. On the history of the notion of the conjuncture in Marxist and neo-Marxist thought, see Koivisto and Lahtinen 2012.

5. See also Sotiropoulos, Milios, and Lapatsioras (2013), who argue that such a conjunctural form of analysis is required for both the 2007–8 financial crisis and the post–financial crisis era.

6. See, for example, the UK's Trades Union Congress (2009) report *Women and Recession* or the research report commissioned by the UK's Equality and Human Rights Commission, *The Equality Impacts of the Current Recession* (Hogarth et al. 2009).

7. This continuousness is the case notwithstanding attempts on the part of social policy scholars to correlate activation strategies with different kinds of welfare regimes (see, e.g., Huo et al. 2008), to make distinctions between different kinds of activation measures in terms of degrees of coercion (see, e.g., Taylor-Gooby 2004), and to correlate different activation measures with varying national employment rates (see, e.g., Kenworthy 2010). Indeed, despite these efforts to find geo-institutional difference across activation policies, it is important to note that welfare-to-work or activation policy has been found to be a common feature of reformed welfare states (see, e.g., Pierson and Humpage 2016). This is not, however, to propose a simple thesis of convergence or homogenization in regard to social policy or reformed welfare states. As Peck, Theodore, and Brenner (2012) have made clear, the process of the reform of welfare states does not follow a unitary path nor does it aim at a single end point. Instead, such reform is open-ended and experimental in character. The spaces of regulatory change that such reform has produced are, nonetheless, "relationally interconnected within a transnational governance system and are linked through fast-moving, transnationalizing circuits of policy formation" (Peck, Theodore, and Brenner 2012, 273; see also Peck and Theodore 2015).

8. On how the take-up and institutionalization of neoliberal principles has involved a multifarious transnational infrastructure, see Mirowski and Plehwe 2009, Stedman Jones 2012, and Van Horn et al. 2011.

9. It is also important to make explicit that activation regimes act as powerful mechanisms for the discipline and control of labor, and in particular, as a mechanism for punishing the poor (Adler 2016; Waquant 2010).

10. Consequently, Denning notes that Marx did not make use of the term "unemployment" and did not refer to the unemployed. In *Capital*, for example, Marx refers to the not-busy and the unoccupied, but not to the unemployed or to unemployment.

11. Bauman also failed to grasp that the experience of unemployment in the welfare state era that he mapped was primarily that of men.

12. There has been an explosion of recordings of the lives of the disadvantaged and marginalized in the post–financial crisis era, including the lives and experiences of the unemployed (see, e.g., Biggs 2015; O'Hara 2014).

13. In this respect, activation policy conforms to the general characteristics of ongoing welfare state reform, especially the characteristics of continuous mutation and roll-out, including mutation and further embedding in the face of constant crises (Peck and Theodore 2015; Peck et al. 2012).

Bibliography

Aalbers, M. 2008. "The Financialization of Home and the Mortgage Market Crisis." *Competition and Change* 12(2): 148–66.

———. 2012. "European Mortgage Markets before and after the Financial Crisis." In *Subprime Cities: The Political Economy of Mortgage Markets*, edited by M. Aalbers, 120–50. Oxford: Wiley-Blackwell.

Abramovitz, M. 1996. *Regulating the Lives of Women: Social Welfare Policy from Colonial Times to the Present*. Boston: South End Press.

Adam, B. 1994. *Time and Social Theory*. Cambridge: Polity Press.

———. 2004a. "Towards a New Sociology of the Future." Accessed April 12, 2017. http://www.cardiff.ac.uk/socsi/futures/newsociologyofthefuture.pdf.

———. 2004b. *Time*. Cambridge: Polity Press.

Adams, V., M. Murphy, and A. E. Clarke. 2009. "Anticipation: Technoscience, Life, Affect, Temporality." *Subjectivity* 28(1): 246–65.

Adkins, L. 2008. "From Retroactivation to Futurity: The End of the Sexual Contract." *NORA: Nordic Journal of Feminist and Gender Research* 16(3): 182–201.

———. 2017. "Disobedient Workers, the Law and the Making of Unemployment Markets." *Sociology* 51(2): 290–305.

Adler, M. 2016. "A New Leviathan: Benefit Sanctions in the Twenty-First Century." *Journal of Law and Society* 43(2): 195–227.

Aitken, R. 2015. "Everyday Debt Relationalities: Situating Peer-to-Peer Lending and the Rolling Jubilee." *Cultural Studies* 29(5–6): 845–68.

Akalin, A. 2007. "Hired as a Caregiver, Demanded as a Housewife: Becoming a Migrant Domestic Worker in Turkey." *European Journal of Women's Studies* 14(3): 209–25.

———. 2015. "Motherhood as the Value of Labour: The Migrant Domestic Workers' Market in Turkey." *Australian Feminist Studies* 30(83): 65–81.

Alessandrini, D. 2014. "Rethinking Feminist Engagements with the State and Wage Labour." *feminists@law* 4(1): 1–15.

Allon, F. 2010. "Speculating on Everyday Life: The Cultural Economy of the Quotidian." *Journal of Communication Inquiry* 34(4): 366–81.

———. 2014. "The Feminisation of Finance: Gender, Labour and the Limits of Inclusion." *Australian Feminist Studies* 29(79): 12–30.

———. 2015a. "Everyday Leverage, or Leveraging the Everyday." *Cultural Studies* 29(5–6): 687–706.

———. 2015b. "Money, Debt and the Business of 'Free Stuff.'" *South Atlantic Quarterly* 114(2): 283–302.

Allon, F., and G. Redden. 2012. "The Global Financial Crisis and the Culture of Continual Growth." *Journal of Cultural Economy* 5(4): 375–90.

Amato, M., L. Doria, and L. Fantacci. 2010. "Introduction." In *Money and Calculation: Economic and Sociological Perspectives*, edited by M. Amato, L. Doria, and L. Fantacci, 1–15. Basingstoke, UK: Palgrave Macmillan.

Amoore, L. 2013. *The Politics of Possibility: Risk and Security beyond Probability*. Durham, NC: Duke University Press.

Amoore, L., and M. de Goede. 2008. "Transactions after 9/11: The Banal Face of the Preemptive Strike." *Transactions of the Institute of British Geographers* 33(2): 173–85.

Amoore, L., and V. Piotukh. 2015. "Introduction." In *Algorithmic Life: Calculative Devices in the Age of Big Data*, edited by L. Amoore and V. Piotukh, 1–18. London: Routledge.

Anderson, A. 2012. "Europe's Care Regimes and the Role of Migrant Care Workers within Them." *Population Ageing* 5:135–46.

Anderson, B. 2000. *Doing the Dirty Work: The Global Politics of Domestic Labour*. London: Zed Books.

Andersson, K., and E. Kvist. 2015. "The Neoliberal Turn and the Marketization of Care: The Transformation of Eldercare in Sweden." *European Journal of Women's Studies* 22(3): 274–87.

Annesley, C. 2014. *UK Austerity Policy: A Feminist Perspective*. Berlin: Friedrich-Ebert-Stiftung.

Aquanno, S. 2009. "US Power and the International Bond Market: Financial Flows and the Construction of Risk Value." In *American Empire and the Political Economy of Global Finance*, edited by L. Panitich and M. Konings, 119–34. Basingstoke, UK: Palgrave Macmillan.

Ascher, I. 2016a. "'Moneybags Must Be So Lucky': Inside the Hidden Abode of Prediction." *Political Theory* 44(1): 4–25.

———. 2016b. *Portfolio Society: On the Capitalist Mode of Prediction*. New York: Zone Books.

Bach, S. 2016. "Deprivileging the Public Sector Workforce: Austerity, Fragmentation and Service Withdrawal in Britain." *Economic and Labour Relations Review* 27(1): 11–28.

Bakker, I. 2007. "Social Reproduction and the Constitution of a Gendered Political Economy." *New Political Economy* 12(4): 541–56.

Banoli, G. 2010. "The Political Economy of Active Labor-Market Policy." *Politics and Society* 38(4): 435–57.

Barad, K. 2010. "Quantum Entanglements and Hauntological Relations of Inheritance: Dis/continuities, SpaceTime Enfoldings, and Justice-to-Come." *Derrida Today* 3(2): 240–68.

Barba, A., and M. Pivetti. 2009. "Rising Household Debt: Its Causes and Macro-economic Implications: A Long-Period Analysis." *Cambridge Journal of Economics* 33(1): 113–37.

Barrett, M., and M. McIntosh. 1980. *Women's Oppression Today*. London: Verso.

Bauman, Z. 1998. *Work, Consumerism and the New Poor*. Buckingham, UK: Open University Press.

———. 2010. *Living on Borrowed Time: Conversations with Citlali Rovirosa-Madrazo*. Cambridge: Polity Press.

BBC. 2011. "Recession Threatening to Turn Back Time for Women." BBC News, July 4. Accessed March 19, 2017. http://www.bbc.com/news/uk-northern-ire land-14007048.

Beasley-Murray, J. 2000. "Value and Capital in Bourdieu and Marx." In *Pierre Bourdieu: Fieldwork in Culture*, edited by N. Brown and I. Szeman, 100–119. Lanham, MD: Rowman and Littlefield.

Beckert, J. 2016. *Imagined Futures: Fictional Expectations and Capitalist Dynamics*. Cambridge, MA: Harvard University Press.

Bennett, F. 2014. "The 'Living Wage,' Low Pay and in Work Poverty: Rethinking the Relationships." *Critical Social Policy* 34(1): 46–65.

Berardi, F. 2011. *After the Future*. Edinburgh: AK Press.

Berlant, L. 2008. *The Female Complaint Durham: The Unfinished Business of Sentimentality in American Culture*. Durham, NC: Duke University Press.

———. 2010. "Affect and the Politics of Austerity: An Interview Exchange with Lauren Berlant." *Variant* 39–40 (Winter): 3–6.

———. 2011. *Cruel Optimism*. Durham, NC: Duke University Press.

Bertram, E. 2015. *The Workfare State: Public Assistance Politics from the New Deal to the New Democrats*. Philadelphia: University of Pennsylvania Press.

Biggs, J. 2015. *All Day Long: A Portrait of Britain and Work*. London: Serpent's Tail.

Bjerg, O. 2016. "How Is Bitcoin Money?" *Theory, Culture and Society* 33(1): 53–72.

Black, W. K. 2013. "Comparing Unemployment during the Great Depression and the Great Recession." *New Economic Perspectives*. April 5. Accessed January 20, 2017. http://neweconomicperspectives.org/2013/04/comparing-unemployment -during-the-great-depression-and-the-great-recession.html.

Blackburn, R. 2008. "The Subprime Crisis." *New Left Review* 50: 63–106.

Blyth, M. 2013. *Austerity: The History of a Dangerous Idea*. Oxford: Oxford University Press.

Boland, T. 2015. "Talk: Nothing to Be Done." In *The Sociology of Unemployment*, edited by T. Boland and R. Griffin, 11–29. Manchester, UK: Manchester University Press.

Boltanski, L., and E. Chiapello. 2005 [1999]. *The New Spirit of Capitalism*. Translated by G. Elliott. London: Verso.

Bourdieu, P. 1977 [1972]. *Outline of a Theory of Practice.* Translated by R. Nice. Cambridge: Cambridge University Press.

———. 2000 [1997]. *Pascalian Meditations.* Translated by R. Nice. Cambridge: Polity Press.

———. 2003 [2001]. *Firing Back: Against the Tyranny of the Market 2.* Translated by L. Wacquant. London: Verso.

———. 2005 [2000]. *The Social Structures of the Economy.* Translated by C. Turner. Cambridge: Polity Press.

Bourdieu, P., et al. 1999 [1993]. *The Weight of the World: Social Suffering in Contemporary Society.* Translated by P. Parkhurst Ferguson. Cambridge: Polity Press.

Brenkman, J. 2002. "Queer Post-politics." *Narrative* 10(2): 174–80.

Brown, W. 2015. *Undoing the Demos: Neoliberalism's Stealth Revolution.* New York: Zone Books.

Bryan, D., R. Martin, and M. Rafferty. 2009. "Financialization and Marx: Giving Labor and Capital a Financial Makeover." *Review of Radical Political Economics* 41(4): 458–72.

Bryan, D., and M. Rafferty. 2006. *Capitalism with Derivatives: A Political Economy of Financial Derivatives, Capital and Class.* Basingstoke, UK: Palgrave Macmillan.

———. 2007. "Financial Derivatives and the Theory of Money." *Economy and Society* 36(1): 134–58.

———. 2010. "A Time and Place for Everything: Foundations of Commodity Money." In *Money and Calculation*, edited by M. Amato, L. Doria, and L. Fantacci, 101–21. Basingstoke, UK: Palgrave Macmillan.

———. 2011. "Deriving Capital's (and Labour's) Future." *Socialist Register* 47:196–223.

———. 2012. "Why We Need to Understand Derivatives in Relation to Money: A Reply to Tony Norfield." *Historical Materialism* 20(3): 97–109.

———. 2014. "Financial Derivatives as Social Policy beyond Crisis." *Sociology* 48(5): 887–903.

Bryan, D., M. Rafferty, and C. Jefferis. 2015. "Risk and Value: Finance, Labor and Production." *South Atlantic Quarterly* 114(2): 307–30.

Bryan, D., M. Rafferty, and B. Tinel. 2016. "Households at the Frontiers of Monetary Development." *Behemoth* 9(2): 46–58.

Burnett, J. 1994. *Idle Hands: The Experience of Unemployment, 1790–1990.* London: Routledge.

Butler, J. 1993. *Bodies That Matter: On the Discursive Limits of Sex.* London: Routledge.

———. 1998. "Merely Cultural." *New Left Review* 227:33–44.

———. 2004. *Precarious Life.* London: Verso.

Calhoun, C. 1993. "Habitus, Field, and Capital: The Question of Historical Specificity." In *Bourdieu: Critical Perspectives*, edited by C. Calhoun, E. LiPuma, and M. Postone, 61–88. Chicago: University of Chicago Press.

———. 2006. "Pierre Bourdieu and Social Transformation: Lessons from Algeria." *Development and Change* 37(6): 1403–15.

Çalişkan, K., and M. Callon. 2009. "Economization Part 1: Shifting Attention from the Economy to Processes of Economization." *Economy and Society* 38(3): 369–98.

———. 2010. "Economization Part 2: A Research Programme for the Study of Markets." *Economy and Society* 39(1): 1–32.

Callon, M. 1999. "Actor Network Theory—The Market Test." In *Actor Network Theory and After*, edited by J. Law and J. Hassard, 181–95. Oxford: Blackwell.

Callon, M., Y. Millo, and F. Muniesa. 2007. *Market Devices*. Oxford: Wiley-Blackwell.

Cameron, D. 2009. "Labour's Debt Crisis." *Conservative Party Speeches*, January 12. Accessed March 21, 2017. http://conservative-speeches.sayit.mysociety.org/speech/601423.

Carrasco, C., and M. Domínguez. 2011. "Family Strategies for Meeting Care and Domestic Work Needs: Evidence from Spain." *Feminist Economics* 17(4): 159–88.

Cavendish, C. 2009. "Insane Spendaholics Are Mortgaging Our Future." *The Times*, March 20, 2009. Accessed March 21, 2017. http://www.timesonline.co.uk/tol/comment/columnists/camilla_cavendish/article5941273.ece.

Charbonneau, M., and M. P. Hansen. 2014. "Debt, Neoliberalism and Crisis: Interview with Maurizio Lazzarato on the Indebted Condition." *Sociology* 48(5): 1039–47.

Chesnais, F. 2014. "Fictitious Capital in the Context of Global Over-accumulation and Changing International Economic Power Relationships." In *The Great Recession and the Contradictions of Contemporary Capitalism*, edited by R. Bellofiore and G. Vertova, 65–82. Cheltenham, UK: Edward Elgar.

Chicchi, F. 2010. "On the Threshold of Capital, at the Thresholds of the Common: Sidenotes on the Ambivalences of Biopolitical Capitalism." In *Crisis in the Global Economy: Financial Markets, Social Struggles, and New Political Scenarios*, edited by A. Fumagalli and S. Mezzadra, 139–52. Cambridge, MA: MIT Press.

Christophers, B. 2015. "The Limits to Financialization." *Dialogues in Human Geography* 5(2): 183–200.

———. 2017. "The Performativity of the Yield Curve." *Journal of Cultural Economy* 10(1): 63–80.

Clough, P. T., and C. Willse. 2011. "Beyond Biopolitics: The Governance of Life and Death." In *Beyond Biopolitics: Essays on the Governance of Life and Death*, edited by P. T. Clough and C. Willse, 1–16. Durham, NC: Duke University Press.

Coco, J. F. 2013. "Evidence on the Benefits of Alternative Mortgage Products." *Journal of Finance* 68:(4): 1663–90.

Cole, M. 2007. "Rethinking Unemployment: A Challenge to the Legacy of Jahoda et al." *Sociology* 41(6): 1133–49.

Coleman, R. 2008. "Things That Stay." *Time and Society* 17(1): 85–102.

————. 2010. "Dieting Temporalities: Interaction, Agency and the Measure of Online Weight Watching." *Time and Society* 19(2): 265–85.

————. 2014. "Inventive Feminist Theory: Representation, Materiality and Intensive Time." *Women: A Cultural Review* 25(1): 27–45.

————. 2016. "Notes towards a Surfacing of Feminist Theoretical Turns." *Australian Feminist Studies* 89(31): 228–45.

Connolly, W. E. 2011. *A World of Becoming*. Durham, NC: Duke University Press.

Cooper, D. 2014. *Everyday Utopias: The Conceptual Life of Promising Spaces*. Durham, NC: Duke University Press.

Cooper, M. 2008. *Life as Surplus: Biotechnology and Capitalism in the Neoliberal Era*. Seattle: University of Washington Press.

————. 2010. "Turbulent Worlds: Financial Markets and Environmental Crisis." *Theory, Culture and Society* 27(2–3): 167–90.

————. 2012. "Workfare, Familyfare, Godfare: Transforming Contingency into Necessity." *South Atlantic Quarterly* 111(4): 643–61.

————. 2015. "Shadow Money and the Shadow Workforce: Rethinking Labor and Liquidity." *South Atlantic Quarterly* 114(2): 395–423.

————. 2017. *Family Values: Between Neoliberalism and the New Social Conservatism*. New York: Zone Books.

Cooper, M., and M. Konings. 2015. "Contingency and Foundation: Rethinking Money, Debt and Finance after the Crisis." *South Atlantic Quarterly* 114(2): 239–50.

Cooper, M., and C. Waldby. 2014. *Clinical Labour: Tissue Donors and Research Subjects in the Global Bioeconomy*. Durham, NC: Duke University Press.

Crotty, J. 2005. "The Neoliberal Paradox: The Impact of Destructive Product Market Competition and 'Modern' Financial Markets on Nonfinancial Corporation Performance in the Neoliberal Era." In *Financialization and the World Economy*, edited by G. Epstein, 77–110. Northampton, UK: Edward Elgar.

Day, P., and T. Cobos. 2012. "Spain Protests Labor Reforms as Hundreds of Thousands Take to Streets." *World Post*, April 20, 2012. Accessed March 21, 2017. http://www.huffingtonpost.com/2012/02/19/spain-protests-labor-reforms_n _1287491.html.

Dean, M. 1995. "Governing the Unemployed Self in an Active Society." *Economy and Society* 24(4): 559–83.

Deeming, C. 2014. "Social Democracy and Social Policy in Neoliberal Times." *Journal of Sociology* 50(4): 577–600.

————. 2016. "Rethinking Social Policy and Society." *Social Policy and Society* 15(2): 159–75.

de Goede, M. 2000. "Mastering Lady Credit: Discourses of Financial Crisis in Historical Perspective." *International Feminist Journal of Politics* 2(1): 58–81.

————. 2012. *Speculative Security: The Politics of Pursuing Terrorist Monies*. Minneapolis: University of Minnesota Press.

———. 2015. "Speculative Values and Courtroom Contestations." *South Atlantic Quarterly* 114(2): 355–76.

Deleuze, G. 1992. "Postscript on the Societies of Control." *October* 59: 3–7.

Denning, M. 2010. "Wageless Life." *New Left Review* 66: 79–97.

Deville, J. 2015. *Lived Economies of Default*. London: Routledge.

Di Feliciantonio, C. 2016. "Subjectification in Times of Indebtedness and Neoliberal/Austerity Urbanism." *Antipode* 48(5): 1206–27.

Dodd, N. 2012. "Simmel's Perfect Money: Fiction, Socialism and Utopia in *The Philosophy of Money*." *Theory, Culture and Society* 29(7–8): 146–76.

———. 2014. *The Social Life of Money*. Princeton, NJ: Princeton University Press.

Dullien, S., H. Herr, and C. Kellerman. 2011. *Decent Capitalism: A Blueprint for Reforming Our Economies*. London: Pluto.

Duménil, G., and D. Lévy. 2014. "The Crisis in the Early 21st Century: Marxian Perspectives." In *The Great Recession and the Contradictions of Contemporary Capitalism*, edited by R. Bellofiore and G. Vertova, 26–49. Cheltenham, UK: Edward Elgar.

Dymski, G. A., and A. Kaltenbrunner. 2017. "How Finance Globalized: A Tale of Two Cities." In *The Routledge Companion to Banking Regulation and Reform*, edited by I. Ertürk and D. Gabor, 351–72. London: Routledge.

Dynan, K. E., and D. L. Kohn. 2007. *The Rise in U.S. Household Indebtedness: Causes and Consequences*. Finance and Economics Discussion Series (FEDS), Working Paper No. 37, Divisions of Research and Statistics and Monetary Affairs. Federal Reserve Board: Washington.

Edelman, L. 2004. *No Future: Queer Theory and the Death Drive*. Durham, NC: Duke University Press.

Ehrenreich, B., and A. R. Hochschild, eds. 2002. *Global Woman: Nannies, Maids and Sex Workers in the New Economy*. London: Granta.

Elliott, J. 2013. "Suffering Agency: Imagining Neoliberal Personhood in North America and Britain." *Social Text* 31(2): 83–101.

Elson, D. 2013. "Austerity Policies Increase Unemployment and Inequality." *Journal of Australian Political Economy* 71: 130–33.

Epstein, G. 2005. "Financialization and the World Economy." In *Financialization and the World Economy*, edited by G. Epstein, 3–16. Cheltenham, UK: Edward Elgar.

Esping-Anderson, G. 1990. *The Three Worlds of Welfare Capitalism*. Princeton, NJ: Princeton University Press.

Esposito, E. 2011. *The Future of Futures: The Time of Money in Financing and Society*. Cheltenham, UK: Edward Elgar.

European Women's Lobby. 2012. *The Price of Austerity: The Impact on Women's Rights and Gender Equality in Europe*. Brussels: European Women's Lobby.

Eurostat. 2015. *Youth Unemployment: Eurostat Statistics Explained*. Eurostat, September 1, 2015. Accessed March 20, 2017. http://ec.europa.eu/eurostat/statistics-explained/index.php/Youth_unemployment.

———. 2017. *Unemployment Statistics: Eurostat Statistics Explained*. Eurostat, March 2, 2017. Accessed March 19, 2017. http://ec.europa.eu/eurostat/statistics-explained/index.php/Unemployment_statistics.

Farrell, D., and F. Greig. 2017. *The Gender Gap in Financial Outcomes: The Impact of Medical Payments*. Washington, DC: JPMorgan Chase Institute.

Farris, S. 2015. "Migrants' Regular Army of Labour: Gender Dimensions of the Impact of the Global Economic Crisis on Migrant Labour in Western Europe." *Sociological Review* 63(1): 121–43.

Fawcett Society. 2013. *Budget 2013: Helping or Hurting Women?* London: Fawcett Society.

———. 2015. "About Us." *Fawcett Society*. Accessed March 21, 2017. https://www.fawcettsociety.org.uk/.

Federici, S. 2012. *Revolution at Point Zero: Housework, Reproduction, and Feminist Struggle*. Oakland, CA: PM Press.

———. 2013. "Permanent Reproductive Crisis: An Interview with Silvia Federici." *Mute* (March): 1–18.

———. 2014. "From Commoning to Debt: Financialization, Microcredit, and the Changing Architecture of Capital Accumulation." *South Atlantic Quarterly* 113(2): 231–44.

Feher, M. 2009. "Self-Appreciation; or, The Aspirations of Human Capital." *Public Culture* 21(1): 21–41.

Ferguson, R. 2003. *Aberrations in Black*. Minneapolis: University of Minnesota Press.

Fine, B. 2010. "Locating Financialisation." *Historical Materialism* 18: 97–116.

Fisher, P. 2015. "We Borrow Too Much from the Future at Our Peril." *Financial Times*, August 18, 2015. Accessed March 21, 2017. https://www.ft.com/content/f9630ee6-3b5e-11e5-bbd1-b37bc06f590c.

Fleck, C. 1971. "Introduction to the Transaction Edition." In *Marienthal: The Sociography of an Unemployed Community*, by M. Jahoda, P. Lazarsfeld, and H. Zeisel, vii–xxx. London: Transaction.

Folbre, N., ed. 2012. *For Love and Money: Care Provision in the United States*. New York: Russell Sage Foundation.

Foucault, M. 2008. *The Birth of Biopolitics*. Translated by G. Burchell. Basingstoke, UK: Palgrave Macmillan.

Fox Piven, F. 2011. "The New American Poor Law." *Socialist Register* 48:108–24.

Fraser, N. 1995. "From Redistribution to Recognition: Dilemmas of Justice in a 'Postsocialist' Age." *New Left Review* 212:68–93.

———. 1997. *Justice Interruptus: Critical Reflections on the 'Post-socialist' Condition*. London: Routledge.

———. 2013. *Fortunes of Feminism: From State-Managed Capitalism to Neo-liberal Crisis*. London: Verso.

Freeman, C. 2014. *Entrepreneurial Subjects: Neoliberal Respectability and the Making of a Caribbean Middle Class*. Durham, NC: Duke University Press.

Freeman, E. 2010. *Time Binds: Queer Temporalities, Queer Histories*. Durham, NC: Duke University Press.

Frisby, D. 2004a. "Preface to the Third Edition." In *The Philosophy of Money*, by G. Simmel [1907], xv–xlvi. Translated by T. Bottomore and D. Frisby. London: Routledge.

———. 2004b. "Introduction to the Translation." In *The Philosophy of Money*, by G. Simmel [1907], 1–49. Translated by T. Bottomore and D. Frisby. London: Routledge.

Fudge, J. 2011. "Global Care Chains, Employment Agencies and the Conundrum of Jurisdiction: Decent Work for Domestic Workers in Canada." *Canadian Journal of Women and the Law* 23(1): 235–64.

Gabor, D., and C. Ban. 2016. "Banking in Bonds: The New Links between States and Markets." *Journal of Common Market Studies* 54(3): 617–35.

———. 2017. "Europe's Toxic Twins: Government Debt in Financialized Times." In *The Routledge Companion to Banking Regulation and Reform*, edited by I. Ertürk and D. Gabor, 134–48. London: Routledge.

Gane, N. 2015. "Central Banking, Technocratic Governance and the Financial Crisis: Placing Quantitative Easing into Question." *Sosiologia* 4:381–96.

Genosko, G., and N. Thoburn. 2011. "Preface: The Transversal Communism of Franco Berardi." In *After the Future*, by F. Berardi, 1–8. Edinburgh: AK Press.

Gerardi, K. S., H. S. Rosen, and P. S. Willen. 2010. "The Impact of Deregulation and Financial Innovation on Consumers: The Case of the Mortgage Market." *Journal of Finance* 65(1): 333–60.

Giddens, A. 1981. *A Contemporary Critique of Historical Materialism*. Vol. 1. Berkeley: University of California Press.

Gilbert, K. W. 2007. "Slowness: Notes toward an Economy of Différancial Rates of Being." In *The Affective Turn: Theorizing the Social*, edited by P. Clough and J. Halley, 77–105. Durham, NC: Duke University Press.

Gilbert, N. 2002. *Transformation of the Welfare State: The Silent Surrender of Public Responsibility*. Oxford: Oxford University Press.

Gill, R., and S. Orgad. 2015. "The Confidence Cult(ure)." *Australian Feminist Studies* 30(86): 324–44.

Gill, S., and I. Bakker. 2006. "New Constitutionalism and the Social Reproduction of Caring Institutions." *Theoretical Medicine and Bioethics* 27:35–57.

Gindin, S., and L. Panitch. 2012. *The Making of Global Capitalism: The Political Economy of American Empire*. London: Verso.

Goodman, A. 2012. "Unions Protest Spanish Labor Reforms." CNN Europe, February 19, 2012. Accessed March 21, 2017. http://edition.cnn.com/2012/02/19/world/europe/spain-mass-protests/index.html.

Graeber, D. 2011. *Debt: The First 5,000 Years*. New York: Melville House.

Granovetter, M. 1985. "Economic Action and Social Structure: The Problem of Embeddedness." *American Journal of Sociology* 91(3): 481–510.

Green, J. 2013. "The Politics of Quantitative Easing: 'Recovery' through Regressive Redistribution." *Speri Comment: The Political Economy Blog*, September 24, 2013. Accessed May 6, 2017. http://speri.dept.shef.ac.uk/2013/09/24/politics-quantitative-easing-recovery-regressive-redistribution/.

Grosz, E. 2000. "Deleuze's Bergson: Duration, the Virtual and a Politics of the Future." In *Deleuze and Feminist Theory*, edited by I. Buchanan and C. Colebrook, 214–34. Edinburgh: Edinburgh University Press.

———. 2004. *The Nick of Time: Politics, Evolution and the Untimely*. Durham, NC: Duke University Press.

———. 2010. "The Untimeliness of Feminist Theory." *NORA: Nordic Journal of Feminist and Gender Research* 18(1): 48–51.

Gutiérrez-Rodriguez, E. 2010. *Migration, Domestic Work and Affect: A Decolonial Approach on Value and the Feminization of Labour*. London: Routledge.

———. 2014. "Domestic Work—Affective Labor: On Feminization and the Coloniality of Labor." *Women's Studies International Forum* 46:45–53.

Guttmann, R. 2015. *Finance-Led Capitalism: Shadow Banking, Re-regulation and the Future of Global Markets*. Basingstoke, UK: Palgrave Macmillan.

Guyer, J. I. 2007. "Prophecy and the Near Future: Thoughts on Macroeconomic, Evangelical and Punctuated Time." *American Ethnologist* 34(3): 409–21.

———. 2012a. "Obligation, Binding, Debt and Responsibility: Provocations about Temporality from Two New Sources." *Social Anthropology* 20(4): 491–501.

———. 2012b. "Life in Financial Calendrics." Accessed March 3, 2016. http://www.culanth.org/fieldsights/338-life-in-financial-calendrics.

Hacker, J. S. 2006. *The Great Risk Shift: The New Economic Insecurity and the Decline of the American Dream*. Oxford: Oxford University Press.

Hall, S. 1978. "Marxism and Culture." *Radical History Review* 18:5–14.

———. 1979. "The Great Moving Right Show." *Marxism Today* (January): 14–20.

———. 1980. "Cultural Studies: Two Paradigms." *Media, Culture and Society* 2(1): 57–72.

Haraway, D. 1991. *Simians, Cyborgs and Women: The Reinvention of Nature*. London: Routledge.

Hardt, M., and A. Negri. 2001. *Empire*. Cambridge, MA: Harvard University Press.

Harrington, A., and T. Kemple. 2012. "Georg Simmel's 'Sociological Metaphysics': Money, Sociality and Precarious Life." *Theory, Culture and Society* 29(7–8): 7–25.

Harvey, D. 2004. "The 'New' Imperialism: Accumulation by Dispossession." *Socialist Register* 40:63–87.

———. 2007. *A Brief History of Neoliberalism*. Oxford: Oxford University Press.

———. 2010. *The Enigma of Capital and the Crises of Capitalism*. London: Prime Books.

Hassan, R. 2003. "Network Time and the New Knowledge Epoch." *Time and Society* 12(2–3): 225–41.

Haywood, M. 2010. "The Economic Crisis and After: Recovery, Reconstitution and Cultural Studies." *Cultural Studies* 24(3): 283–94.

Hemmings, C. 2011. *Why Stories Matter: The Political Grammar of Feminist Theory*. Durham, NC: Duke University Press.

High, H. 2012. "Re-reading the Potlatch in a Time of Crisis: Debt and the Distinctions That Matter." *Social Anthropology* 20(4): 363–79.

Highmore, B. 2002. *Everyday Life and Cultural Theory*. London: Routledge.

———. 2011. *Ordinary Lives: Studies in the Everyday*. London: Routledge.

Hobsbawm, E. 1983. "Introduction: Inventing Traditions." In *The Invention of Tradition*, edited by E. Hobsbawm and T. Ranger, 1–14. Cambridge: Cambridge University Press.

Hochschild, A. R. 2000. "Global Care Chains and Emotional Surplus Value." In *On the Edge: Living with Global Capitalism*, edited by A. Giddens and W. Hutton, 130–46. London: Jonathan Cape.

———. 2012. *The Outsourced Self: What Happens When We Pay Others to Live Our Lives for Us*. New York: Picador.

Hogarth, T., D. Owen, L. Gambin, C. Hasluck, C. Lyonette, and B. Casey. 2009. *The Equality Impacts of the Current Recession*. The Equality and Human Rights Commission Research Report Series, Manchester, UK: The Equality and Human Rights Commission.

Huber, G. 2017. *Sovereign Money: Beyond Reserve Banking*. Basingstoke, UK: Palgrave/Macmillan.

Humphrys, E., and D. Cahill. 2017. "How Labour Made Neoliberalism." *Critical Sociology* 43(4–5): 669–84.

Huo, J., M. Nelson, and J. D. Stephens. 2008. "Decommodification and Activation in Social Democratic Policy: Resolving the Paradox." *Journal of European Social Policy* 18(1): 5–20.

Husserl, E. 1931. *Ideas: General Introduction to Pure Phenomenology*. Translated by W. R. Boyce Gibson. London: Allen and Unwin.

Immervol, H. 2012. "Activation Policies in OECD Countries: An Overview of Current Approaches." *Labor Markets* 14:1–8.

International Labour Organization. 2013. *Global Wages Report: Wages and Equitable Growth*. Geneva: International Labour Office.

———. 2015. *World Employment Social Outlook: The Changing Nature of Jobs*. Geneva: International Labour Office.

International Monetary Fund Survey. 2010. "Interview with Olivier Blanchard." *International Monetary Fund Survey Online*, September 2010. Accessed January 19, 2017. https://www.imf.org/en/News/Articles/2015/09/28/04/53/sonew090910a.

Jahoda, M., P. Lazarsfeld, and H. Zeisel. 1971. *Marienthal: The Sociography of an Unemployed Community*. London: Transaction.

Jasarevic, L. 2014. "Speculative Technologies: Debt, Love and Divination in a Transnationalizing Market." *Women's Studies Quarterly* 42(1–2): 261–77.

Jeong, B. 2016. "The Production of Indebted Subjects: Capitalism and Melancholia." *Deleuze Studies* 10(3): 336–51.

Jessop, B. 2002a. *The Future of the Capitalist State*. Cambridge: Polity Press.

———. 2002b. "Liberalism, Neoliberalism and Urban Governance: A State-Theoretical Perspective." *Antipode* 34(3): 452–72.

Joseph, M. 2014. *Debt to Society*. Minneapolis: University of Minnesota Press.

Juventud Sin Futuro. 2011. *Juventud sin Futuro*. Barcelona: Icaria Editorial.

Kakissis, J. 2012. "Greeks Worry That a Future of Austerity Is No Future at All." *McClatchy DC*, February 13, 2012. Accessed March 21, 2017. http://www.mcclatchydc.com/news/nation-world/world/article24724120.html.

Kananen, J. 2012. "Nordic Paths from Welfare to Workfare: Danish, Swedish and Finnish Labour Market Reforms Compared." *Local Economy* 27(5–6): 558–76.

———. 2014. *The Nordic Welfare State in Three Eras: From Emancipation to Discipline*. London: Routledge.

Karamessini, M., and J. Rubery, eds. 2013. *Women and Austerity: The Economic Crisis and the Future for Gender Equality*. London: Routledge.

Karpik, L. 2010. *Valuing the Unique: The Economics of Singularities*. Princeton, NJ: Princeton University Press.

Katz, L. F. 2010. "Long-Term Unemployment in the Great Recession." Testimony to the Joint Economic Committee, U.S. Congress, April 29, 2010. Accessed March 22, 2017. http://scholar.harvard.edu/files/lkatz/files/long_term_unemployment_in_the_great_recession.pdf.

Kenworthy, L. 2010. "Labour Market Activation." In *The Oxford Handbook of the Welfare State*, edited by F. G. Castles, S. Leibfried, J. Lewis, H. Obinger, and C. Pierson, 435–47. Oxford: Oxford University Press.

Kerr, I., and J. Earle. 2013. "Prediction, Preemption, Presumption: How Big Data Threatens Big Picture Privacy." *Stanford Law Review Online* 66(65): 1–8.

Khan, M. 2015. "A New Disease Is Spreading across Europe: Hysteresis." *The Telegraph*, October 27, 2015. Accessed March 20, 2017. http://www.telegraph.co.uk/finance/economics/11955566/A-new-disease-is-spreading-across-Europe-hysteresis.html.

Kingsley, P., L. Hickman, and E. Saner. 2011. "What It's Like to Be Young and Looking for Work in Britain." *The Guardian*, November 1, 2011. Accessed March 13, 2017. http://www.guardian.co.uk/society/2011/nov/01/young-looking-for-work-britain.

Koivisto, J., and M. Lahtinen. 2012. "Historical-Critical Dictionary of Marxism: Conjuncture, Politico-historical." *Historical Materialism* 20(1): 267–77.

Konings, M. 2010. "Rethinking Neoliberalism and the Crisis: Beyond the Re-regulation Agenda." In *The Great Credit Crash*, edited by M. Konings, 3–30. London: Verso.

———. 2014. *The Development of American Finance*. New York: Cambridge University Press.

———. 2015. "State of Speculation: Contingency, Measure, and the Politics of Plastic Value." *South Atlantic Quarterly* 114(2): 251–82.

———. 2016. "Governing the System: Risk, Finance, and Neoliberal Reason." *European Journal of International Relations* 22(2): 268–88.

———. 2018. *Capital and Time: For a New Critique of Neoliberal Reason*. Stanford, CA: Stanford University Press.

Kowalewska, H. 2015. "Diminishing Returns: Lone Mothers' Financial Work and Incomes Incentives under the Coalition." *Social Policy and Society* 14(4): 569–91.

Krinsky, J. 2007. *Free Labor: Workfare and the Contested Language of Neoliberalism*. Chicago: University of Chicago Press.

Krippner, G. 2005. "The Financialization of the American Economy." *Socio-economic Review* 3(2): 173–208.

Krugman, P. 2009a. "Fighting Off Depression." *New York Times*, January 4, 2009. Accessed March 21, 2017. http://www.nytimes.com/2009/01/05/opinion/05 krugman.html.

———. 2009b. *The Return of Depression Economics and the Crisis of 2008*. New York: Norton.

La Berge, L. C. 2014a. "The Rules of Abstraction: Methods and Discourses of Finance." *Radical History Review* 118:93–112.

———. 2014b. *Scandals and Abstractions: Financial Fiction of the Long 1980s*. Oxford: Oxford University Press.

Lang, C., I. Schömann, and S. Clauwaert. 2013. *Atypical Forms of Employment Contracts in Times of Crisis*. Brussels: European Trade Union Institute.

Langley, P. 2008. "Sub-prime Mortgage Lending: A Cultural Economy." *Economy and Society* 37(4): 469–94.

Lansley, S. 2011. *Britain's Livelihood Crisis*. London: Touchstone.

Lansley, S., and H. Reed. 2013. *How to Boost the Wage Share*. London: Touchstone.

Lapavitsas, C. 2009. "Financialized Capitalism: Crisis and Financial Expropriation." *Historical Materialism* 17(2): 117–48.

———. 2011. "Theorizing Financialization." *Work, Employment and Society* 25(4): 611–26.

Lash, S. 2007. "Capitalism and Metaphysics." *Theory, Culture and Society* 24(5): 1–26.

———. 2010. *Intensive Culture: Social Theory, Religion and Contemporary Capitalism*. London: Sage.

Latour, B. 2005. *Reassembling the Social: An Introduction to Actor-Network Theory*. Oxford: Oxford University Press.

Law, A. 2009. "The Callous Credit Nexus: Ideology and Compulsion in the Crisis of Neoliberalism." *Sociological Research Online* 14(4). www.socresonline.org .uk/14/4/5.

Lazzarato, M. 1996. "Immaterial Labour." In *Radical Thought in Italy: A Potential Politics*, edited by P. Virno and M. Hardt, 133–47. Minneapolis: University of Minnesota Press.

———. 2004. "From Capital-Labour to Capital-Life." *Ephemera: Theory and Politics in Organization* 4(3): 187–208.

———. 2009. "Neoliberalism in Action: Inequality, Insecurity and the Reconstitution of the Social." *Theory, Culture and Society* 26(6): 109–33.

————. 2011. *The Making of the Indebted Man*. Los Angeles: Semiotext(e).

————. 2015. *Governing by Debt*. South Pasadena, CA: Semiotext(e).

Leonard, S., and N. Fraser. 2016. "Capitalism's Crisis of Care." *Dissent* (Fall). www
.dissentmagazine.org/article/nancy-fraser-interview-capitalism-crisis-of-care.

Lewis, G. 1996. "Welfare Settlements and Racializing Practices." *Soundings: A
Journal of Politics and Culture* (Autumn): 109–20.

Lewis, J. 2001. "The Decline of the Male Breadwinner Model: The Implications
for Work and Care." *Social Politics* 8(2): 152–70.

Livingston, J. 2011. *Against Thrift: Why Consumer Culture Is Good for the Economy,
the Environment and Your Soul*. New York: Basic Books.

Long, S. 2009. "Governments Warned: 'Don't Mortgage the Future.'" *Lateline*,
Australian Broadcasting Corporation, June 6. Accessed March 21, 2017. http://
www.abc.net.au/lateline/content/2008/s2611909.htm.

Lutz, H. 2011. *The New Maids: Transnational Women and the Care Economy*. London:
Zed Books.

Mackenzie, D. 2007. "Is Economics Performative? Option Theory and the Construction of Derivative Markets." In *Do Economists Make Markets? On the Performativity of Economics*, edited by D. Mackenzie, F. Muniesa, and L. Siu, 54–86.
Princeton, NJ: Princeton University Press.

Mackenzie, D., F. Muniesa, and L. Siu, eds. 2007. *Do Economists Make Markets? On
the Performativity of Economics*. Princeton, NJ: Princeton University Press.

MacLeavy, J. 2011. "A 'New Politics' of Austerity, Workfare and Gender? The
UK Coalition Government's Welfare Reform Proposals." *Cambridge Journal of
Regions, Economy and Society* 4(3): 355–67.

Mahmud, T. 2013. "Debt and Discipline: Neoliberal Political Economy and the
Working Classes." *Kentucky Law Review* 101(1): 1–54, 69–89.

————. 2015. "Neoliberalism, Debt and Discipline." In *Research Handbook on Political Economy and Law*, edited by U. Mattei and J. D. Haskell, 69–89. Cheltenham, UK: Edward Elgar.

Marazzi, C. 2007. "Rules for the Incommensurable." *SubStance* 36(1): 11–36.

————. 2010. *The Violence of Financial Capitalism*. New York: Semiotext(e).

Martin, R. 2002. *Financialization of Daily Life*. Philadelphia: Temple University Press.

————. 2013. "After Economy? Social Logics of the Derivative." *Social Text* 31(1):
83–106.

————. 2015. "Money after Decolonization." *South Atlantic Quarterly* 114(2):
377–93.

Marx, K. 1979 [1891]. *Wage Labour and Capital*. Moscow: Progress Publishers.

————. 1981 [1894]. *Capital: A Critique of Political Economy*. Vol. 3. Translated by
D. Fernbach. Harmondsworth, UK: Penguin / New Left Review.

————. 1983 [1867]. *Capital: A Critique of Political Economy*. Vol. 1. Translated by
S. Moore and E. Aveling. London: Lawrence and Wishart.

Massumi, B. 2007. "Potential Politics and the Primacy of Preemption." *Theory and
Event* 10(2): n.p.

———. 2015. *Ontopower: War, Powers, and the State of Perception*. Durham, NC: Duke University Press.

Maurer, B. 2015. *How Would You Like to Pay? How Technology Is Changing the Future of Money*. Durham, NC: Duke University Press.

Maurer, B., and L. Swartz. 2015. "Wild, Wild West: A View from Two Californian Schoolmarms." In *Moneylab Reader: An Intervention in Digital Economy*, edited by G. Lovink, N. Tkacz, and P. De Vries, 221–29. Amsterdam: Institute of Network Culture.

McDowell, L. 1991. "Life without Father and Ford: The New Gender Order of Post-Fordism." *Transactions of the Institute of British Geographers* 16:400–421.

———. 2004. "Work, Workfare, Work/Life Balance and an Ethic of Care." *Progress in Human Geography* 28(2): 145–63.

———. 2008. "The New Economy, Class Condescension and Caring Labour: Changing Formations of Class and Gender." *NORA: Nordic Journal of Feminist and Gender Research* 16(3): 150–65.

McFall, L. 2009. "Devices and Desires: How Useful Is the 'New' Economic Sociology for Understanding Market Attachment?" *Sociology Compass* 3(2): 267–82.

McRobbie, A. 2002. "Clubs to Companies: Notes on the Decline of Political Culture in Speeded Up Creative Worlds." *Cultural Studies* 16(4): 516–31.

———. 2007. "Top Girls? Young Women and the Post-feminist Sexual Contract." *Cultural Studies* 21(4–5): 718–37.

———. 2013. "Feminism, the Family and the New Mediated Maternalism." *New Formations* 80: 119–37.

———. 2015. "Notes on the Perfect: Competitive Femininity in Neoliberal Times." *Australian Feminist Studies* 30(83): 3–20.

Mehrling, P. 2005. *Fischer Black and the Revolutionary Idea of Finance*. Hoboken, NJ: John Wiley and Sons.

Mirowski, P. 2013. *Never Let a Serious Crisis Go to Waste: How Neoliberalism Survived the Financial Meltdown*. London: Verso.

Mirowski, P., and D. Plehwe, eds. 2009. *The Road from Mont Pèlerin: The Making of the Neoliberal Thought Collective*. Cambridge, MA: Harvard University Press.

Mohanty, C. T. 2002. "'Under Western Eyes' Revisited: Feminist Solidarity through Anticapitalist Struggles." *Signs* 28(2): 499–535.

Montgomerie, J. 2009. "The Pursuit of (Past) Happiness? Middle-Class Indebtedness and American Financialisation." *New Political Economy* 14(1): 1–24.

Morini C. 2007. "The Feminization of Labour in Cognitive Capitalism." *Feminist Review* 87: 40–59.

Morris, L. 1990. *The Workings of the Household: A US-UK Comparison*. Cambridge: Polity Press.

Nesvetailova, A. 2015. "A Crisis of the Overcrowded Future: Shadow Banking and the Political Economy of Financial Innovation." *New Political Economy* 20(3): 431–53.

Norfield, T. 2012. "Derivatives and Capitalist Markets: The Speculative Heart of Capital." *Historical Materialism* 20(1): 103–32.

North, P. 2007. *Money and Liberation: The Micropolitics of Alternative Currency Movements*. Minneapolis: University of Minnesota Press.?

Nowotny, H. 2005. *Time: The Modern and Postmodern Experience*. Cambridge: Polity Press.

O'Carroll, A. 2008. "Fuzzy Holes and Intangible Time: Time in a Knowledge Industry." *Time and Society* 17(2–3): 179–93.

O'Connor, J. S., A. S. Orloff, and S. Shaver. 1999. *States, Markets, Families: Gender, Liberalism and Social Policy in Australia, Canada, Great Britain and the United States*. Cambridge: Cambridge University Press.

OECD. 2014a. "Household Debt." *OECD Factbook 2014: Economic, Environmental and Social Statistics*. Paris: OECD Publishing.

———. 2014b. "Active Labour Market Policies and Activation Strategies." OECD, July 15. Accessed January 27, 2017. http://www.oecd.org/employment/emp/ac tivelabourmarketpoliciesandactivationstrategies.htm.

———. 2016. "Household Debt." *OECD Factbook 2015–2016: Economic, Environmental and Social Statistics*. Paris: OECD Publishing.

Offe, C. 1985. *Disorganized Capitalism: Contemporary Transformations of Work and Politics*. Cambridge: Polity Press.

O'Hara, M. 2014. *Austerity Bites*. Bristol, UK: Policy Press.

Orgad, S. 2017. "The Cruel Optimism of *The Good Wife*: The Fantastic Working Mother on the Fantastical Treadmill." *Television and New Media* 18(2): 165–83.

Panitich, L., and S. Gindin. 2005. "Finance and American Empire." *Socialist Register* 41:46–81.

Panitich, L., and M. Konings. 2009. "Demystifying Imperial Finance." In *American Empire and the Political Economy of Global Finance*, edited by L. Panitich and M. Konings, 1–13. Basingstoke, UK: Palgrave Macmillan.

Parisi, L. 2013. *Contagious Architecture: Computation, Aesthetics and Space*. Cambridge, MA: MIT Press.

Pearson, R., and D. Elson. 2015. "Transcending the Impact of the Financial Crisis in the United Kingdom: Towards Plan F—A Feminist Economic Strategy." *Feminist Review* 109:8–30.

Peck, J. 2001. *Workfare States*. New York: Guildford Press.

Peck, J., and N. Theodore. 2000. "'Work First': Workfare and the Regulation of Contingent Labour Markets." *Cambridge Journal of Economics* 24(1): 119–38.

———. 2001. "Exporting Workfare / Importing Welfare-to-Work: Exploring the Politics of Third Way Policy Transfer." *Political Geography* 20:427–60.

———. 2012. "Politicizing Contingent Labor: Countering Neoliberal Labor-Market Regulation . . . From the Bottom Up?" *South Atlantic Quarterly* 111(4): 741–61.

———. 2015. *Fast Policy: Experimental Statecraft at the Thresholds of Neoliberalism*. Minneapolis: University of Minnesota Press.

Peck, J., N. Theodore, and N. Brenner. 2012. "Neoliberalism Resurgent? Market Rule after the Great Recession." *South Atlantic Quarterly* 111(2): 265–88.

Pew Charitable Trusts. 2017. "How Income Volatility Interacts with American Families' Financial Security: An Examination of Gains and Losses and Household American Experiences." *The Pew Charitable Trusts Research and Analysis Issue Brief*, March 9, 2017. Accessed May 15, 2017. http://www.pewtrusts.org/en/research-and-analysis/issue-briefs/2017/03/how-income-volatility-interacts-with-american-families-financial-security.

Pierson, C., and L. Humpage. 2016. "Coming Together or Drifting Apart? Income Maintenance in Australia, New Zealand and the United Kingdom." *Politics and Policy* 44(2): 261–93.

Piketty, T. 2014. *Capital in the Twenty-First Century*. Cambridge, MA: Harvard University Press.

Piskorski, T., and A. Tchistyi. 2010. "Optimal Mortgage Design." *Review of Financial Studies* 23(8): 3098–140.

Polanyi, K. 2001. *The Great Transformation: The Political and Economic Origins of Our Time*. Boston: Beacon Press.

Pollin, R., and S. Luce. 1998. *The Living Wage: Building a Fair Economy*. New York: New Press.

Poon, M. 2009. "From New Deal Institutions to Capital Markets: Commercial Consumer Risk Scores and the Making of Subprime Mortgage Finance." *Accounting, Organizations and Society* 34: 654–74.

Poovey, M. 2015. "Understanding Global Interconnectedness: Catastrophic Generic Change." In *The Material of World History*, edited by T. M. Chen and D. S. Churchill, 150–65. London: Routledge.

Poppe, C., R. Lavik, and E. Borgeraas. 2016. "The Dangers of Borrowing in the Age of Financialization." *Acta Sociologica* 59(1): 19–33.

Postone, M. 1993. *Time, Labor, and Social Domination: A Reinterpretation of Marx's Critical Theory*. Cambridge: Cambridge University Press.

Povinelli, E. A. 2011. *Economies of Abandonment: Social Belonging and Endurance in Late Capitalism*. Durham, NC: Duke University Press.

Power, N. 2009. "Non-reproductive Futurism: Rancière's Rational Equality against Edelman's Body Apolitic." *borderlands* 8(2): 1–16.

Pryke, M. 2017. "'This Time It's Different' . . . and Why It Matters: The Shifting Geographies of Money, Finance and Risks." In *Handbook on the Geographies of Money and Finance*, edited by R. Martin and J. Pollard, 105–24. Cheltenham, UK: Edward Elgar.

Radway, J. 1983. "Women Read the Romance: The Interaction of Text and Context." *Feminist Studies* 9(1): 53–78.

Rafferty, M., and S. Yu. 2010. *Shifting Risk: Work and Working Life in Australia—A Report for the Australian Council of Trade Unions*. Sydney: Workplace Research Centre, University of Sydney.

Rake, K. 2009a. *Are Women Bearing the Burden of the Recession? A Fawcett Society Report*. London: The Fawcett Society.

———. 2009b. "Women Must Not Go Back to the Kitchen." *The Guardian*, March 7, 2009. Accessed March 19, 2017. https://www.theguardian.com/commentisfree/2009/mar/06/women-workplace-equality-recession.

Regan, A. 2014. "Europe's 'Structural Reform Agenda' Is Little More than a Fairytale." *EUROPP*, January 21, 2014. Accessed March 21, 2017. http://blogs.lse.ac.uk/europpblog/2014/01/21/europes-structural-reform-agenda-is-little-more-than-a-fairytale/.

Reinhart, C. M., and K. S. Rogoff. 2009. *This Time Is Different: Eight Centuries of Financial Folly*. Princeton, NJ: Princeton University Press.

Roberts, A. 2013. "Financing Social Reproduction: The Gendered Relations of Debt and Mortgage Finance in Twenty-First-Century America." *New Political Economy* 18(1): 21–42.

———. 2015. "Gender, Financial Deepening and the Production of Embodied Finance: Towards a Critical Feminist Analysis." *Global Society* 29(1): 107–27.

Rose, N. 1996. "The Death of the Social: Refiguring the Territory of Government." *Economy and Society* 25(3): 327–56.

Samers, M. 2011. "Towards a Critical Economy of Workfare." In *The Sage Handbook of Economic Geography*, edited by A. Leyshon, R. Lee, and L. McDowell, 202–14. London: Sage.

Sanford, M. 2009. "Don't Mortgage Our Children's Future." *CNN Politics*, February 13, 2009. Accessed March 21, 2017. http://edition.cnn.com/2009/POLITICS/02/13/sanford.economy/index.html.

Sassen, S. 2000. "Countergeographies of Globalization: The Feminization of Survival." *Journal of International Affairs* 53(2): 503–24.

Scanlon, K., J. Lunde, and C. Whitehead. 2008. "Mortgage Product Innovation in Advanced Economies: More Choice, More Risk." *European Journal of Housing Policy* 8(2): 109–31.

Sennett, R. 2006. *The Culture of the New Capitalism*. New Haven, CT: Yale University Press.

Sevenhuijsen, S. 2003. "The Place of Care: The Relevance of the Feminist Ethic of Care for Social Policy." *Feminist Theory* 4(2): 179–97.

Sewell, W. H. 2005. *Logics of History: Social Theory and Social Transformation*. Chicago: University of Chicago Press.

Siegel, R. 1996. "'The Rule of Love': Wife-Beating as Prerogative and Privacy." *Yale Law Journal* 105:2117–207.

Simmel, G. 2004 [1907]. *The Philosophy of Money*. Translated by T. Bottomore and D. Frisby. London: Routledge.

Slocock, C. 2013. *The Big Society Audit 2013*. London: Civil Exchange.

Smith, A. M. 2002. "The Sexual Regulation Dimension of Contemporary Welfare Law: A Fifty State Overview." *Michigan Journal of Gender and Law* 8(2): 121–218.

———. 2007. *Welfare and Sexual Regulation*. Cambridge: Cambridge University Press.

———. 2008. "Neoliberalism, Welfare Policy, and Feminist Theories of Social Justice." *Feminist Theory* 9(2): 131–44.

Smith, H., H. McDonald, and G. Tremlett. 2012. "Across Europe, There's a Generation with Its Future on Hold." *The Guardian*, October 22, 2012. Accessed March 21, 2017. https://www.theguardian.com/society/2012/oct/22/europe -generation-future-on-hold.

Soederberg, S. 2014. *Debtfare States and the Poverty Industry: Money, Discipline and the Surplus Population*. London: Routledge.

Sotiropoulos, D., J. Milios, and S. Lapatsioras. 2013. *A Political Economy of Contemporary Capitalism and Its Crisis: Demystifying Finance*. London: Routledge.

Spivak, G. C. 1978. "Feminism and Critical Theory." *Women's Studies International Quarterly* 1(3): 241–46.

———. 1985. "Scattered Speculations on the Question of Value." *Diacritics* 15(4): 73–93.

Standing, G. 2011. *The Precariat: The New Dangerous Class*. London: Bloomsbury.

Staples, D. 2007. *No Place like Home: Organizing Home Based Labour in an Era of Structural Adjustment*. London: Routledge.

Steans, J., and L. Jenkins. 2012. *All in This Together? Interrogating UK Austerity through Gender Lenses*. Department of Political Science and International Studies Report, University of Birmingham, Birmingham, UK.

Stedman Jones, D. 2012. *Masters of the Universe: Hayek, Friedman, and the Birth of Neoliberal Politics*. Princeton, NJ: Princeton University Press.

Stockhammer, E. 2012a. "Financialization." In *Handbook of Critical Issues in Finance*, edited by J. Toporowski and J. Michell, 121–26. Cheltenham, UK: Edward Elgar.

———. 2012b. "Financialization, Income Distribution and the Crisis." *Investigation Economica* 21(279): 39–70.

———. 2013. *Why Have Wage Shares Fallen? A Panel Analysis of the Determinants of Functional Income Distribution*. Geneva: International Labour Office.

———. 2015. "Rising Inequality as a Cause of the Present Crisis." *Cambridge Journal of Economics* 39(3): 935–58.

Streeck, W. 2014. *Buying Time: The Delayed Crisis of Democratic Capitalism*. Translated by P. Camiller. London: Verso.

Struyven, L., and G. Steurs. 2005. "Design and Redesign of a Quasi-market for the Reintegration of Jobseekers: Empirical Evidence from Australia and the Netherlands." *Journal of European Social Policy* 15(3): 211–29.

Sunderland, R. 2009. "The Real Victims of the Credit Crunch? Women." *The Observer*, January 18, 2009. Accessed March 19, 2017. http://www.guardian.co.uk/lifeandstyle/2009/jan/18/women-credit-crunch-ruth-sunderland.

Swanson, J. 2005. "Recognition and Redistribution: Rethinking Culture and the Economic." *Theory, Culture and Society* 22(4): 87–118.

Tadiar, N. X. M. 2013. "Life-Times of Disposability within Global Neoliberalism." *Social Text* 31(2): 19–48.

Taylor, D. R., M. Gray, and D. Stanton. 2016. "New Conditionality in Australian Social Security Policy." *Australian Journal of Social Issues* 51(1): 3–26.

Taylor, J. 2016. "Laptops and Playpens: 'Mommy Bloggers' and Visions of Household Work." In *The Post-Fordist Sexual Contract*, edited by L. Adkins and M. Dever, 109–28. Basingstoke, UK: Palgrave Macmillan.

Taylor-Gooby, P. 2004. "New Risks and Social Change." In *New Risks, New Welfare: The Transformation of the European Welfare State*, edited by P. Taylor-Gooby, 1–28. Oxford: Oxford University Press.

Thompson, E. P. 1967. "Time, Work-Discipline and Industrial Capitalism." *Past and Present* 39:56–97.

Thompson, G. F. 2016. "Time Trading and Algorithms in Financial Sector Security." *New Political Economy*. DOI: 10.1080/13563467.2016.1183116.

Thorne, B. 2011. "The Crisis of Care." In *At the Heart of Work and Family: Engaging the Ideas of Arlie Hochschild*, edited by A. I. Garey and K. V. Hansen, 149–60. New Brunswick, NJ: Rutgers University Press.

Thrift, N. 2008. *Non-representational Theory: Space, Politics, Affect*. London: Routledge.

Tiessen, M. 2015. "The Appetites of App-Based Finance." *Cultural Studies* 29(5–6): 869–86.

Trades Union Congress. 2009. *Women and Recession*. London: Trades Union Congress.

———. 2011. *Women's Unemployment Will Rise as Public Sector Job Cuts Kick In*. Press release, September 5, 2011. Accessed March 19, 2017. https://www.tuc .org.uk/economic-issues/economic-analysis/womens-unemployment-will-rise -public-sector-job-cuts-kick.

———. 2013. *TUC General Secretary Frances O'Grady's Address to Congress 2013*. Press release, September 9, 2013. Accessed April 12, 2017. http://www.tuc.org .uk/about-tuc/congress-2013/tuc-general-secretary-frances-ogradys-address -congress-2013.

Triantafillou, P. 2011. "The OECD's Thinking on the Governing of Unemployment." *Policy and Politics* 39(4): 567–82.

———. 2012. *New Forms of Governing: A Foucauldian Inspired Analysis*. Basingstoke, UK: Palgrave Macmillan.

van der Tuin, I. 2015. *Generational Feminism: New Materialist Introduction to a Generative Approach*. Lanham, MD: Lexington Books.

van der Zwan, N. 2014. "Making Sense of Financialization." *Socio-economic Review* 12(1): 99–129.

Van Horn, R., P. Mirowski, and T. A. Stapleford. 2011. *Building Chicago Economics: New Perspectives on the History of America's Most Powerful Economics Program*. Cambridge: Cambridge University Press.

Vidal, M. 2013. "Postfordism as a Dysfunctional Accumulation Regime: A Comparative Analysis of the USA, the UK and Germany." *Work, Employment and Society* 27(3): 451–71.

Vosko, L. 2002. *Rethinking Feminization: Gendered Precariousness in the Canadian Labour Market and the Crisis in Social Reproduction.* Robarts Canada Research Chairholders Series. Toronto: York University.

Wacquant, L. 1999. "Urban Marginality in the Coming Millennium." *Urban Studies* 36(10): 1639–47.

———. 2009. *Punishing the Poor: The Neoliberal Government of Social Insecurity.* Durham, NC: Duke University Press.

———. 2010. "Crafting the Neoliberal State: Workfare, Prisonfare and Social Insecurity." *Sociological Forum* 25(2): 197–220.

Wainwright, T. 2012. "Building New Markets: Transferring Securitization, Bond Rating and a Crisis from the US to the UK." In *Subprime Cities: The Political Economy of Mortgage Markets*, edited by M. Aalbers, 97–119. Oxford: Wiley-Blackwell.

Walby, S. 1984. *Patriarchy at Work.* Cambridge: Polity Press.

Waldby, C., and M. Cooper. 2010. "From Reproductive Work to Regenerative Labour: The Female Body and the Stem Cell Industries." *Feminist Theory* 11(1): 3–22.

Walters, W. 2000. *Unemployment and Government: Genealogies of the Social.* Cambridge: Cambridge University Press.

Weber, M. 1930 [1905]. *The Protestant Ethic and the Spirit of Capitalism.* Translated by T. Parsons and A. Giddens. London: Unwin Hyman.

Whitworth, A., and J. Griggs. 2013. "Lone Parents and Welfare-to-Work Conditionality: Necessary, Just, Effective?" *Ethics and Social Welfare* 7(2): 124–40.

Williams, R. 1961. *The Long Revolution.* London: Chatto and Windus.

———. 1977. *Marxism and Literature.* Oxford: Oxford University Press.

———. 1989 [1958]. "Culture Is Ordinary." In *Resources of Hope: Culture, Democracy, Socialism*, by R. Williams, 3–18. London: Verso.

Wills, J. 2009. "Subcontracted Employment and Its Challenge to Labor." *Labor Studies Journal* 34(4): 441–60.

Wills, J., and B. Linneker. 2014. "In-Work Poverty and the Living Wage in the United Kingdom: A Geographical Perspective." *Transactions of the Institute of British Geographers* 39(2): 182–94.

Wilson, E. 1977. *Women and the Welfare State.* London: Tavistock.

Wisman, J. D. 2013. "Wage Stagnation, Rising Inequality and the Financial Crisis of 2008." *Cambridge Journal of Economics* 37(4): 921–45.

Women's Budget Group. 2012. *The Impact on Women of the Budget 2012.* London: Women's Budget Group.

———. 2016. *A Cumulative Gender Impact Assessment of Ten Years of Austerity Politics.* London: Women's Budget Group.

Women's Resource and Development Agency. 2011. *The Northern Ireland Economy: Women on the Edge?* Belfast: Women's Resource and Development Agency.

Yeates, N. 2004. "Global Care Chains." *International Feminist Journal of Politics* 6(3): 369–91.

Zaloom, C. 2006. *Out of the Pits: Traders and Technology from Chicago to London*. Chicago: University of Chicago Press.

———. 2009. "How to Read the Future: The Yield Curve, Affect and Financial Prediction." *Public Culture* 21(2): 245–68.

———. 2010. "The Derivative World." *Hedgehog Review* (Summer): 20–27.

———. 2017. "Finance." *Correspondences, Cultural Anthropology* website, August 7, 2017. Accessed October 11, 2017. https://culanth.org/fieldsights/1163-finance.

Index

Page numbers in italics refer to figures.

CURRENCIES

New Thinking for Financial Times
Melinda Cooper and Martijn Konings, Series Editors

In the wake of recent events such as the global financial crisis, the Occupy Wall Street Movement, and the rise of anti–student-debt activism, the need for a more sophisticated encounter between economic theory and social and political philosophy has become pressing. The growth of new forms of money and finance, which has only accelerated since the financial crisis, is recognized as one of the defining developments of our time. But even as finance continuously breaches limits and forces adjustments, much scholarly commentary remains focused on the limits of the market and the need to establish some prior state of political stability, thus succumbing to a nostalgia that blunts its critical edge. Not content to adopt a defensive posture, books in this series move beyond well-rehearsed denunciations of out-of-control markets and seek to rethink the core institutions and categories of financialized capitalism. *Currencies* will serve as a forum for work that is situated at the intersection of economics, the humanities, and the social sciences. It will include conceptually driven historical or empirical studies, genealogies of economic ideas and institutions, and work that employs new or unexplored theoretical resources to rethink key economic categories and themes.

Martijn Konings, *Capital and Time: For a New Critique of Neoliberal Reason*